MARKIE'S
BOX

Peter Holroyd

Published by

MELROSE BOOKS

An Imprint of Melrose Press Limited
St Thomas Place, Ely
Cambridgeshire
CB7 4GG, UK
www.melrosebooks.com

FIRST EDITION

Copyright © Peter Holroyd 2005

The Author asserts his moral right to
be identified as the author of this work

Cover designed by Geoff Hobbs Design

ISBN 0 9548480 6 3

Printed and bound in Great Britain by:
Bath Press Limited, Lower Bristol Road,
Bath, BA2 3BL, UK

MARKIE'S
BOX

Peter Holroyd

17TH JUNE, 2000

Marion and I were enjoying a weekend in a holiday flat in Fleetwood. We had been out to a local pub to watch England play Germany at football, the pub was filled to capacity and as the game progressed the crowd got louder and louder so when it finished, with a win for England, we decided to make a quick exit. On our way back to the flat we bought a chicken supper. We had just settled down to enjoy our meal when my mobile phone rang; it was my daughter's boyfriend.

"Not good news I'm afraid," there was a slight pause before he continued, "your Mark has had an accident and he has been rushed off to Preston Royal Infirmary."

"Why Preston Royal?"

"Because he has a head injury and Preston Royal are specialists in this type of accident."

The shock of that nightmare statement was too much for me; I was very confused and dazed. Suddenly I became very angry, and lost control of my actions – for some strange reason I took it out of the wall by smashing my fist through it. Fortunately, it was a plasterboard partition, so all I achieved were two gaping holes and a very sore right hand.

It is very difficult to be rational in a situation like this. Regardless of my service background where I was trained to take an on-the-spot reaction in any situation, I found myself struggling to make a positive decision. This was completely different from anything I had experienced in my life to date, but I had to be realistic and positive. Easier said than done in this sort of situation. Slowly I composed myself and decided that we must go to be with our son Markie.

Regardless of the fact that I had had several drinks, I felt sober. I know now that I could not have been but I had to get to Markie and I had to get to him now. Without hesitation Marion and I dropped everything and sped off to be with him. The drive to the hospital was a silent affair. Neither of us had anything to say, not even words of comfort, just a feeling of numb isolation and the fear of the unknown.

My mind was on Markie all the way. Funny how Mark always gets called Markie – the family adopted this a long time ago – perhaps he got that name due to being very small right up to his turning sixteen. Only family could call him this affectionate name and he would correct others if they used it.

5

Preston Royal Hospital is an old Victorian building, which has been added to and altered; now covering a massive area of land with old and new buildings. Never having had cause to go there in the past, I found it most daunting as it was almost in total darkness when we entered the grounds from the only entrance I knew. I jumped out of the car and tried several doors only to find them locked. By now I felt I was 'losing it' but sense seemed to prevail and I slowly pulled myself together. Surely I wanted the Accident and Emergency Department. Back in the car and as calmly as I could, we exited the entrance we had taken and set about circling the hospital seeking the now very familiar A and E road sign.

Probably only a couple of minutes later, the road into the Hospital appeared on our left. We followed the signs for Accident and Emergency. As we approached Main Entrance, I spotted a security guard. I abandoned the car, jumped out and quickly explained our plight, and he instructed me to park the car in a space close to the entrance and follow him inside. From a massive site plan of the Hospital, he gave us directions to the Intensive Care Unit.

When I said that the hospital was large, it was a slight understatement, it was huge. Long, seemingly endless corridors and dozens and dozens of signs. Most named departments I had never heard of or understood their meanings. Only the sign guiding us to Mark stood out in my mind as we rushed along on our serious mission.

Almost there and I started to get a fear building up in me. What was I going to be greeted with? Would Mark have survived the journey here? If he had, what would we have of him? The expected outcome was completely unknown and too frightening to even hazard a guess.

At last we were there, not a soul in sight, just the sign on a locked door and an intercom system to communicate with someone inside. I hesitantly pushed the button and a lady's voice came back to me.

"Hello can I help you?"

"Yes, I believe you have my son Mark Holroyd." She seemed to hesitate for a few minutes. "Yes, Mr Holroyd, we have your son, please come in."

The door clicked and we entered to find a small waiting room with the customary table covered in dated magazines. The door to the Emergency Department opened and a female nurse appeared.

First she explained that Mark was in surgery at that very moment and told us to make ourselves comfortable, and they would keep us informed should there be any further development.

"Would you like tea or coffee?"

"I would like black tea."

"May I have coffee with milk and one sugar please?" said Marion.

The lady re-appeared after what seemed only a few minutes with our drinks.

Left to our thoughts, Marion and I sat in that small room in total silence, not even attempting to read a magazine or a paper, as we both knew we would not be able to concentrate on anything other than our son Markie.

My mind started to drift and it took me back to when I was but a small boy and to when my father was killed on the night of 7/8th June, 1944. I was only four at the time when the news came that my father was missing, presumed dead.

My father was a rear gunner in a Lancaster Bomber – a very dangerous place to be, I am told. Dangerous in that you have to crawl down a very small tunnel in the aircraft to reach the gun position. This tunnel is so small that you need to be both lithesome and of slight stature to even consider making the passage. My father was both of these, along with also being a very brave person.

You had to be brave or mad or both to even consider being a rear gunner. I have been led to understand that a rear gunner (or tail end Charlie, as they were known) was not accompanied by his parachute in the action station; it had to stay behind in the main part of the aircraft, as the gun position was so confined that it would not accommodate both man and parachute.

I am the youngest of a family of seven. When father was killed, it was a dashing blow to us all, not so much me, as I consider I was too young to be greatly affected. It was of great impact on my three brothers and three sisters, not to mention the grief my mother must have gone through. Funny though as, even up to the time when she passed away, she always said. "That Dad of yours won't be dead, I know him, he will be gadding it up with some tart in the South of France."

Without warning I was snatched out of my dreaming. The sister had returned to announce that the operation was over and that Mark had survived the trauma and would be returning to Intensive Care shortly.

It was 05 30 hrs. "What can I expect," I asked myself not wanting to pose the question on Marion as she to was deep in her own thoughts.

Suddenly the door buzzer sounded and the same sister followed the same routine, and carried out the same procedure, as she had done for us. Again, another grief-stricken family; this time it was the mother and father of a young man who, like Mark, had suffered head injuries. After a short time, when they had become to accept where they were and what had happened and had a 'brew' from the good nurse, the young man's father explained that the car his son had been driving had left the road.

That saying always strikes me as a strange one, as from my experience cars do not leave the road without some assistance. Obviously, I said nothing on this subject but, for some reason, it came into my mind. Was this man blaming the car for the reason that his son was here?

It was now 06 00 hrs. And there was a lot of activity going on. New staff were appearing and it became apparent that the main part of the day was about to get into full swing. Or was there really a main part of the day in a place like this. There was not, as I found out later; victims of these disasters have no time-scale.

Still waiting and all of us sitting in silence, I let my eyes wander to the glass panel in the door leading to the ward. There was, as I have said, quite a lot of activity going on. Doctors in masks and gowns, nurses and ward workers, people passing to and fro. Then I saw a body pass the glass panel being pushed along on a bed by at least four people, faces masked out and looking quite sinister, posts fastened to the bed with lots of bags, bottles and other equipment hanging from them. Other bodies pushing more posts on wheels with even more bottles hanging from them. I clearly remember what I felt and I tried not to show my emotions to Marion, as she had not been in a position to witness what I had seen. I knew at that moment that the bundle on the bed was our son, Markie.

Grief overcame me and I could feel the fear welling up inside me. I could not control myself any longer and uncontrollably I started to cry.

To be consoled and comforted by total strangers is a very touching experience. Not one I relished on this occasion. The man whose son's car had left the road put his arm around me and said,

"Let it come out lad, you'll feel a lot better for it." I wished I had never had the silly thought about that man's son and the 'self-driving car'.

Sister arrived with a brew of strong black tea and a comforting smile. Marion just stared in what looked like total disbelief. Was it because her ex-Royal Marine Commando husband was crying or was it a look of 'I am not here, am I'?

At last composed but under a great deal of stress, I was ready to go forward. I needed to know how Markie was. Supporting each other, Marion and I were guided from the waiting room into this 'new world' of Medical Technology, the passageway festooned with equipment whose use was out of my comprehension.

As we drew nearer to the Intensive Care Ward, we clung tighter to each other. The fear was again building up in me, "I have to be strong," I kept telling myself, and try to radiate some confidence for the sake of Marion.

We turned into the ward; it had five beds. We were taken to the bed in the far right-hand corner and there he was. "Oh my God, Mark, what have you done." I heard myself say. Looking back, I cannot think of a sillier question.

If I had any feelings at all that moment, it was one of mistaken identity. This person on the bed had his head covered in bandages, I thought, "This is not our Markie, it can't be, Mark's head is nowhere near the size of the one in front of me, this head is massive." All the time these thoughts were going through my mind, I knew I was seeking blindly for any excuse so as to lessen the inevitable blow I was going to have to accept.

It was Markie; I just did not want it to be.

ADEN

For some strange reason my thoughts strayed away again. Perhaps it was the fear of having to accept what you are presented with. I drifted back to when I was in 45 Commando Royal Marines and the frightening experience of when I first came under fire.

It was in 1961, I was in the mountains of Aden close to the Yemen border and I was leading a small patrol when suddenly we came under fire. Regardless of the intensive training you get in the Royal Marines and the arduous activities at Commando School, nothing can prepare you for the real thing. When you first come under fire, you are suddenly hit with a massive pump of adrenaline and fear smacks you like you cannot imagine. The fear on that occasion was the same frightening feeling I was getting now, as I knew and accepted that the person on the bed was, in fact, Markie.

Probes were sticking out of his head, tubes and pipes up his nose and down his throat, with monitors attached to various parts of his body. There was the strange sound of various machines and pieces of equipment buzzing away keeping our son alive.

"So this is what a life support machine is all about", I thought.

I suddenly thought of Marion, "What is she feeling? Why am I ignoring her?" I turned to find her frozen faced and transfixed on the person on the bed. I later learnt that her thoughts had been very similar to mine, that of having to accept that the person there in front of you is your son.

The lovely and very caring Sister was standing by us; she explained what most of the equipment was for and what is was doing. The probe in the head was there to set off an audible warning should the pressure in the skull start to increase. The big machine was doing the breathing for Mark, and so on, and so on. I became quite deaf to her explanations, as my thoughts were with Markie.

"Would you like to speak to the surgeon, Mr Holroyd?"

Suddenly and sadly I was back in the real world. I lingered over my reply.

"Yes please."

I was still feeling slightly detached from all the goings-on. It would be some time before the surgeon would be free, so Marion suggested we take in some fresh air.

We wandered through that maze of corridors and finally reached the outside. We made our way across the car park and sat on a grassy bank. The sun was glowing in the sky and the place was coming alive with people busy starting another day.

"This is some day, I thought, probably the worst one I will have in this lifetime."

Sitting there on the grass feeling the warmth of the sun, my thoughts drifted back to Aden.

THE KILLING HILLS

After getting over the initial fear of knowing that someone has compromised you and that his intentions of wanting to kill are real, the training starts to come into its intended use. We could not just get up and walk away from this person; he was not prepared to accept that. He was out there unseen, just waiting for us to make the next move. Training told me that we had to draw his fire somehow and the only way to achieve this was for one of the patrol to get up and make a very short dash before taking cover again. All the rest of the patrol must observe the area suspected of housing the enemy.

With luck we hoped to get a sight of him or even a sign like a puff of smoke from a rifle. We had to attempt something, as the alternative was to wait for dark and crawl out of it.

Reluctantly, I gave the order, knowing full well a comrade may be killed,

"Roberts, I want you to make the move, go on the count of three, the rest of you observe, one, two, three go."

Roberts leapt to his feet and dashed about 20 feet, then hit the ground and crawled for cover. Nothing, absolutely nothing; maybe we took the enemy by surprise. I decided to try it again, this time another man must be chosen or 'Robo' would think I didn't like him.

"Barlow, your turn, on the count of three, one, two, three go."

Barlow did a carbon copy of Robo's action but unlike his attempt Barlow managed to draw some enemy fire and was lucky to live to tell his tale. This time we got the desired result. Bang–bang–bang, three shots rang out from the enemy position and smashed into the ground close to us.

"Seen." bawled out Mason and Stewert more or less in chorus.

"Return the fire."

They did so, soon to be joined by Barlow and I when we saw their fall of shot.

"Don't you think we should go back in?" It was Marion.

"Yes, of course."

We had to make our way back to what had now become a dreadful reality. We arrived at the unit and I pressed the button on the intercom system to announce our presence.

"Please come in."

This time, another Sister greeted us; she was really a clone of the first one. I realised at that moment that you to be a very special person to do a job such as theirs. Again another brew and another wait. My friend, the father of the boy who was injured in the car accident, came back from the ward to report that his son was still comatose but did not appear to be badly injured. I sincerely hoped he wasn't and told him so.

"Mr Holroyd, Mr ???????? (the surgeon) will see you now."

It was the second Sister. Marion remained seated.

"Are you coming, love?" I enquired.

She didn't reply. She just gave me that knowing look that means, no thanks. I followed number two to a very small room next to the ward and was greeted with a positive handshake from the Surgeon.

"Sit down, Mr Holroyd, I will explain the situation so far."

Number two kindly brought me yet another cup of tea. Mr? went on to tell me that Mark had been unfortunate enough to sustain a severe blow to the head. Sadly, Mark's skull had not been fractured and that bleeding within the skull had taken place, causing pressure to build up within the head. He explained how he had had to open up Mark's skull to remove a blood clot, which in his own words, "was as big as my fist."

"What is the worst-case scenario. I need to know as I have to tell the family; please don't pull any punches."

"If your son survives the next 48 hours, he will probably live on; however, owing to the size of the blood clot and the pressure placed on his brain, he will only have an existence and not a full life."

I was completely gutted with his reply, but I had asked for the worst with no punches pulled and that was exactly what I got. I just hoped no one would ask me the same question, especially one of the family.

With a feeling of being totally out of control of what the future would hold, or what to do next, I returned to the waiting room, collected Marion and together we left for home.

As with our apprehensive trip to the hospital, the journey home was also a very silent one.

Back home at last to face Julie and Wendy, Mark's twin sister. They were very much in a state of shock and hungry for good news, of which I had none.

How can I tell them what Mr ?? has told me. I couldn't just say,

"Sorry, girls, but if Mark is lucky and manages to survive the next couple of nights, we will be left with a body in a vegetated state."

No way could I subject them to that sort of talk. I had be positive.

It was then that I decided that I was only going to have a positive attitude, and I wanted this to 'rub off ' onto the girls and Marion. I debarred myself from thinking in a negative sort of way, as others might pick up these vibes.

I decided that I would have to lie if I were asked what went on in the meeting with Mr ? Thankfully, no one asked. It was as if they knew what had gone on and they did not really want to know what my answer would be.

That evening I went over to see Mark; the girls had already been over in the afternoon. There was obviously no change in Mark, but I did have a very interesting chat to a lady who was visiting her brother. He was in the next bed to Mark and she went on to tell me that this was his second encounter with a severe head injury. His first one was when he had a motorbike accident from which he had made an amazing recovery. His second accident, if you can call it that, was when he was beaten almost to death by a bunch of youths in a subway. He had been kicked about the head and body until he lost consciousness. The remarkable thing about the chat with this lady was her attitude. She was so calm and collected and talked in a very positive manner. She said confidently,

"I got him back the last time and I am sure I can do it again."

My thoughts were that I must 'take a leaf out of her book' and it was then that I set my mind on doing my utmost to get Markie back.

It's odd, but in a situation like this your whole world is turned around. Your attitude to life changes. Things that were very important to you become quite insignificant. Your mind tells you will get through this but inside you don't know how.

Friends and others change. Some become cautious of you and appear afraid to ask

"How is Mark?"

Some come out with utterly stupid statements like

"Don't worry it will be alright."

You feel like replying

"How the fuck do you know, are you a fucking Doctor?"

Or they may say,

"I know how you must feel."

Again, you want to offend them by saying

"Don't be fucking stupid, you have not got a fucking clue how I feel."

I never did reply in this manner but the temptation to do so was not easy to hold back. After all they only ask you these questions to try to comfort you.

Sleep too avoids you in this sort of situation. You feel a bit like a child again, having to go to bed when you are told to, even when you are not a bit tired. Only this time it is not your Mam who sends you to bed, it is yourself, as you know you must have sleep but it just goes on avoiding you.

I found that my ability to go back in time was much stronger. I am not sure why. Was I trying to escape from this terrible situation?

I became aware of this when I was alone with Mark whilst he was in Preston. It was Monday evening about 36 hours after the operation.

12

THE BALLOON

I was sat with Mark just looking at his motionless body and silently praying for his recovery. My mind became blurred and I drifted back to my childhood.

I was about 5 years old. We lived on Piccadilly Road in Burnley. It was quite a large house, and we needed it, for at home were my three brothers and three sisters, watched over and looked after by our Mam.

Mam had little money and we used to entertain ourselves by sitting around the 'wireless' or playing simple games.

Being the 'baby' of the family meant that I was a little spoilt by my elder sisters, Joan, Norma and Pamela, in order of seniority.

Mam used to teach piano to provide a bit of income and our 'front room' was dedicated to this task. It was most certainly out of bounds to us children.

In those days every household had a 'front room', a room set aside for when you had company or there was a death in the family. I can recall many occasions when someone local had a death in the family. The coffin would be placed on a table in the front room with the lid off and people were expected to call and pay their respects. It could be there for days waiting for funeral arrangements to be made.

I was an adventurous sort of boy and on one occasion whilst exploring on our back street I found a 'balloon'. Strangely enough it was deflated and had a knot in it, so I thought I would take it home and test that it was okay.

Into the kitchen, which housed an old set boiler and oven which had to be 'black leaded' by my senior brothers, Granville, Raymond and Fred in that order. The kitchen was where we took all of our meals; we would sit at a long wooden table, which had to be given a good scrubbing after every meal, and this day it was our Pam's turn to carry out the task.

I managed to undo the knot and decided to inflate the balloon with water. I put it over the tap end and I let it dangle into the big pot sink. I turned on the water and it started to swell and swell as more and more water went into it. Pam called out,

"Norma, Joan, come and see what Peter has got ."

They stood there watching me wrestle with this now massive balloon. For some reason they were in fits of laughter. They were so loud that our Mam broke off from giving a piano lesson to see what the commotion was all about.

She charged into the kitchen and stood there, mouth open with her eyes fixed on my now enormous balloon. Then, bang, the balloon burst and I stood there like a drowned rat with bits of my precious balloon all over the place.

The girls were still roaring with laughter. I didn't understand what was so funny for I had lost my lovely big balloon and got a good soaking.

It was years later when I found out just what my lovely balloon must have been. No wonder the girls were in fits of laughter. It also explains the surprise on my Mam's face.

THE CRASH

That evening's drive back home from Preston was a strange one. My thoughts were with Mark and I kept thinking and wondering if we would still have him in the morning.

I was alone, travelling from the traffic lights on the Preston–Blackburn Road, heading towards Whalley. I found myself last in a line of four cars heading the same way. We were approaching the entrance to Samlesbury Aircraft Factory; fortunately for me I had left a distance of about one hundred yards between my car and the one in front. Suddenly a car appeared travelling at very high speed heading towards us on the wrong side of the road. There, in front of my very eyes, it was happening. The speeding car smashed into the lead car, bounced off it into the second car, and the third car crashed into all three of them. I managed to stop but I was frozen. I just could not believe the carnage there in front of my very eyes; within seconds there was an eerie silence.

Debris was strewn all over the road; two people had been thrown from their cars into the road. One car had no side in it at all, and I could see an elderly gentleman hanging by his seat belt, very still and looking gaunt, his head and eyes seemed transfixed on me.

I can remember his face even today. I am quite ashamed that I could not offer him, or any of them, any assistance whatsoever, as I was totally frozen.

I must have been in total shock as it is not in my 'make-up' to ignore anyone in need but I did. I carefully drove through the debris, my eyes fixed forward trying to turn a 'blind eye' on those poor souls. When I got clear, I managed to pull into a lay-by very close to the accident but out of sight, and again that 'losing it' feeling hit me and I burst into tears.

It took me about 20 minutes to control myself and in the background I was aware of the emergency services with their bells and horns wailing as they attended the scene of the accident.

They were obviously tending to those poor souls. I hope they can forgive me for not helping them in their time of need. I am not very proud of my actions that night but for some reason I could not have done anything else. Every time I pass the scene of this tragedy, my thoughts go back to that terrible night. For, at the side of the road, some bereaved person has placed a wooden cross with a small brass nameplate on it. I often wonder if it is for the old man with the staring eyes.

TUESDAY 20TH JUNE, 2000

Up early, having had a bad night. I have been 'cat napping' most of it as I have been expecting the phone to ring with some dreadful news. I am only too thankful that it hasn't.

The old saying "No news is good news" – certainly in this instance it turned out to be true, as surely they would have called me if Mark had not got through the night. I had to know how Markie was, so I took up the phone then paused and thought,

"What am I going to say and how will I react if the news is not good?" I had to force myself to make the call.

"Good morning, I am Mark Holroyd's father, can you please tell me how he is?"

"Mark has had a peaceful night and there is little change in his condition."

I learnt later that this reply is standard procedure, generally used when someone enquires as to the state of a patient. They have to be very conservative as to how much information they can disclose over the phone.

Julie and Wendy went to see Mark during the day as I still had my company to run. That may seem a bit alien to some people but it is fact. I needed a distraction or I would have 'cracked up'; work gives me this as it occupies my mind, plus I have to keep telling myself

"There is nothing I could do for Mark even if I were there at his side."

The evening visit was easier as Markie had cleared the magic 48-hour hurdle. We found him in the same room, in the same position with the same probes and tubes and all of that 'foreign to me' machinery, which was doing Mark's breathing for him. The first good news was from the Sister in charge; she explained that the life support machine was now only doing 90% of his breathing. Mark was actually contributing 10% of his needs himself. Whilst we were watching Mark he moved his head, just a little, but the important thing to us was that he moved his head.

WEDNESDAY 21ST JUNE, 2000

My birthday, one I will never forget. From waking up I had decided that I would have no more birthdays until Mark could say "Happy Birthday Dad." So we put a hold on presents and celebrations.

To assist Mark in breathing, it was considered that a tracheotomy had to be performed. (That, in layman's terms, means a tube would be placed into Mark's windpipe via a hole in the lower front of his neck.) A simple procedure or so I was led to believe, but not for our boy. For no obvious reason, when Mark was taken to the theatre he suffered some sort of a trauma, so they had to call off the operation.

He was taken back to his ward and once again placed back on full ventilation, as he had lost the ability to contribute his 10%. A decision was made to try again when he had recovered from this setback.

Some birthday, I thought, as I drove home, then I remembered I'm not having any more birthdays.

Thursday 22nd June, 2000

I had a good meeting today at the hospital with a Senior Neurosurgeon. He spent a good hour talking about how complex the brain is and what the possibility was of Mark making a full recovery. He did not give me any great hopes but he did say,

"As Mark is a young man and by the looks of him a very fit one, he has a reasonable chance that he will improve from his present state."

"What sort of improvement can we expect and over what period," I enquired.

"That, sir, is a question that no-one can answer; not enough is known of the brain to even hazard a guess. There is one thing I can assure you of and that is that it will take a long time. I have known people to continue to improve for five to eight years before recovery stops."

"Five to eight years", I thought, "that is a hell of a long time. It looks like we are at the start of a very long and dusty road. I just hope that I and all the family are up to this massive challenge."

Marion preferred not to be present at the meeting, so on the way home she asked what we had talked about and what the Specialist's views might be as to the future. I had to give her an answer, as after 35 years of marriage you cannot tell lies and hope to get away with it.

"What do I tell her? Do I try to 'paint a pretty picture'? Or do I tell the truth as it was given to me earlier?"

I was in a total quandary. When I tried to speak, I couldn't; the words would not come out. Once again that dreadful feeling was welling up inside me. "I must stop the car," I thought, "or I am going to lose control." Thankfully a layby appeared and I quickly turned in and stopped.

I was too late now to control myself, but suddenly, in my mind, I was convinced that Markie was going to die. Sadly I blurted out,

"Marion, I know we are going to lose him, he is going to die."

Then once again I was overtaken with total grief and I 'lost it'. All I wanted to do was cry and cry and I did.

Regardless of Marion's presence and not considering how she must feel, I just cried and cried. She left me to my 'pain' and got out of the car, knowing she would have to let the situation take its course.

FRIDAY 23RD JUNE, 2000

Tracheotomy completed this morning. When I first saw it I thought, "I don't like the look of that."

It seems so alien to see someone you love dearly having to have his or her body mutilated just to stay alive. I will have to get used to it, as I am sure that things will probably get a lot worse before we get to the end of this journey.

Mark, I was told, performed like a hero in surgery and was back to providing something towards his breathing They didn't tell me how much but even a small contribution was better than nothing.

On the evening visit we got quite a shock, as until then Mark's head had been heavily bandaged. Tonight, the nurse had removed them and, silly as it sounds, his head looked even bigger. The scars from the operation were visible. He was a mess, to say the very least. Standing over him I felt so helpless.

"Oh God", I thought, "why my Markie?"

I was staring into his face when suddenly I noticed that his eyes were moving under his eyelids; this gave me quite a buzz Is this the first sign of recovery?

I found myself holding my breath, "Is Mark going to open his eyes? Is he about to come out of the coma?" A thousand and one thoughts passed through my brain.

"Mr Holroyd, are you all right, do you want a chair?" It was the Sister, the first one I had met on the night of the accident.

"Yes please, I just feel a bit peculiar. I thought for a few seconds that Mark was about to open his eyes."

She invited me to sit down, then vanished to get one of her now famous brews; she knew exactly when a strong cup of tea was called for. She joined me and we had a short chat.

"May I call you Peter?"

"Please do."

She got a chair and sat beside me. We talked for a short while about the family situation. She was so reassuring, explaining how she had found that people need signs of some sort of recovery to help them through the trauma.

"You will be willing things to happen and sadly all too often these signs are in your imagination." I nodded to affirm my understanding.

"You may be seeing things that aren't there. Please, only believe positive signs of improvement that you yourself have seen, and you know that it definitely happened."

"Good advice", I thought. She went on to say,

"Try not to get excited at what people tell you."

Again, I gave a nod of confirmation.

"If possible, try not to visit alone, as if there are signs of something positive happening you need to have someone to confirm that. Only believe the indisputable and never let your imagination run riot with you, just actual events and positive signs are what you need, never try to see something that does not exist."

Fine words of wisdom from a very kind and learned lady. I will remember her advice.

I must tell the girls all she has told me. Hopefully, we will all endeavour to follow her advice and accept it as our new benchmark. It was then that I decided to keep a diary to allow the family to record all events and observations relating to Markie's recovery.

Saturday 24th June, 2000

Arrived at about 13 00 hrs to find Mark had been placed on a much smaller ventilator.

"Good news, I thought, it means that he has cleared the first hurdle."

"He is now providing about 50% of his breathing requirements." Sister told me. She went on to say,

"The sooner we can get a patient breathing for themselves the better, as we do not want the sufferers to become too dependent on the ventilator to do all the work."

All this good transfer of vital information on subjects unfamiliar to us, but very important, enabled us, the family, to feel part of the 'team'. We felt good to be involved and 'kept up to speed' with the events, whilst on this journey down the already familiar dusty road.

SUNDAY 25TH JUNE, 2000

Wendy and I went to see Markie today, as some of Marion's family were down from Scotland. Good of them to come down and offer their support in our time of need.

We were doing our silent vigil by Mark's bed when suddenly his body jerked violently, so much so that it startled us to the extent of making us both gasp with shock. Funny really, as when you are performing a bedside wait, you are willing something to happen and when it does you get one hell of a kicking, or should I say one hell of a buzz? Whatever it is, it certainly 'jump starts' you.

Mark is doing a lot of coughing today; I suppose it is a good sign, as at least he is reacting to clear whatever it is that is making him cough. Sister asked,

"Was Mark a smoker?"

"Yes," Wendy confirmed.

"How would you class him, moderate, normal or heavy?"

"About 20 to 30 a day I would say, how would you class that?"

"Heavy, I think we had better try to clear his lungs a little."

"How?" I wondered.

We did not have to wait long to find out. Sister returned with a strange contraption which had a pipe connected to a large glass container, which was empty, but not for long. The pipe was carefully inserted into Mark's lungs via the tracheotomy and the contraption was turned on. Shock upon shock, this machine was a sort of vacuum cleaner or suction pump. I would never have guessed how effective such a gadget is. It was working okay, as globules of phlegm were sucked from Mark's chest and deposited in the glass receptacle.

"Not a pretty sight. If I had seen this contraption working years ago, I would have found it very easy to stop smoking. The sight of all this 'grunge' coming of Mark's chest would, I feel, be enough to encourage any smoker to stop," I thought. When I stopped smoking, it took over a year to get rid of the urge to have the odd fag. We left after seeing this performance as it made us both feel quite sick. Not just the fact of what we had seen, but the feeling of being so helpless to do anything positive for Mark.

MONDAY 26TH JUNE, 2000

I visited Mark in the evening; no noticeable change. Sister informed me that they were seeking a bed at The Intensive Care Ward at Burnley General Hospital. So Mark might be moved there at short notice.

TUESDAY 27TH JUNE, 2000

Got a phone call in the afternoon to say that they had got a bed for Mark at Burnley. As Wendy was off to visit Mark today, I called her to give her the news prior to her visit. When she was ready to leave Preston, the Sister rang me to say that the probe in Mark's head had been removed, as it was no longer required to monitor the pressure. She also said that the feed pipes had been re-routed; they were now entering his body via his nose rather than his mouth. She closed after telling me that the ambulance had just turned up to transport Mark back to Burnley.

Visited Mark that night to find him in the Intensive Care Ward. He was fast asleep so we did not stay.

THE WAITING GAME

Life slipped into a routine for the next few days, as Mark appeared to be sleeping a lot. It made me recall what my Mam used to say.

"If you're not well, go to bed; sleep's best cure in't world."

As Mark was in the Intensive Care Unit, it seemed inappropriate to have a conversation whilst in the Ward. So we kept our visiting to a minimum, a difficult thing to do, as you suffer from the terrible urge to be by his side. So, rather than keep a bedside vigil, I used to go to the hospital and sit in a small seating area by the ward. All this waiting and thinking kept me drifting back to the past. One night I was back in Aden again to when a Quteibe tribesman or men brought us under fire.

Regardless of the amount of firepower we directed at our target, it was to no avail, as just as we were about to move on, our 'friend' decided we were staying put. The Quteibe or 'Wolves of the Radfan' were, and still are, very adept at fieldcraft, shooting and generally knowing the land they work in. They strut about with their rifles over their shoulders, holding the gun by the muzzle, their clothing loose and baggy, drawn in at the waist with a strong belt on which would hang a curved dagger. All finished of by rounds and rounds of ammunition in bandoleers across their bodies; a formidable enemy and difficult to take on. We treated them with a lot of caution and secretly with a degree of respect. These men know nothing other than a life of fighting someone Who they fight does not seem important to them just so long as the cause seems right.

We were in a pretty tight spot and there would be little doubt that our position would have been relayed back to other tribesmen looking for a kill.

A quick referral back to my 'boss' on the radio and I was given the okay for more support. This man or men were in for one hell of a shock, as my boss had given me the 'rubber stamp' to call an air strike.

Our co-ordinates were relayed back to H.M.S. Ark Royal, a strike aircraft carrier lying just off Aden. We very gingerly crawled about, laying down high visibility cloths to direct the aircraft to the target. All we could do now was wait. When you consider that the pilots have to scramble their aircraft, take off, find your location and then hit the delegated target, you could probably estimate an hour's wait.

Don't believe it. Twenty-one minutes later, explosive rockets and heavy gunfire devastated the whole of the target area.

Strange how you see the results of your request being fulfilled before you hear the aircraft. The noise is something I cannot describe, other than to say it is horrendous; the planes pass over you so low that I felt I could jump up and touch them. Then came the re-run, and again I watched in awe at the devastation that these aircraft and their pilots inflicted.

A much higher fly past over our position, a wiggle of the wings, and then total silence.

Decision time and I didn't need a lot of persuading, as to stay here would not be wise, since there is a strong possibility that 'old baggy pants' could have survived the air strike.

"Stand by to move back."

The lads started to crawl away from their existing position as our friend could have set his weapon upon any of us.

"Barlow, Sandy, prepare to lay down smoke to our left, let me know when you are ready."

I watched and waited for them to get their smoke grenades from their pouches.

"Ready," shouted Barlow. Sandy echoed the call.

"Stand by to lay smoke to our left on three, one, two three."

We waited for the grenades to explode and emit their thick grey cloud to obscure our movements from our friend.

"Okay, stand by, follow me."

Again, no persuasion necessary. In unison we were on our feet and running as fast as our cumbersome gear would allow. No fire came in from the enemy; maybe the air strike had been successful.

Sadly, I felt no remorse for that poor soul at that point in time, as my only interest was to put as much space between him and me as I could.

We made good progress, as we were all very high on adrenaline created by our encounter with the enemy: an encounter that we would have to re-live on many more occasions.

I never thought I would be glad to get back to Fort Dhala, our make-shift home on the top of a high feature in the Radfan Mountains.

Mark continued to improve very slowly for the rest of the week. With just the tiniest of signs of movement from Markie, I found that I got a little excited. Not just me, but Julie and Wendy also.

Marion was a little more cautious than us in accepting any signs of improvement. She probably had the right approach; she did, however, find it very difficult to visit Mark on her own.

Little signs, like Mark moving his feet slightly. On one occasion whilst taking a blood sample, the needle penetrated his skin and he jerked his arm. Sad to see but at least I knew Mark had retained the feeling of pain.

One of the things that tended to stress me was his tracheotomy. On occasions it used to get really messy but I had a horrible urge to try to clean it. I was not allowed to do this, so I kept asking the nurses to clean it for me. They must have found me a right 'pain in the butt', but on no occasion did they refuse to comply with my requests.

Sunday 2nd July, 2000

Mark had improved so much since arriving at Burnley that it was thought that his life was no longer in danger. So, on the move again, this time to the High Dependency Ward.

A promotion, as I cared to look at it. He was out of the forest now but he was still in a dense wood.

Off the ventilator completely now and Mark is supporting his own breathing. This he does via his tracheotomy, by placing a facemask over the hole in his neck. Moisturised oxygen is then sent to the mask. This not only ensures that oxygen gets into Mark's blood and the fact that it is moisturised is helping to break up all the phlegm on his chest. They are still clearing out his lungs with the horrible 'lung vacuum', as I call it, and it is not a pretty sight.

It was the final of the Euro 2000 Cup that day, and one of the nurses found a radio from somewhere and put it on Mark's side cupboard. What a nice gesture, I wonder how she knew that Markie enjoyed a good football match. I remember thinking at the time,

"What a very kind and lovely thing to do."

Monday 3rd July, and that week

Wendy got a great surprise today as, when she was with Mark in the afternoon, his right eye opened, just a little but enough to get her quite excited. I must admit that it gave me a good feeling too when she rang me with an update on her visit.

On our evening visit, Mum was holding his hand when she got quite emotional, she turned to me and said,

"He is squeezing my hand, not hard but he is definitely squeezing it." Her voice was slightly broken with emotion and we both stood over Markie watching the slight twitching movement of his hand.

Tuesday and Wednesday saw little change in Mark.

His scalp and his skin condition had started to become terribly dry and flaky, so we agreed to ask for the dermatologist to see Mark. He duly came and examined Mark and prescribed a strange concoction like a sticky oily cream for his problem. This had to be rubbed onto his scalp daily. He provided a big tub of cream for his skin. Both worked fine.

Up to now we had requested that only family could visit Mark. The only exception was on Tuesday. Mark's best mate, another Mark, better known to us all as Enty, called to say he had a day off. So Mum and I took him in to see Mark. I know it came as quite a shock to poor old Enty but he 'took it on the chin'. He watched over Mark for some time before saying,

"Hiya, Mark, don't worry about owt, I'll sort things out, and if you want owt, just ask."

Cracking words, I just wished that Mark could ask for something.

Whilst still on the High Dependency Ward, we attempted to cap off Mark's tracheotomy but failed miserably. He lasted only a minute before he started to show trauma and the cap had to be removed. They informed us that they must continue trying to get him to breathe naturally and the only way to achieve this is to keep trying.

"We will keep trying and we will get there, rest assured."

Beds in High Dependency Wards are always in great demand. As Mark was improving it was decided to move on yet again. Yes! More promotion, this time to Ward 22, a recovery ward. Patients come to this ward to get over accidents and operations. As Mark still needed a lot of nursing care, he was placed in a small room of his own, suitably sited close to where the nurses could keep an eye on him.

By now we had got a good routine going for Mark. Julie would visit through the morning, Wendy in the afternoon whilst Marion looked after Wendy's baby, Georgina, followed by Mum and me in the evening.

HORSES, CARS AND COPS

On occasions when I visited Mark alone, I would tell him all sorts of tales from my past. I remember on one occasion, I felt determined to get a smile or some reaction from him. So off I went back in to my past to find something that might do the trick.

It was 1958. I was almost through my training; and I was in the King's Squad, stationed at Eastney Barracks, Southsea, near Portsmouth.

A chum and I had been out on the town, seeking some female company. We must have been total optimists, hoping to find female company in a Naval Port. The only women that were free were the ones you had to pay for, and that was not what we wanted or could afford.

So, during our search for true love, we managed to get somewhat 'three sheets to the wind' and very happy. Derby, my mate, called that because he came from Derby, and I, were wending and weaving our way back to Barracks when we came across a travelling fairground.

As it was quite late, and the fairground was in darkness, the temptation to have a go on it was too great.

We decided that we should enjoy a free session. I rather took a shine to a small black and white horse so I promptly got astride the poor thing. Derby, being an ex-car mechanic, went for a small Noddy type car.

Just having a play on these soon turned to boredom. So, we thought nothing more but to take them back to the barracks with us. They detached easily from the carousel and off we went along the seafront, me carrying my trusty steed and Derby pedalling his car.

We were making great progress when our world suddenly became illuminated. The flashing lights of a police van and a police car approached us from opposite directions. The thought entered my head to escape, but to where? The only way to go was in the sea, and I was not that desperate. The van mounted the wide promenade and stopped alongside the horse and me.

"Good morning, Royal," bellowed a massive Police Sergeant ('Royal' or 'Bootneck' are terms used by serving or ex-Royal Navy personnel when referring to a Royal Marine).

"May I ask why you are carrying your horse?"

Stuck for words and wanting some banter, I replied, "It's knackered, Sergeant, and I am taking it to the knackery."

"Well done, lad, what a good Royal you are, I'll give you a lift." With that I was swiftly helped into the back of the van along with my horse, whom I had christened 'Trigger'.

"Can I presume that the 'bootneck' in the car up ahead is your mate?" asked the Constable who was driving the van.

"Yes, he's my chum, Derby." The other police vehicle was keeping a 'watching brief' over the actions. Slowly, the Constable manoeuvred the van in front of Derby, who was happily pedalling away along the 'prom'. A quick call from the siren and on went the 'Stop Police' sign.

I sat on the tail of the van whilst the Sergeant approached the car. Derby was a star, he waved his right arm, giving the slowing down signal, then he came to a halt.

"Excuse me, 'Royal', is this your car?"

"No, it belongs to a mate of mine and he has lent it to me to go home in."

"Are you aware that your lights are not working?"

"Oh! Yes, replied Derby, that's why I am on the promenade. There's a lot less traffic on here."

By now, the policemen from the other car had joined us. One in particular could not stop laughing. His laugh was so infectious that it got us all going. I had tried to get over to Derby to help him out of the car but due to the amount of ale I had drunk and the situation we were in, I found that I could not stay on my feet. I fell to the ground, pulling Derby on top of me. We all just rocked about laughing for a good 10 minutes.

The end came, or should I say the first part ended, with Derby and I being dropped off near the Barracks by our new friends, the Constable and the Sergeant. They didn't drop us too close to the Barracks, as they felt it fit to overlook the incident. The Sergeant said they would take 'Trigger' and Noddy Car back to the fairground and explain to the owner that it was just a harmless prank. They seemed convinced that they would see the funny side of the incident. However, that was not to be the case.

Mark seemed to have been listening to my story but sadly I got no reaction from him in this instance.

"Could he hear me?" I wondered. "Had he completely lost most of his senses? Was he damaged that badly that he could not understand what I had been telling him? Who knows? God might, but God, he seems to be keeping his cards very, very close to his chest." All these thought were going through my mind.

I went home that night with a sad, sad, heart but with the determination to keep trying and trying. "I must get Markie back, at any cost."

THURSDAY 6TH JULY, 2000

Ward 22 had some amazing staff. On one occasion I noticed a lady who looked very familiar. It turned out that she used to work in a shop that I supplied. Allison, the lady in question, used to call and collect goods at our warehouse and she and Mark got on ever so well. She was very upset about Mark's accident; you could see the sadness in her face whilst working with him.

Another girl, who had very special qualities, was Olive Oil (not her real name I hasten to add). She was so special, that I cannot remember her names, only her nickname. Nurse Olive Oil's speciality was looking after Mark's feet. An unenviable task, as his feet were a mess, to say the least. Besides her other duties and when she had time, she would spend hours working on his feet to rid them of dead skin.

Mark had lived in his own house with some of his 'so-called friends' (more on that subject later).

As a young man he was not the best at looking after himself. He was fond of fast cars, fast food and even fast women; all the things young men enjoy. The last of most young men's priorities is personal hygiene. Mark's feet were at the bottom of all lists, so Olive was a Saviour and a Godsend.

Ivan, a male nurse in Ward 22, was also 'a doer'. His aim was to get Mark off his tracheotomy and, on a daily basis, or at least when he was on duty, he would try to cap it off. I remember, on one occasion when he had placed the cap on the end of the 'trachea', he was standing at the foot of the bed with a confident smirk on his face,

"Almost a minute now," he said proudly. He spoke too soon; as no sooner had the words left his mouth, than Markie gave an almighty cough. The cap fired off like a bullet from a gun and it was bang on target, it smacked into Ivan's forehead leaving him 'gaucking' in great surprise and shock. If Mark had been aware of what he had done he would have been in fits of laughter, along with all who witnessed the incident.

Still a lot of concern over Mark's chest. He was still 'rattling' away, and coughing up globules of phlegm. Doctors examined his chest at regular intervals and their advice was to continue using the mask with the moisturised oxygen, and this should eventually break it all up.

Firing the cap off 'trachea' became Mark's 'party piece'. I seriously don't think he was aware of what he was doing. When new members of staff got appointed to look after Mark, we would forget to warn them of his trick. It was written on the Daily Regime that 'capping him off' had to be carried out at least once during their shift. They were instructed to cap him off, start the timer, and stand at the foot of the bed and watch Mark for any signs of stress. If he got agitated in any way, then the cap had to be removed and the length of time capped off had to be recorded. As a member of the family was usually with Mark, there was no danger involved other than to the poor nurse being 'shot' by Markie's new weapon. The look of surprise on their faces was a treat when they 'got smacked' and it gave us an 'uplift' in those trying times.

If Mark is aware of what he is doing, then he deserves a lot of credit for his new improved 'party piece'.

His chest was still very loose and on occasions he would cough up some phlegm. He soon learnt that he now had a very lethal weapon. He has now become very adept at firing out the phlegm in the same way as he fires off his cap. I became convinced that he could target people. His favourite one was 'Olive', not because he objected to his feet being massaged but because she always stood at the foot of the bed to carry out this task.

When Olive was not available to do his feet, Wendy, Mark's twin sister would apply the oil. She had a canny way of knowing when a 'bullet' was on its way and would duck before it hit her.

TUESDAY 11TH JULY, 2000

Mark is beginning to show more signs of improvement today. I gave permission to shave his head yesterday, and he certainly looks different. He has not been shaved bald but I cannot recall his hair being this short, ever. I think our Markie looks 'well fit'; he looks more composed somehow and at peace with himself. Other little 'pluses' have appeared; there is now a slight movement in his legs. His left eye is open a fraction more. Little things to some people but giant improvements as far as I am concerned. The 'physio' people had tried to sit Mark on the edge of his bed today to see if that might stimulate something. He only managed a few minutes and he required a lot of support, but it is all going forward. We have to try everything conceivable to bring Markie forward, and bring him forward we will.

Told Mark the results of the story about 'Trigger', my horse, and Derby's car whilst I sat with him that night.

"Left right, left right, left right," the Royal Marine Regimental Sergeant Major bellowed out as we were quickly marched into the Adjutant's Office.

Derby and I had been 'rumbled'. It turned out that the fairground owner was not too pleased about our antics with his horse and car. When 'our new-found' friend, the Police Sergeant, took them back and explained what had gone on, the man insisted that he wanted to press charges against us. This left the Sergeant no alternative but to seek us out.

The morning parade of all ranks was delayed by the R.S.M. to allow the Sergeant to walk along the lines of men in the hope that he would point us out. He was not that much of a 'new-found friend', as if he had been he would have turned a 'blind eye' to Derby and me. He didn't and picked us out with great ease. The result was that we were speed marched off to the Guardroom to await our fate.

In incidents such as this you are looked upon as bringing the Corps into disrepute, something frowned upon and taken very seriously in the Royal Marines.

Being on a charge always seems a little unfair, as the only voices you hear are first, the R.S.M., who shouts loud commands at you, then the voice of the Adjutant giving you your sentence. We were not clamped in irons or anything that drastic, but we given extra duties in the 'galley' (that's the kitchen) for the next seven evenings. I had never ever thought about how many potatoes can be consumed in one mealtime. I am now an expert in this field: the answer is a hell of a lot.

News of our pending Court Case came through sooner rather than later. In secret I had been hoping that it had been overlooked. No such chance.

Off to Court we went, escorted by two guards and an Officer.

I felt so stupid standing there in my best uniform with Derby by my side. The case against us was read out, and I heard a few sniggers from within the court. Well, it is not every day you have two Royal Marines in court on charges such as this,

"Marine Holroyd, is this the horse in question?" The question came from the bench.

"At this distance I could not be certain, Sir. I find it difficult to be certain."

"Perhaps if you got closer you could recognise it?"

"I believe with a closer look I might be able to confirm if it is the horse in question."

At this stage I was invited to give the horse a close examination.

"Well?"

"Sir, I am confident that this is the horse that I know as Trigger." More sniggers.

I thought to myself, "I'm beginning to enjoy this."

Derby was put to the same test but, unlike me, he was asked to get into the car. If you have never seen a Royal Marine in his 'best blues' trying to get into a roundabout car you have never lived. After a lot of grunting and squeezing he finally managed it.

That did it, one person started to laugh and it spread like a forest fire. The whole court was in an uproar; even the people presiding over the case could not restrain themselves from a smile.

A break for 15 minutes was announced.

When we convened, the room was back to normal. Whilst we had been out, the wise men on the bench had deliberated our case and decided on a verdict.

"Marine Holroyd, we find you guilty."

"Marine Derby, you also have been found guilty. I sentence you both to pay five shillings each."

I could have kissed the Judge but thought the better of it, "I am in enough trouble for one day, without going mad and kissing the Judge." I felt such relief as we were marched out of court. Someone outside shouted, "Well done lads, that was bloody good 'crack'."

Left, right, left, right, left, right. The R.S.M. was marching us back in to see the Adjutant.

"I believe the court case was a very humorous occasion; perhaps another 14 days' extra duties will wipe the smile off your faces."

The R.S.M. bellowed out,

"About turn, quick march, left right, left right, left right."

'Spud bashing' didn't seem as bad the second time around, as we kept bursting out into fits of laughter when we talked about the court case.

Mark seemed to have listened to the story, as he stayed awake all the time I relayed it to him. He showed no positive reaction, not even a slight movement The only thing I did notice was his left eye seemed to move about a little, or was I imagining this? As I am alone with him I cannot ask for a second opinion.

Sunday 9th July, 2000

Mark opened his right eye a fraction today. He has developed a hell of a cough and his chest is 'rasping' away. It sounds pretty rough and on occasions he is fetching more phlegm.

"Better out than in" my Mam would have said. I have to agree with that. I just wish it didn't make me feel a little sick when he does it.

Monday and that week

Feet moved slightly on my visit, Wendy had noticed that when she was here. Again, all little bits but I suppose that's how he will progress, very slowly and just a little bit at a time. It is so frustrating at times, you feel like saying.

"Come on, Markie, give us something positive, sit up and say something, even if it is to tell me to F off."

On Wednesday they 'wired' Mark up to a new monitor. This machine would 'keep an eye' on Mark's heart rate and his oxygen blood levels. I find in this sort of situation that you collect information and get told lots of things. On occasions, because of your lack of knowledge of nursing, hospitals, medical terms, names of drugs and the names of various forms of treatments, you get very confused and start to 'drown'.

"I don't want to know all of this jargon, I just want our Markie to get well and come home."

The urge to say that is difficult to control, you feel like saying it but you don't. These people who are giving you all of this information are doing it for you. They just want to 'keep you in the picture'. So you have to accept it and get used to it, as it is not going to go away, not overnight anyway.

Mark's scalp and his skin have improved over the past week. The Dermatologist who came up with the creams and concoctions is certainly a very learned person.

The Great Escape

I was always a lad with a 'wanderlust'. My first introduction to education was when my Mam took me to Rosehill Junior School, a distance of about 3 miles away. I am not sure what age I was, but there was something I was certainly positive about and that was 'I hated it'. I was probably about four or five. The school rules were that we had a compulsory sleep in the afternoons and that was not really 'my cup of tea'.

"Come along, children, it's time for your nap." I can hear her now

The small beds were in a long passage-like room, which was glass-fronted with sliding doors onto our play area outside. Curtains were drawn, but they were very thin and it did not go dark when they were drawn.

On the first 'Escape'

I call it that because I felt that I was a prisoner. As soon as the teacher had left the room, I put my pre-arranged plan into action. On with my shoes, then I moved down to the last of the sliding doors. I knew it would be open, as I had checked it earlier. Carefully I opened the door, just enough to slip out. Inside, I was full of the fear of getting captured, but I found that I was enjoying it. Butterflies were racing about in my belly. I understand now that this was my first 'sight' of adrenaline. Into the bushes, then carefully and slowly moving towards the road, taking great care not to disturb them. Any movement of them may alert one of my mentors. If they did, I would probably be captured. The alternative would be to give myself up.

"Surrender", I thought. "No way, if they come near, I will just have to run for it."

Dropping down the small wall onto the pavement:

"I'm free, but where do I go from here? I know, I will make my way home down the track leading to Scotts Park via a small farm and farmyard."

All was going to plan until I got to the farm, then all hell was let loose. Geese, they came from out of nowhere and raced towards me at high speed.

"I must run or I am dead!"

So run I did, just as fast as my little legs would carry me. Out through the gate down a track heading for a bridge that would take me into the Park. I was running as fast as I could, but I knew I was not going fast enough. The beasts were getting closer and closer all the time, looking bigger and bigger and 'shouting' louder and louder.

"What will they do if they get me?"

By now the adrenaline had turned to fear.

"I have never heard of anybody being killed and eaten by a goose," was just one of my thoughts.

The gate to the bridge looked massive, as it loomed closer.

"Would it be locked? Would I be able to push it open?"

Two of the geese had got in front of me by now.

"Oh no, they are going to cut me off!"

I finally got to the gate, but by now these 'hissing' monsters surrounded me.

"There's nothing for it, I am going to have to get my back to the gate and fight them off whilst I open it."

I was lashing out with my feet and shouting out as loud as I could. I must have done enough. I got to the gate, turned to push it open with my back, whilst still kicking out and shouting. The geese had backed off and were walking back to the farm. Safely on the bridge now with the gate firmly shut, I stood and watched as the beasts retreated. In fear or relief, I found myself shouting abuse at them.

"If my Mam heard me using such words, she would 'kill me'," I thought, "but that would be better than being eaten by a herd of geese."

Mark had certainly been listening to me. I don't know how I know, but I just had a gut feeling that he had.

"I'll continue tomorrow night, Markie, that's if you're up to it."

Thursday 13th July, 2000

Julie was first to visit today and she got herself very excited. She rang me to say

"Markie squeezed my hand really hard Dad. He squeezed it that hard that I burst into tears," she added. "It was not with pain I cried, it was with great joy, as it is the very first positive thing that Markie has done to me since the accident."

"That's wonderful, my Jewel," (my pet name for her).

"Dad, does it mean he is going to be okay?"

"Too early to say, Julie, and I don't want you getting too high, as if you fall it will hurt. So just a bit at a time and I will be a 'happy chappy'."

Wendy got quite excited too. She wrote in the diary that Mark had opened his eye a little more and that on close inspection it was much clearer. He also gave her three good yawns and moved his legs a little.

I talked to Alison (the nurse) that evening and she said

"Your Mark has had a good day today, not 100 per cent though, as when I was cleaning his teeth, he closed his mouth on the swab and wouldn't let go. I bet it took me a good 10 minutes to persuade him to let me have it."

"Good for you, Markie," I thought.

As Markie was reasonably aware, I concluded the Great Escape Story.

Now safely in the Park, I had to decide where to go from here.

"My Mam always collects me from school; how am I going to get around that?" I thought. "Perhaps I could get back near the school and pretend I have been there all of the time and just appear when she comes to get me. How can I do that, the geese will get me and kill me? There must be another way to school, but I don't know it."

I sat on a bench near the Band Pavilion pondering my future. At last I decided that I would go home and try to bluff my way through it.

"Hi ya, Mam, I wasn't feeling very well, so the teacher brought me home."

"Oh yeah, that's funny because your teacher has just been here to tell me that you had vanished from school, you little bugger."

"Oh heck, what do I say to that?" I thought.

"What's more, young man, the Headmaster had to bring her here in his car and he is not very pleased. He wants us both at school tomorrow to decide what he should do with you. You've done it now lad, get yourself upstairs while I ponder on it."

"You've done it now, Peter." It was my sister Pam. "I reckon you will get the strap for that."

'The strap' was a big leather 'picking strap'. It had come off a weaving machine. The part it played was to fling the shuttle across the machine. My Mam had another use for it and that was to discipline her seven offspring.

"Don't get me wrong, Markie, my Mam was far from being a bully. In fact, she was more like a judge as she would seek the views of the innocent ones in the family before deciding what to do with the wrong doer."

Our Fred came for me.

"Come on, Pete, me Mam wants you in the front room."

"Front room. Oh heck, this is serious."

My Mam was sat on her piano stool with the dreadful smelly picking strap across her knees. (It used to smell of onions, why I never knew.) Granville, Raymond, Joan, Norma, Pam and our Fred all stood in a semicircle in front of her.

"We all feel that you have let the family down with what you have done today and we want a proper explanation as to why you did it."

I then told them my tale from start to finish. They all looked on as I told them in detail of how I had averted being killed by the geese. No one laughed, as Mam would not have allowed that. When I had finished, they all looked at Mam to see what she would say.

"Peter (she always gave us our full name when she was serious), what you have done is wrong, very wrong. You have frightened your Headmaster and your teacher by vanishing. You have cost me money (not good news), as I have had to telephone the school to put their minds at rest and you have put the Holroyd name to shame. We have all talked as to what should be done, but in the light of your 'Great Escape' from the killer geese, I think you have been put through enough fear for today."

"What a relief," I thought.

"Now get out, the lot of you."

I felt quite special that day, as my brothers and sisters made me tell them about my adventure over and over again and, every time I did, I made it a little glossier.

Again, not too sure what Mark made of my story. I know he can hear me and I know I am doing him no harm just talking to him. I bet, in the not too distant future, he will quiz me about the truth of my stories. One thing I know is that he would never 'catch me out', as there is no way I could tell him lies. The stories are all true. They have to be. Hate to think what he would think of me when he does recover enough to ask me about my tales on his road to recovery. I can say to him in all honesty:

"Every story I have told you, Markie, has been perfectly true. They are all about me, not all nice things, some very scary, but all true, believe me."

Markie's doing extremely well with the capping off of his trachy. By Friday 14th July, we were able to cope with it capped off for 3 hours. Not a lot of action over the weekend, other than that Mark is slightly more active with his left arm. Abdullah (he is the big coloured nurse), seems to enjoy the same TV characters as Mark does. Star Trek, South Park and the Simpsons are among their favourites, so he has agreed to put them on if he is on duty. He also suggested that a photograph of Dannielle might be a good idea. Wendy has agreed to sort that out.

Kellie is the mother of Dannielle, but sadly she and Mark split up some time ago (more on that later). She said that 'Danni', as we affectionately call her, has been asking,

"When can I go to see my Daddy?"

I rang Kellie when I got this request and explained:

"Kellie, Mark is not a pretty sight yet and we don't want little Danni to go to see her Dad just yet. Can you tell her that he is sleeping most of the time, or that children are not allowed on the ward he is on? Tell her that Grandad will take her in as soon as they move Daddy. I feel that whilst Mark has the feed tube up his nose and the noisy trachy in his throat, it may be too much of a shock for her."

Thankfully, Kellie agreed with our views.

MONDAY 17TH JULY, 2000

Wendy and Enty went in this afternoon. Wendy rang me to say,

"Dad, it was brilliant today. I took Enty in to see Markie and when Enty said 'Hi ya Mark', he opened his eye to about twice its normal state. I bet it was 80%." She was very excited over this.

On our evening visit, the Sister explained that they had not capped off his trachy as he had been very tired today. Wendy and Enty must have had the best out of Mark today.

TUESDAY 18TH JULY, 2000

I got a big brick in my throat today. When I went to visit Mark that evening, he was fast asleep, so I took up the diary to update myself on the day's events. It was Wendy's entry that did it. It goes as follows:

"When Enty and I went to see Mark today, he already had his eye open, about 95%. He also kept moving his eye, as if trying to look at me. When I moved closer to him to stroke his face, it was as if he was really looking at me. It was as if he knew that it was I close to him, stroking his face. The emotion I felt was overwhelming, I had a mixture of emotions, hope and my real love for him. I nearly cried. I told him how proud I was that he had done this, and for the first time since the accident, I was able to kiss his lips. You could tell he was tired as his eye kept rolling as Georgina's do when she is tired."

Talk about nearly crying, I did when I read this. It is so compassionate and true; she has said exactly what we feel. Wendy's feelings must be very strong as she is Mark's twin, so their affiliation to each other must be different, having shared Mum's womb must make their bonding much stronger.

The duty sister brought me up to speed on the day's events and told me that the doctor who did the rounds that morning has said it was time that Mark should move from the nursing care ward to Rakehead Rehabilitation.

"Rakehead Rehabilitation, where is that?"

"Come look out the window."

We moved over to look out, the sister pointed down to a group of low-lying bungalow-type buildings.

"That is Rakehead, but to get a bed in there is virtually impossible, as there are only a few rooms and a long, long waiting list. You have now got Mark to the point where it is sink or swim, and you will find from now on that you are going to have to fight all the way. I can tell you this from past experience.

No-one likes the situation, but it is happening all the time now. We are short on three main ingredients. One, Nurses, two, Doctors and three, Money. So, don't give in, Peter, and don't accept second best, you must fight for Mark's sake."

"Thanks luv," was about all I could come back with at that moment.

"If my bosses heard me talking to you in this manner, I would be 'down the road', so please keep this conversation to yourselves."

"Don't worry, Sister," Marion said. "I've known that bugger for over 30 years and he can and will fight. Rest assured Markie would get what he needs."

With that vote of confidence coming from Marion, who has always been a woman of few words, it seems I have no alternative but to fight.

THE FIGHT

Let the battle commence was what I felt the following day. I started by going to Rakehead and requesting an interview with the man in charge. I then spent most of the day phoning and pestering his secretary. I kept getting 'fobbed off' with a myriad of excuses. My persistence continued the next day. I know that she thought I was a pain in the arse, but that was of no consequence. I didn't care what she thought. Eventually we got to know each other quite well and even got on first-name terms.

"I'm winning her over," I thought.

On the third day I won. I did not call her, she actually called me.

"Peter, I have got you an appointment with Doctor A. He will see you on Friday morning at 10.30."

"You're a darling. Thanks J."

You are probably thinking that I have a bad memory for names. This is not the case. I am purposely not using their names nor the correct ones, as it would be unethical to do so, especially where the Health Care and nursing staff are concerned.

I pondered during the time up to having the meeting of how I was going to approach Dr A. Marion and I agreed that we would have to go with our 'begging bowls' thrust out and try to get some compassion out of him. This was not my normal way of getting things done but then again it is far from a normal situation. It is our Mark's future life at stake.

THURSDAY 20TH JULY, 2000

RUN ASHORE

Mark was quite awake on my visit, so I decided that I would try to humour him in some way.

It was late December or early January 1961 and trouble had broken in Dar-Es-Salam, Tanganyika. The President's army had revolted and had taken over. At this point, what we could do about it had not yet been sorted out. Forty-five Commando were shipped out of Aden on an Aircraft Carrier. We met up with the Carrier in Mombasa Harbour and joined the crowded ship. Beds were non-existent, so we had to adopt any free space we could find to sleep. With no specific timetable to stick to, we were allowed shore leave but not before the whole of the Ship's Company and the embarked Commando had been lectured by the ship's Medical Officer. We were advised that the 'ladies' of Mombasa who earned their living selling sex, were to be given a wide berth, as they were famous for carrying just about every venereal disease known to man.

"So do not be lured into their beds or you will possibly meet your maker and I don't mean your parents."

"Going ashore, Ollie?" It was Bungy Williams, an old squaddy of mine.

"Why not, I'm bored shitless on this thing."

We had a good wander around and checked out all the places of interest. The most impressive to me were the giant tusks spanning the road leading into Mombasa. Soon bored with our sightseeing, we decided on a few beers. The bars were filthy and haunted by the now infamous ladies of leisure, all trying to sell their wares.

"Sorry, Bungy, I can't put up with this shit hole."

"Me neither, let's see what we can find."

"Here is a man who will know the score."

Coming up the track/road was an old three-badge matelot. (That's one who has seen at least 12 years' service.)

"Hi, Jack. (An affectionate name used by marines when addressing a sailor.) What's the crack with entertainment in this crap hole?"

"Follow me, Royal, the only decent ale is in the night clubs and I am heading for the best in town."

We latched onto our newly found friend and soon arrived at the club Its name was 'The Best In Town'. We soon made ourselves at home, well not really at home because this club had its share of 'Ladies of the night', but these were of higher standard than those in the bars.

"Look at the arse on that," said Bungy as he 'eyed up' a very rounded young coloured girl.

"Some farting tool there, Bungy, but it's look not touch and I'm going to make certain of that as I happen to be your minder tonight. I know how your brain thinks when you get full of ale. So none of your antics, like 'Lead on Dick, I'll follow'." That was one of Bungy's favourite sayings when he was seeking some poor unsuspecting female for his pleasure and hopefully some physical relief.

I think I must be boring Markie as he has fallen asleep.

"Not to worry, son, you rest. I'll catch up on that tale later. God bless you." With that I left and made my way home, having a little chuckle to myself as I re-lived the time in Mombasa.

The door entry system at Rakehead took me back to that dreadful first visit to Preston Royal. I introduced our arrival to the metal microphone on the wall.

"Come in please."

The door clicked and we entered. We were met by J., she is the assistant to Mr A.

"Good to see you, Mr Holroyd, you are a very persistent man."

"Hello J, thanks for what you have done, this is my wife Marion. Unlike me, Marion is a much more tolerant person."

"That's probably just as well. Come on I will take you in to see Mr A."

Mr A. was a small man, I seemed to dwarf him when he stood up and offered his hand. We sat down and prepared ourselves for the battle to commence.

"Thank you for giving us the opportunity to come along and explain our plight."

"I am very much aware of your reason for being here, as I have looked at your son's case notes and I feel that we must offer him a bed and soon."

"What no fight?" I thought.

"First, I must explain what Rakehead is all about. Mark has suffered an acceleration injury. This is so called due to the head coming to a sudden stop. The brain is 'floating' in fluid and continues to thrash about in this type of accident. When the accident takes place, the brain crashes into the front of the head then hurtles to the back. This causes excessive stress on the nerve fibres, arteries and veins, which pass through the area; they often become torn and separated. Thus, great swelling of the brain occurs in a space, which has no spare capacity. This is known as 'intercranial pressure' and, if the patient does not get early treatment, the blood in the arteries can be 'cut off' causing the brain to die. This was Mark's problem, he was bleeding within the skull, a 'Subdural Haematoma' or a blood clot forming from a ruptured artery."

At this stage, Marion burst into tears and was shaking uncontrollably. He noticed her state and reacted by trying to console her. He spoke to J on his intercom and asked her if she would make us a drink. Drink appeared and the three of us sat in silence. I broke the silence by saying,

"Doctor, I know we are all aware that Mark has had a serious accident and that as a family we must do our utmost to get him back to us. Your kind explanation is very professional but I am sorry, we are not students listening to your lecture. We are Mark's Mum and Dad and all we want is a future, not to dwell on the past. I don't even know how or where Mark received his injury. It is not relevant at this stage." That said, I thought, "Oh shit, I've blown it."

"Okay, I will find you a bed and I will attempt to do that within the next 7 days. I must add, however, that you will have to find alternative accommodation for him."

We were shocked with his decision, no fighting or arguing. We had got him in. The 6- months' stay did not seem important at that time. Believe me, 6 months is nothing, as we soon found out. He is a straight to the point man. We now refer to him as Mr Black and White, as that is the sort of world he lives in. Very little compassion, no humour, and always straight to the point. Yes, Mr Black and White suits him down to the ground.

Wendy seems to be finding our problem very difficult to cope with, and appears to be hurting more than we are, if that's possible. The problem is, there is no hiding place. You live, work, eat, sleep and generally get on with your life, but there lurking in the darkness at the back of your mind is Mark. Not that we want him to go away, that is the last thing on your mind. We need him to recover so much that, if we are not careful, other events or your feelings for other people could drift away. We have talked about this and we are all in agreement that united we stand and, if divided, Mark will fall.

SATURDAY 22ND JULY, 2000

"Do you feel it is time to open up visiting to others? Mark's mate, Albert, has called me about three times now." Wendy turned to us waiting for a reply. Marion gave that 'okay' look.

"Wendy, you can take the devil in if you feel it will do some good. Just one thing I must insist on is that whoever goes to visit, there must be one of us there. Oh, and warn them not to say anything emotional or emotive as I know that Mark is listening to all that is said."

"Thanks, Dad, I'll give Albert a bell later."

"Wendy, can you make sure that we will restrict visiting to one of us and no more than two mates at a time."

THE POOL

That night when Mark and I were alone, I took him back to Mombassa. It was good to go out with Bungy again as we came through training together. We settled on stools at the bar. It was a long one, running almost the full length of the room. In front of the bar were lots of tables and chairs; beyond them was a dance floor and then a large swimming pool, complete with a high diving board. I was telling Bungy about my day.

"Had a cracking day today, Bungy. I was the comedian who got 'lost at sea'."

"I thought it would be one of you lot. You're all fucking crackers. How did you get lost anyway?"

"After breakfast, I asked to borrow one of those sailing boards. You know, those tiny flat planks with a mast and sail. They're called Piccolos. Well those things go like 'a bat out of hell' when you get the hang of them. I was 'tear arsing' around the harbour, fighting to keep it upright, not a care in the world, pissed wet through and doing the thing I like best. Playing with boats."

"Come on, come clean, how did you manage to stay away over 6 hours? You didn't half cause a panic on board. The rumour on the ship was that some arse hole with no experience had got off with a boat and had probably drowned."

"That's not so, Bungy. The truth is, on one of my ups and downs with the boat, I managed a full turn over, mast down so to speak. Could I get the bastard upright? No way, the mast was firmly embedded in the sand. Nobody about, only big ships and they don't have lookouts in harbour."

"Them buggers don't have them at sea", said Bungy with a chuckle. "Go on what did you do next?"

"Well I smoked a packet of fags."

"You lying git, you don't smoke and if you did they would have been pissed wet through."

I was getting a bit under the weather by now as I was beginning to slur a little.

"I'm winding you up, you dick head. There was nothing I could do, only wait and sit it out. Probably 2 hours later I could sense that the tide must be coming in, as by rocking the boat the mast seemed to be moving. One hour later and after about 100 shakes of the boat it released. I was unprepared for this and I fell backwards. The boat was coming over so I stepped on the short keel, got a good grasp of the mast, gave a heavy lean back, and up she came. I stepped off the keel onto the boat. You know Bungy, I didn't even get my feet wet."

"Come on, you prick, it'll be daylight before you finish your tale."

"Not much more to it now. I sailed her back to the carrier and got one of the best bollockings of my life from a young Second Lieutenant. Imagine a young 'subby' bollocking a 'bootneck'. I deserved at least 'Jimmy the one', if not the skipper himself. I didn't tell them I had been stuck in the sand; I just said it was so exciting and enjoyable that I totally lost my sense of time. You must try it some day, Sir, you might like it."

"Get out of my sight, Royal, you have caused enough panic for one day."

Whilst I had been telling the tale, more marines had joined us.

"Thought you would have been banged up for it, Pedro, after your antics today. You're a crafty bastard getting away with that. If it had been me, all I would have heard would have been 'Mind your fingers, Royal' and then the slamming of the cell door." It was Sticks Weekes, another old chum.

"Anybody for a swim," someone suggested.

No one replied. It was a very sticky night and the thought of a dip in the pool was an excellent idea. In total unison every marine in the place carefully stripped naked, folding up their gear into neat piles and leaving it on the bar or their tables. Like a small army we 'fell in' and marched in line to the pool via the dining area and the dance floor. We lined up on the edge of the pool.

"On three gentlemen. One, two, three." In we went.

Mark had fallen asleep again. I thought that tale would have kept him awake.

SATURDAY/SUNDAY 22ND/23RD JULY, 2000

Wendy is having a bad time again. Her entry in the diary says,

"Come on, Markie, wake up, hug me, and give me a kiss and tell me you love me. I tell you I love you and miss you every time I come here. Please Markie help me."

She goes on to say that she tried to be tough with him and 'boss' him into trying harder, but says she failed. Julie took Kellie in for the first time on Saturday afternoon. Poor Kellie got a shock. She just stood and stared at Mark as if she was frozen. I knew it would be that way. I won't go into why they parted, as it is not relevant to Mark's recovery. It is sad though, as at one time they were very much in love, hence the production of our loving grandchild Dannielle.

Mark was very sleepy on Saturday night, so Mum and I only stayed about half an hour. He was obviously out for the night, so we left him at peace.

Mum convinced Wendy to have a day off on Sunday and to spend the day over at her boyfriend's parents' home. They were having a barbecue, so the change would be good for her. She was very reluctant to go, but I was very pleased when she agreed to it.

SUNDAY EVENING

CASIVAC

Good, Mark was awake when I got here, so I decided to go on nattering. I am convinced he listens to me when I tell him stories. He peers at me, with his open eye as if he is trying to concentrate on what I am saying.

"The swim was great, Mark. You would have loved it had you been with us. The pool had filled up pretty well. We even got some of the girls to join in, but not for long as Bungy and a couple more lads were like dogs on heat. The boys were touching and grabbing at the girls. I must say it was a hell of a temptation to join them, but sense prevailed and I could still hear the words from the Medical Officer."

"High diving board, just my cup of tea," I thought. Up I went and it was high. From the top, the pool looked quite small. "I can't chicken out, they will take the piss out of me if I do." So it had to be down. It seemed ages before I hit the water, but I did it and I was quite chuffed with myself.

"Anyone for some seamanship training. When I was at the diving board, I noticed a boat just over the wall."

"I'm game," someone said. "Let's go for it lads."

They did and with a lot of grunting and groaning, we got the ancient clinker-built wooden boat in the pool. We had about a good hour messing about, then we split up into teams of four and had timed races doing four lengths of the pool, just paddling with our hands. By 5.00 am we were all shattered. Bungy and Sticks were still messing about in the boat, so I climbed back up the high board.

"Bungy, Sticks, prepare to repel boarders. I'm coming aboard."

Too late, I was on my way down. The only problem was I didn't land on the boat I went straight through it. Feet first, of course. I surfaced to a roar of applause and laughter.

"Ollie, you're fucking crazy," Sticks shouted.

We had to be back on board before 06 00 hrs, so we hadn't a lot of time.

"Come on, Bungy, we can't afford to be late."

"Piss off, Ollie. I'm in love and I'm going to have a quickie with this bird."

She was clinging to him like a magnetic mine.

"Bungy, just come here a minute."

He did.

"Remember what the M.O. said: all these women are carrying some sort of disease or other. I bet you haven't even got a French letter, have you?"

He nodded. No.

"So come on back with me. That black bitch is just not worth it, she's a whore."

Unbeknown to me she was stood behind me.

Crack.

"What the fuck was that?"

She had taken off her stiletto shoe and smacked the heel through my beret and into my head. Blood was pouring from the half-inch deep wound.

"You bastard." I grabbed her by her hair and her arse, bashed my way across the dining area, scattering tables and chairs with her body and flung her into the pool.

"Come on, Bungy, you have a 'casivac' (casualty evacuee) on your hands and he needs a doctor fast."

Back we went at great speed. As the M.O. was tending to my wound, I said,

"I started the evening with you, Sir, but I didn't dream of ending it with you."

He gave a little laugh and replied,

"You bootnecks are a pain in the arse sometimes. You have just ruined my beauty sleep and at my age, I need it, desperately."

MONDAY /TUESDAY 24TH/25TH JULY, 2000

Wendy has done a good job of mustering Mark's mates. Albert, Christian and Enty accompanied by Wendy went in to see Mark on both days. On Monday night, Christian and Albert were speechless. They just stood at the foot of the bed staring at Mark.

"Come on you two, say something. I was hoping that the sound of your voices would trigger something." Wendy tried to encourage the lads to speak.

Still no reaction.

Enty did his bit by trying to encourage Mark.

"Come on, Ollie, say some'at. Lads are 'ere to see ya."

No reaction from Mark.

On our evening visit, Mark was once again a very tired boy.

Albert, Enty and Wendy went in again on Tuesday. This time Wendy suggested that they leave Albert with Mark in an effort to give him the opportunity to have a private few minutes. Not a good idea, as no sooner had Wendy and Enty left the room, than the alarm on Mark's feed started to sound. A normal action and one you get used to. Albert panicked and when a nurse arrived to attend to the feeder, he was as white as a ghost and rooted to the spot. The nurse explained that the feed had finished, hence the reason for the alarm. I learnt later that Albert has a fear for hospitals and that his Grandad was very ill in another hospital.

WEDNESDAY 26TH JULY, 2000

Mark, Wendy and Dannielle's birthday today.

Mark responded to the occasion by being more active than he has in the past. We all seemed to notice it, even though we visited at varying times. I had a hell of a guilty feeling for the first time in 31 years. I had not bought Mark a present. I did set off to the shops, but I found I was getting too upset, so I had to call it off. I sat in the car park for about 1 hour trying to compose myself, enough to go back to work. Maybe like me, it will be better if we shelve birthday cards and presents until Markie is well again.

FRIDAY 28TH JULY, 2000

Mark had his nasogastric tube removed today. (That's the tube up the nose and down into the stomach.) It has been replaced by another tube, inserted through the stomach wall directly into the stomach. All feed and medication will be given to Mark via this tube. Wendy and Julie say that Mark was heavily sedated and was 'sleeping off' his operation, so they only stopped a short while.

Our evening visit was somewhat of an occasion. Stuart, one of our drivers at work, is a bit of a macho man and loves to pose and brag. Having said that, he is a great man and a hell of a good fellow to have around. He had said earlier in the day,

"I'll come in and see my mate Mark tonight."

"Great stuff, we'll meet you down there."

I gave him instructions as to where we would meet. Marion and I met Stuart at the prearranged spot and off we went up in the lift to Ward 22. Mark was pretty much out of it. Not surprising, as the operation had only been 8 hours ago.

"God, doesn't he look different with short hair. You know, I think he looks better."

"I have to agree with that, not just the short hair, but the removal of that tube which was up his nose is a big improvement."

"What was the tube up his nose for?"

"It went up the nose and right down to his stomach, to feed him and to give him his drugs."

"So is he eating now?"

"No, they have put a tube through his body straight into his stomach. I think I'll have a look at it."

I pulled back the bedding and there it was, protruding from his body. Marion meanwhile had turned her back to us and was admiring the conkers on the tree across the road from Mark's room.

"I've never seen so many conkers on a tree before."

I knew what she was doing as I knew she would not want to look at Mark's new tube. Stuart too was standing back.

"Just look at this, Stuart, it's amazing what they can do today. Just think that a little pipe is Mark's lifeline to living."

He peeped over my shoulder and said

"Yeah."

I was putting the covers back over Mark.

"Peter, quick look at Stuart."

I whipped round and there was Stuart, as white as a sheet, back to the wall and eyes rolling in his head. I managed to grab him as he slid to the floor. Marion shot out of the room to get help. Stuart by now was coming round a bit, so Sister and I got him sat on a chair.

"Don't be ashamed, this often happens. It is just the shock of seeing a patient on your first visit."

When the colour returned to his cheeks, Marion said,

"Come on, Stuart, let's go downstairs and have a fag."

Off they went in the lift, but before it got to the ground floor Stuart did his party piece again. This time he was out cold. Not wanting to leave Stuart in the lift to go back up, Marion wedged the door open with her handbag and went to seek help. Help came in the form of two male nurses, followed by another nurse with a hospital wheelchair. Back up to Ward 22, our Sister came quickly over and carried out a blood pressure test.

"It's casualty for you, young man, and I'm personally going to take you there. There is no way you are leaving here without a proper check-up."

With that, she wheeled him off to casualty. He never did have that check up. He sat in his chair as he was told, but when his wife Dianne turned up, he jumped out of the chair into the car and off they sped.

Saturday 29th July, 2000

Now almost 6 weeks into the accident and I still have to keep pinching myself, hoping that I will wake up from this nightmare. No chance, Pedro. It's here and you have to learn to live with it. Betty and Crawford are staying the weekend with us. Funny relationship really. Betty is Marion's sister and Crawford (his nickname is Crackers) is her boyfriend. It seems funny to call a man of 60 years 'boyfriend'. Wendy took them in to see Mark. When she got back she was on a bit of a high.

"Mark has been holding my hand today. I asked if I could hold his hand and I carefully put my hand in his, like having a handshake. It was minutes later before he did anything, but slowly he started to move his fingers and thumb and gripped my hand. I am over the moon."

And she was. I was so pleased for her as she is in so much pain and she needs all the help she can get. Her partner who lives with Wendy is not offering her any support at all. He is too content on getting drunk just about every night down in the Four Alls, our village pub.

Mark is still getting physio every day. This is absolutely essential, as without someone working on his body, the muscles can become to feel redundant and seize up. Some days he can be quite limp, but other days, he may be extending an arm or a leg or both. Getting these muscles to relax or 'chill out' as the trade calls it, is an art in itself, as to force a muscle to chill out can result in damage to the ligaments. I am watching and learning as I feel that I want to be more 'hands-on' with Mark.

Since the accident, Mark has been particularly bad with his psoriasis. This shows up as red, itchy, scaly patches. Thankfully I have never had it, but Mum, Wendy and Mark have always had it. The dermatologist has agreed to give Mark a little more attention, with the hope of clearing it up.

The rest of that week was not a good one. Mark seemed to be sleeping for more than he had been. It is as if he has no energy at all. I have asked the dietician if she could review Mark's drip feed in order to give him a bit more energy. I have also been pestering J and Mr A. (Black and White) regarding the bed for Mark, as it is over a week since he made me the promise. I actually got an apology from him via Jane, to say that, when he made me the promise, he had forgotten that the decorators were moving in to decorate the bedrooms. So at the moment they are juggling around with the rooms they have.

The following week, Mark showed slight improvement. His feed had been changed. He was now on 75% feed and 25% energy. It could be the reason for his slight improvement. Mark is slight on moisturised oxygen, as he still has a considerable amount of 'grunge' in his lungs and, on occasions, they have to use the lung vacuum on him to suck it out as it breaks up. Claire, Wendy's friend from the village, went in with her this week for the first time. Normally a 'bubbly lass', but not on this visit. She only managed a few words. She managed to survive that first visit, as on Thursday she went again and this time coped with it very well. Claire is no stranger to hospitals. At 18 she was diagnosed as having cancer. Chemotherapy and lots of other treatments worked and thankfully she has fully recovered.

We have got to address letting Dannielle go to see Mark, as Kellie told me that she had said to her Grandmother (Kelly's Mum),

"I don't think I am ever going to see my Daddy again."

It was decided that when Mark got down into Rakehead, we would take her in to see him.

FRIDAY 11TH AUGUST, 2000

Wendy was not too pleased today as she says that Mark's rash is due to him not being washed regularly. How she found out I do not know, but I believe what she says is true. Mark is not even getting a bed bath. Apparently, they wipe him down with an Aqueous Cream. Wendy has the same problem and she explained to the nurses that the only way she keeps this at bay is to give her body a good scrub with vegetable oil soap. So she has 'put them in the picture'.

Julie has been a complete hero since the accident. She has been to see Mark every day. I think out of all of us, she is the one who can 'take it on the chin'. I say this with a feeling that she is hurting just as much as the rest of us, but she hides it much better. That evening, Mum and I went to see Markie, only to find him in a state of stress. He appeared to be in pain as he was doing a lot of moaning and the odd tear was coming from his eyes. Even his left eye was slightly open, a joy to see, but not with tears flowing down his cheek. That night was a bad one for us both. We slept in separate rooms and, in my case, I cried myself to sleep.

SATURDAY 12TH AUGUST, 2000

Mark seems much better today. Whatever was troubling him seems to have passed on.

SUNDAY 13TH AUGUST, 2000

Typical of Markie's weekend. Sleep, sleep and more sleep.
Visitors this weekend were obviously us but also Claire and Enty.

MONDAY 14TH AUGUST, 2000

Good news today, we are going to move to Rakehead on Wednesday. I just hope we are not disappointed with it, as secretly we are all expecting a miracle when we get in there. Deep down inside, I know it won't happen but at least we will be on a firm footing to help Markie forward.

That evening I noticed blood in his urine bag, which caused me great concern. I found Sister and pointed the matter out, but apparently it is not unusual for this to happen when you have a catheter in situ. This is a tube inserted down the penis into the bladder. Short term this is fine but long term, it can cause problems. Sediment can block the pipe causing urine to by-pass the blocked tube and create bed wetting, which obviously is distressing. It can also cause inflammation in the bladder, hence, blood in the bag. The other bodily function cannot be controlled. You may get a signal that it is about to happen, other than that you have to take it as it comes.

THE MOVE

Rakehead Rehabilitation Unit is what the name implies: a place where people are housed whilst they receive treatment, such as physiotherapy, speech therapy, occupational therapy and, of course, good nursing care.

The original name of this Unit was Young Disabled Unit. It is now far from being that; however, I do not want to get into this subject as it is a little political, and a man in my position has to be careful what one says and to whom you say it.

I keep thinking back to my Mam's famous words of advice in situations like this.

"There's always a time when you have to say your piece lad, but there are other times when you need to keep your gob shut.'

Another bit of sound advice she would come out with was,

"Make sure that your brain's in gear before you open your gob."

On this occasion both sayings are to be adhered to, as I am always the one to 'fire the first round' when I feel things are not quite in order. Now I like to think of my Mam's sound advice before I 'squeeze the trigger'.

The move down to Rakehead went as smooth as could be. Mark seemed to take it in his stride and he was soon settled in a very cosy and private room of his own. There were four such rooms all situated close to the nurse's rest room and were described as 'the high dependency bedrooms'.

Nurse A. was the appointed senior nurse for Mark; her responsibility is ensuring that Mark's nursing follows a strict routine all day every day. I don't mean she has to be there all the time but she is the one who 'carries the can', should something go a 'bit pear-shaped'.

Visiting is very flexible indeed, you can call just about anytime. Times we found to avoid were early mornings, as everyone was very busy preparing patients for the day, and meal times, as again everyone is busy. The best time is the evening, as there is no pressure to get out of the way as most patients are bedded down reasonably early.

On the second day Julie and Wendy visited Markie and commented on how pleased they were that he had reached a more permanent 'home'. Marion and I left the day visit to the girls and we called to see Markie that evening. On arrival, you have to go through a similar door entry system to the one at Preston. Sad that the door had to remain locked but, as Rakehead stood apart from the main hospital in its own grounds, security was a bit of a problem. It was said that, on several occasions in the past, unwelcome visitors and even thieves had been found in the home.

Once we had gained entry, we headed for Mark's room, the third on the right. On approaching the first room, we became aware of a strange noise coming from it. Curiosity took the better of me. As the door was open, I looked in. What I saw came as one hell of a shock. There on a strange-looking mattress, similar to a cat's basket, was a twisted, deformed body of a person. To say that this came as a shock would be a gross understatement.

"Why am I looking in on this poor soul's private world, and what gives me the right to remain here looking at it."

I remained in the doorway riveted to the spot, unable to take my gaze from the bed and its contents.

"Come on, Peter, come on." Marion insisted as she pulled me away from the open doorway and guided me to Mark's room.

I got into his room and plonked myself onto the nearest chair and started to fight to recover my composure.

" God, is my Markie going to end up like that thing?"

Thoughts like that were racing through my mind along with the terrible feelings I felt for that 'body'.

"God, if that is all the future you have in store for my son, please take him now, this very instant."

I look back at this incident and I feel ashamed at having such thoughts. How could I have wished my son's death? I know why now, and I am sure that other people placed in the same situation would probably react in a similar way. To wish his death was a terrible thing and to ask God to do it, now, was something I will not be proud of for the rest of my life.

Suitably recovered and two cups of tea later, I was ready to get on with what I was going to find the most difficult task that I am ever going to encounter. That of getting Markie back.

FRIDAY 18TH AUGUST, 2000

Mark is going through all of the settling-in procedures today. He is being assessed by all who are going to take part in his rehabilitation.

Physiotherapy, Speech Therapy, Occupational Therapy to name but a few, all are getting together to build up a programme of how they are going to allocate their activities and where Mark will fit into their day. He will also be viewed by the Dietician to sort out what feeding is to take place and how it will be done. They will also weigh and measure Mark to ensure that there is little, if any, change to his body weight and muscle build. Lots and lots of other things have to be considered when setting up what they refer to as 'Mark's Regime' to ensure that he is going to have a trouble-free recovery.

On the evening visit Bob and Sheila called to see Mark. They brought him a bottle of Holy Water to keep by his bed. Nice thought on their part, let's hope it works.

Saturday night and I have Markie to myself.

ANTIQUES AND FAIRIES

"Where are we off to tonight, son," I asked. Sadly, no verbal reply only a slight opening of his right eye.

"A winks as good as a nod", I thought, but I suspect that's the wrong way round.

"Can I buy you a drink, Royals?"

The offer came from a 'Fairy' (pet Naval name for a homosexual).

"Very nice of you, mine's a pint of cider, what do you want, Cock", I asked my friend Mike.

"Cider is fine for me thanks."

"What's with this 'cock' thing then me lover?" asked the Fairy.

So I carefully explained to him that the name Cock was a way of referring to a friend up in Lancashire. It could be used when talking to a stranger if you didn't know their name. It is not out of order for two people meeting to say,

"Ello, Cock, arya all rete?" To which the reply would probably be,

"I, am as rete as a clock, ow ar you, Cock?"

"Am ore rete."

I looked at Mike and the 'fairy' to see what their reaction was; it was one of bewilderment I went on to say,

"Dus ta undrestan me, Cock."

"Hi a do, Cock", replied our fairy friend.

"Now that's not bad for a Plymouth Puffter," I thought.

"I thank you, kind Sir, for the lesson of the Lancashire dialect but can we now speak Queen's English. My name's Melvyn, what is yours?"

Introduction over and we all seemed to be getting on very well; in fact we were having a good laugh, mainly at Melvin's expense.

" What's with this Queen's English, Melvin, is it exclusive to a Plymouth Gristle Grabber like you?" asked Mike.

(Gristle Grabber is another pet name for a Homosexual along with others like 'Whoofter', 'Puffter' and 'Brown Hatter' to mention but a few.)

"You are a shower of bastards you 'boot necks', but you do make me laugh and you are always good for the 'crack'."

(Crack is again a bit of navy slang meaning laugh or fun and not a part of a 'bootneck's' anatomy.)

I explained to Markie that Mike and I were based at Stonehouse Barracks in Plymouth. We were the initial batch of Royal Marines coming together for the re-formation of 43 Commando Royal Marines.

Stonehouse Barracks is at the far end of Union Street, an area known to be the favourite haunt of ladies of ill repute and their male counterparts. Contrary to some belief, prostitutes and homosexual men get on very well together, as they have a common aim. That is, to lure some 'thick' or unsuspecting Matelot or bootneck into considering having sex in one form or another or perhaps an alternative to it, depending on the hunter's preference and, of course, the consent of any willing prey.

"Don't get me wrong, Mark." I hastened to tell him. "Your dad has always been quite normal where sex is concerned."

To this, Markie opened his right eye just a little bit more than usual, and did I notice a slight rising of his eyebrow?

Anyway, big do's and little do's, the night wore on and our conversations got sillier and sillier. Suddenly Melvin made a proposal.

"I've got a bottle of Dimple Haig whisky and some lovely steaks back at my place, would you like to join me for a drink and some supper?"

"I'm going for a piss, are you coming, Ollie?" Mike strode off with me in tow.

"Should we go back, eat his steaks, sup his whisky and then piss off?"

"Sounds okay to me, but for fuck's sake let's not get separated. I don't want to have to crack the Fairy" (crack means smack or punch), I replied.

"Well, are we going?" he made a slight pause, then added "Cock."

"Yea, come on", I paused then said, "Cock."

We all chuckled as we made our way down Union Street, heading for Melvin's place. We halted outside a very classy antique shop, crammed 'Jack full' of memorabilia. There were uniforms, tables and chairs, carpets, old clocks and a suit of armour, which stood at the turn in the stairs. You name it and it was in there.

The flat upstairs was something to be admired. In honesty, I was dumbfounded.

"Fucking hell, Mike, this is some pad."

He didn't reply, as he too was in awe at what was in the place.

"Here we are, boys, one bottle of Dimple as promised. There's a crate of Pale Ale by the fridge if you want a beer chaser. I'll get on with the steaks." With that, Melvin vanished.

Ten minutes and half of the Dimple gone, and he returned. Three lovely steaks, bread and butter and with Melvin squeezed between Mike and I on the leather sofa, we tucked in.

"Oh that was lovely, time to clean up." Melvin gathered up the plates and cleared the table and left Mike and me to finish off the whisky.

"I don't know about time to clean up, I reckon it's time to clear off." With that Mike was on his feet and rushing for a quick exit with me close on his heels.

"You can't leave me now," shouted Melvin, as he chased after us.

Mark's lamps went out at this point, so I decided it was wise to let him rest as Nurse Allison had advised us.

"Head injured people need lots and lots of rest. So when Mark decides he wants to sleep, let him do so."

Those words reminded me of my mam, she always said,

"If ya not rete, gu to bed an sleep, it's best cure in't world."

I felt a bit sorry for myself on the way home. In fact, I got a bit tearful. That too reminded me of one of Mam's famous quotes:

"Go on lad, av a good 'scrick' tha'll piss less."

What a learned lady my mam was. That thought cheered me up and the tears were forgotten.

SUNDAY 19TH AUGUST, 2000

Julie first to see Mark today and her report reads:

Got to Markie at 13 15hrs to be greeted by Nurse Allison.

"Mark has had a very good morning, we got him onto his shower tray at 10 and gave him a good clean-up. I really think he enjoyed it, as on two occasions he tried to grab the sponge off me."

After the shower, Markie has been dressed, plonked back on his bed and deposited in the Day Room to await his visitors.

Wendy next to call, with Amy, a friend of our family, who lives in our village, followed by myself. Mark looking very relaxed and seemed to be concentrating on what was going on. When Amy spoke to Mark, I had a gut feeling that he was aware of her presence and that he was 'taking in' what was being said. When Wendy spoke to him, he made an effort to turn his head in her direction. Nurse J came to have a chat to us.

"I have given Mark a new tracheotomy tube today, a much smaller one, this should encourage him to try to breathe more in his normal manner. We will continue to cut down on size but we don't want him off his moisturised oxygen, at least not yet. His chest is far from clear and we are a little afraid of moisture building up in his lungs."

Suddenly it hit me, moisture, lungs = pneumonia. Shit! We don't want that, not after coming all this way. My picture of pneumonia is someone getting too much fluid or 'pus' in the air sacks in the lungs. This I believe can cause death. I had to interrupt Nurse J to ask.

"Could Markie get pneumonia?" Straightforward question I thought.

"Yes, in short, but very unlikely now he is under 24-hour care." Straightforward reply, but not a 'No'.

I found that if you ask a question of that nature, you rarely get a positive answer. Doctors, Nurses and all involved are instructed not to be too specific with any answers for fear of being sued. Hence her answer: it was a non-committal reply. Not a Yes, or a No.

Mark had settled into a routine now and I think he accepted that he was restricted to his bed. Every 3 hours, in would come a pair of staff to keep Mark on the move. This is to ensure that he does not get 'pressure points' on his body, which could result in bedsores. I tried to put myself in his place being disturbed all the time and not being in a position to move oneself. I just couldn't imagine how it must feel.

TUESDAY @ 13 45HRS

"Dad, it's me, Julie. Mark is sat up in a wheelchair out in the Day Room."
She was so excited she could hardly get the words out.

One hour later the phone rang again.

"Dad, he has done a full hour in the chair and he is just going back to bed.
You need to see him in his chair, he looks terrific."

Her enthusiasm spun off onto me and I remember feeling uplifted.

"My lad sat out in a wheelchair, this is terrific." I shouted out, but I had
no-one to hear me, as I was alone in my office. I had a feeling of being very
proud of Markie and I wanted the world to know that my lad was trying so
hard to get back to us.

The settling-in period at Rakehead was a big learning curve for all of us.
This is the place where it is all going to happen, like talking, walking and
getting back to normal for Mark. I think that one has to give out positive vibes
when with Mark and I have asked everyone never to feel negative, as I am
sure that Mark will pick up on negative talk or thoughts. In my own mind,
especially when I have Mark to myself, I feel that he is with me, understanding
what is going on and what is being said. So again I have to keep the family
assured that all would turn out fine, providing we stick together and all push
or pull Mark in the same direction. This became more apparent when Mum,
Mark's Auntie Norma and I were around Mark's bed one night. We were
talking over Mark and I could feel that he had now got back some sort of
voice recognition, as when Norma said something from her side, I noticed a
slight movement of his right eye towards where the sound was coming from.
Then when Mum or I spoke, his eye would move, ever so slightly towards
us. I was not on my own with this viewpoint; the girls Julie and Wendy had
said individually to me that they felt the same. Wendy was probably the most
affected as she was of the opinion that Markie was still in some sort of coma;
a point of view I found very difficult to accept. My feelings were that Mark's
injuries were far more serious than any of us could imagine. There I go, not
practising what I am preaching. I hope to God that these negative vibes are
not getting to anyone else, especially Markie. In bed at night, I feel so sad
that, on occasions, I find it so difficult to stop myself from having a good cry.
I cannot risk getting Marion upset over my emotions, as I know that she too
is finding the situation very difficult to cope with.

63

WEDNESDAY 23RD AUGUST, 2000

Had a good opportunity to take a close examination of Mark's wheelchair. When I say Mark's wheelchair, I don't exactly mean that. The chair is one acquired by G, the head of physio, as even though Mark was measured for a chair back in July, there is still no sign of it appearing. As wheelchairs are not my strongest subjects, I had to go from what I could observe. My conclusion was that this chair had not been acquired by Mr G. but that it was a chair made up from lots of other chairs or should I say parts of chairs. I was pleased that G. had got Mark a chair of sorts, but this 'thing' in all fairness is a wreck.

So, into battle I must go. When I say battle, I don't mean I donned my Royal Marine camouflage suit, grabbed my rifle and got 'cam cream' on my white bits and prepared to assault some unsuspecting enemy. That would have come quite natural to me; this was totally different. I would have to adopt a more tactical role.

"Remember the old mob's motto, Ollie." I told myself. "Not by strength but guile."

I repeated this a few times to myself and I promised to try to abide by the old rule. To take this attitude is a little alien to me, as most of my life I have had to fight for just about everything. Fight not as a Commando but fight to acquire a decent way of living, a nice home, and a good and loving family. Look back on anybody's life and you will understand where I am coming from. Life is not easy and there are many occasions when you have to take a hardstand and fight.

To get a wheelchair for Mark I thought would be a simple operation. Don't believe it! The wheelchair people are, in all fairness, nice people, but sadly they are short of resources, mainly money. When I finally got to speak to them, I found out that 'our Mark' did not exist to them. They denied any knowledge of anyone having measured Mark up for his chair. I told them I had been present when it occurred and that I would recognise this person should I be allowed to enter their midst. An offer they declined, perhaps because someone had 'cocked up'. An accusation they failed to understand. So we were back at square one. They promised to set some sort of priority on to getting Mark a chair but clearly stated that it could be some time. In the interim, I decided that I would attempt to make 'a silk purse out of a sow's ear' and set about scrounging bits of chair from every available source. A foot-rest here, an arm rest there, a cushion from somewhere else. I even had to improvise and make a decent head-rest for Mark out of some discarded foam rubber. The end result wasn't too bad, even if I say so myself.

In the evening I was alone with Mark, as Marion had been to see him earlier in the day. He was propped up in bed and appeared to be quite alert. It was very quiet and the only positive sound was Mark breathing via his tracheotomy. It was a 'rasping' or 'gurgling' sound as Mark's chest was not at its best.

I felt my thoughts drifting back to the frightening episode at Melvin's flat.

Suddenly Melvin went for me; he grabbed me around the neck and we both fell down the first flight of stairs. No sign of Mike, the bastard had fled. Fear was welling up in me as I fought to get away. This now seemed more serious than I ever imagined, as Melvin tightened his grip around my neck. We crashed into the wall of the small landing where the stairs turned. In fear, I reached behind me over my head and got a firm grip of Melvin's hair but still he tightened his grip. Nothing for it but to fling myself down the next flight. As we fell, he retained his grip until we crashed into the full suit of armour that lived in the corner of this stairs. The shock of his precious antiquity falling down the final flight made Alvin let me go and he raced after this 'clanking' load of junk.

"I must get away," I thought, so I dashed down the stairs only to be confronted with Melvin. In fear, I lashed out at him several times until he backed off. The door to the street was wide open behind Melvin so I made for it. Again, he tried to stop me and again I lost control and reigned more blows to him. He fell to the ground and I went for it. He still fought on as he had grabbed my leg as I tried to get over him. He was clinging to me with both hands and trying to pull me back. I dropped onto my bottom and kicked him anywhere with my free leg. I was in sheer panic. Suddenly he let go and started a strange moaning sound. Free at last, I raced down the street. Then I heard loud footsteps behind me. I knew they were getting closer as they were becoming louder and louder.

"Oh God, no, he is closing in on me."

I remembered from training that the best time to escape is as close to capture as possible and I could not get closer than this. So I stopped, turned round and smashed my fist into the face in front of me.

"Fucking hell, Ollie, what's that for?"

It was Mike; he was flat on his back with blood flowing from his mouth and nose.

"Mark, wake up, you are going to miss the best bit."

He didn't, so I decided to tell him the rest of the tale another night. On my drive home I couldn't stop laughing. The thought of Mike flat on his back was so vivid, I could almost see him.

Thursday 24th August, 2000

Julie was on a high again. She reported that, when she was pushing Mark back to his room, she accidentally banged his knee on the side of the bed. The impact had the amazing result of making him fully open his right eye. Up to present, it had never been more than two thirds open. I just wish it had been the other eye as it is only slightly open. On my visit at 16 00 hrs he was fast asleep on his bed. He looked very relaxed. As an experiment I touched the palm of his left hand with a small piece of paper, he twitched. So I tried it on the other hand and then on his feet. Nothing from his right hand but a very positive result from both feet. All seems very trivial but when you are faced with such a trauma, you tend to start 'looking under stones' to get a kick. The natural reaction of a twitch, in my eyes, is a very positive one. It tells me that Mark is aware of the tickle. His limb sends this 'tickle' to the brain and the brain tells the limb to 'twitch'. Anyone with a medical mind would probably laugh at me but I don't care, as I prefer to interpret what I see into fact.

For a long time now, we have been rubbing olive oil into Mark's feet and for the last few weeks we have been rubbing it into his scalp, as his head is completely covered with dry skin. A dermatologist called to see Mark at our request and she kindly prescribed a concoction of coconut oil and coal tar to rub into his scalp each night, with the hope of clearing it up. I have never considered just how much has to go into looking after, and physically handling, someone in Mark's condition. Just getting him into his chair can take about 10 minutes for two people. Mark, sadly, cannot offer any help in what is going on. At first I used to get very stressed when watching him being handled, as I felt so strongly for him.

"What is happening to me, why am I here, who are these people, why can I not move, see, hear, eat, drink, control my bowels, where are my family and friends?"

These are only my thoughts of what could be going on in Mark's mind and if this is as I imagine, then I hurt like hell for my Markie. This pain does not get better; it gets worse as the days go by. The only way I can handle it is by 'letting off steam' in as many ways as I can. I obviously conceal all of this and only try to 'let go' when I am alone. Often, whilst out on business in the car, I can find myself wanting to shout out and swear loudly or even pray to God for his help. The only way I can control these strong emotions is to go with it and do it. So, I often shout out at the top of my voice and say out loud as many swear words that spring to mind. I often say the Lord's Prayer and ask him for help. Other days, I am not so nice to God as I want to blame someone for our plight. I find myself asking God,

"Why, Mark, why us, why anybody, why do you do it God, there is no reason to inflict such pain on anyone."

I hate these days, but they won't go away. Funny really, how it is natural to want to blame someone else and, sadly, most of us want to blame God.

"Who else is there?" I often ask.

Mark is now getting more hands-on treatment from the physio people. Not heavy-handed stuff, more manipulation of his limbs to try to stop them seizing up. Not letting Mark stay in one position for long periods is essential, especially when in bed. As Mark cannot tell us when he wants to change position, we have to assume that he does. Again, a two-person job and a simple device made of nylon placed under the middle of his body to help you slide him across or even up and down the bed to get him into a new position. His body has to be carefully inspected to ensure he is not getting any pressure points, or, dread the thought of it, bedsores.

A TYPICAL DAY IN MARK'S LIFE, AUGUST 28TH, 2000

Julie, Enty and Lauren arrived at 2.15 p.m.

Mark was in bed on his back and seemed to have a rattle on his chest. Both eyes were open very wide. His left eye was open wider than I've seen before. The staff put him in his chair and we took him outside to get some fresh air. His chest seemed to be better when he was in his chair; the upright position seemed to help. Not tensed, seemed very relaxed. A nurse said he was mumbling earlier.

Dad at 15 25 hrs.

Mark in his wheelchair in the day room with Julie, Enty and Lauren. They left at 15 30 hrs. and I decided to take Mark on a tour of the establishment. We went round the internal corridor a couple of times and finished off in the garden. He was wide awake the whole time; I tried to get him amongst the flowers to enjoy the fragrance. His eyes were very active and reacting to the light changes when the sun was playing 'hide and seek' with the clouds.

Mum, Wendy and Georgina arrived at 17 00 hrs. just as the nurses had decided that Mark had had enough, as he had spent two and a half-hours in his chair without even a 'head nod'. Some achievement I feel. I left at 17 20 hrs.

Mark knows that Georgina and I are here and he got quite upset for a few minutes. We actually had a few tears, he had a really strange look on his face when Georgie was making her usual sounds. He also drew his knees up slightly a couple of times, which is the most active response that Markie has had when I have been around him.

19 15 hrs.

Mum and Dad again. Mark woke up for us when we spoke to him. Both eyes open and quite a lot of leg movement. He kept drawing his knees up and then stretching out his legs. Mark is back on 'Nutricia' drip feed, he was on that in Ward 22 but they changed it to 'Pepti'.

Bob and Sheila we got here at 20 30 hrs. Mum and Dad had left at 20 15 hrs, When talking to Mark, his left eye opened as wide as his right eye. Then he dozed off at 20 35 hrs. So we left at 20 40 hrs.

SATURDAY 2ND SEPTEMBER, 2000

Good day for Marion today, as she has plucked up enough courage to visit Mark on her own. This is some achievement for her, as she has a terrible feeling that something could happen to her boy while she is alone with him. I have tried and tried to convince her, but Marion is a very strong-willed person and try as you may to change her, she won't until she is ready.

That night, I caught Markie in good form. I think he is looking forward to more stories.

Back to Plymouth, Union Street and our local, the United Services Pub. Sunday lunch the day after the saga with Melvin.

"Mornin, Peter, mornin Mike. What are you drinking?" It was Ron the landlord.

"Two pints of 'Scrumpy', Ron, please."

Ron pulled the cider, took payment and came back with the change.

"You know that queer you were talking to last night?" Ron asked, "did you go back to his place when you left?"

"Piss off", said Mike, "do you think we are a pair of fucking fairies?"

"Just wondered", said Ron, and off he went to serve someone else.

The pub had a very eerie silence about it, not the usual noisy place. After the one very silent pint, I ordered two more. When Ron brought the drinks, curiosity took the better of me.

"Ron, why did you ask us if we went back to the queer's place?"

"Well about 4 o'clock this morning, all hell let loose down at Melvin's shop. That's the queer you were talking to."

"Oh! What was that all about?"

"The police found Melvin dead in the doorway of his shop. They say his head had been kicked in."

"Dead, Doorway, Melvin," was all I really heard. I suddenly wanted to fall, as my legs turned to water. I clung onto the bar rail for support. Mike was in a similar pose and was staring straight at me. When Ron retreated Mike got close to me and whispered,

"You arse hole, you never said you kicked his fucking head in. What the fuck are we going to do?"

I had no answer as I was in too much shock. All I could imagine was going on trial and going to jail. The shame, the pain, what would my mam think of me now? No longer her hero son, I was now probably banished from her life forever. Ten, maybe 15, minutes passed by in stony silence. Mike and I sat in

69

the bar, drinks untouched and a terrible feeling that all eyes were fixed on us. I was frozen to the spot and Mike, like me, was glued to the bar rail.

"Well I hope that teaches you two bastards a lesson."

It was Melvin and he was making the finest appearance of his life. He swaggered towards us with his hands on his hips. Without hesitation I flung my arms around him and shouted:

"You bastard. You had me shitting myself there."

Hours later, and as 'drunk as a mops', Mike and I staggered back to Barracks. The Corporal on the gate cast a watchful eye, shouting,

"What have you two rascals been celebrating then?"

"Getting away with fucking murder, Corporal, yes fucking murder," I shouted at the top of my voice as I punched the air with a clenched fist.

I turned my eyes to look straight into Mark's eyes, or should I say to look straight into his good eye. It was wide open and was staring back at me. I had a positive feeling that Mark had been listening intently to what I had been telling him. In fact, at that point, I was certain, as our eye contact was so strong. Suddenly I knew we were in communication with each other. My emotions overtook me on the way home, so I stopped in a layby on Barden Lane and had a good cry.

SUNDAY 3RD 13 05 HRS

Nice day today, so Mum and I took advantage of it and took Mark for a good walk around the grounds. All the time you find yourself watching Mark for any reactions. A change of smell, a sudden noise, the icecream man's music bellowing out across the grassy area to the rear of Rakehead, 'It's now or never' by Elvis. I always wondered why the icecream man selected that song. I don't think it would make me rush out to buy one. Anyway, the people he was trying to attract were the small ones and I cannot imagine any of them knowing who Elvis was. Not important though as it was a sound, and if Mark recognised that, it would make me a happy man. I picked up some conkers, broke them open and placed them under his nose to see if he had any recognition. Sadly, no. I really thought it might, as Mark and I collected conkers every year when he was small. He did, however, grow out of it when he was about ten years old. That night, when Nurse L. had got Markie to bed, he came out of his room 'grinning' like the original Cheshire cat.

"Mark has just given me a cracking smile," he said, "It has made my day."

We left at 20 07 hrs leaving Markie very much at peace.

MONDAY 4ᵀᴴ SEPTEMBER, 2000

Julie a bit concerned about the area around Mark's tracheotomy today as she noted this on her visit at 13 55 hrs. I have to agree with this, as it does look very angry around the hole. She also reports that G. (the physio) said that Mark had had a very good session today and that he appeared to be getting stronger.

TUESDAY 5TH SEPTEMBER, 2000

My sister Pam visited Mark today, she reports that Mark appears to be aware of people's presence and says he looks to be trying to focus on who is talking to him.

Physio today was again a good one. G., A. and R. helped by male nurse L. managed to get Mark into a standing position. Not for very long, but nevertheless, a stand. L. said he was shocked as to how tall Mark is. He thought it quite funny to see everybody looking up into Mark's face as they got him into the full standing position.

WEDNESDAY 6TH SEPTEMBER, 2000

Arrived at 1.40pm – slightly earlier than normal, Mark was having physio so I joined in with the session. Giles had Mark standing earlier but, when I went in, Mark was sitting leaning on Andy while Giles concentrated on Mark holding his head himself. He did really well, holding it himself for about a minute. When Giles and Andy put Mark back in his chair, he got really upset and began to cry. This upset me but Giles explained that this was really good. If Mark didn't show any emotions, then there would be cause for concern. Looking over the last 2 days of notes, Mark is smiling more. I think he's found a bit of the 'sparkie' inside himself that we all miss and love so much.

FRIDAY 8TH SEPTEMBER, 2000

Mr G. of physio has told Julie that Mark has had a good physio session today. It made her feel good, as it did when she told Mum and myself.

Rab, an old friend of ours, called to see Mark and he was very pleased with Mark's improvement. Unbeknown to me, Rab had called to see Mark when he was on Ward 22. Mark was very much awake on the evening visit, so Mum and I had a good natter to him and for a good hour he tolerated us, or was he just being nice? The only way he could shut us up was to close his eyes. This he did and he kept them that way, so we left.

SATURDAY 9TH SEPTEMBER, 2000

Mark managed 5 hours in his chair today. That is some achievement, well done, Mark.

On the evening visit, Margaret, an old friend and partner to Ian, a very good friend of mine, called in to see us. She had been visiting Ian's Dad who is on Ward 22. With Margaret was her grand-daughter, a sweet little thing. Strangely, she looks and sounds very much like Dannielle. With a little coaxing, she said 'hello' to Mark. His reaction was quite alarming. He opened his eyes much wider than he had done before and he appeared to be trying to mouth a reply. Sadly, no sounds came out, but he was, for those few seconds, aware of the child's presence.

Monday 11th September, 2000

Physio again today and Mark put on an average performance or so I am informed by Julie and Enty who had been present.

In the evening, visit. Smack! Problems! Felt it straight away when we arrived at 19 00 hrs. L. the male nurse was 'stressed up to his eye balls' when we arrived.

"Sorry, Peter, but Mark has developed a pretty serious waterwork's problem. It happened when we were turning Mark, we must have pulled on his catheter (the pipe down Mark's 'willy' into the bladder). He has started passing quite a lot of blood. We have sent for the Urologist."

"Just how serious is this?" I asked Nurse A, when she arrived with the Urology man.

"Not a problem, Sir. Something I see and deal with every day. All I need to do is replace his catheter with a new one. Rest assured, he will be fine after a good night's rest." The Urologist told us this in a very calm and collective way, so much so that he made us feel less stressed from that point on.

"Thank you, Doctor. I just thought it was another disaster happening. You have reassured me no end."

With that, he and nurses L. and A. went into Mark's room and closed the door behind them. I looked at Marion. She looked pained and shocked and by her expression I must have looked the same. Mark was moved to a medical ward, to ensure he could have constant observation throughout the night. I was assured of this, by a lovely Irish nurse whom we met when we accompanied Mark on his move. Her words to the porters were,

"Put Mark there in front of the night station where we can see him."

She then turned to Marion and me and said,

"Please go home and be at peace, I and God are looking over him tonight, so have no fears."

We left feeling drained and tired, but at peace, due to the Irish lady's lovely words.

TUESDAY 12TH SEPTEMBER, 2000

THE SMACKING

The notes the girls made during their day visits say that he has slept most of the time. He was totally different when I arrived. Sitting upright in bed, hair nicely groomed and looking hungry for a story.

"Mark, I want you to picture the scene. It's about Aden and just what it was like."

Mark looked straight at me, so I went on to set out the picture.

We were serving with 45 Commando in Little Aden, about 15–20 miles out of Aden city. A big camp made up of small single-storey huts and a large air-conditioned recreation and dining building. It used to belong to one of the big oil companies for accommodating their workers. The whole of the area of the camp was dominated by a large tower, which had a large flame burning at the top, something to burn off pressure from the nearby refinery.

"We are going up country tomorrow, lads," explained the Company Sergeant Major. "So an early start for this trip and let's just hope that we get there without incident."

"Up at first light into the trucks for our journey to Fort Dhala," I explained to Mark.

"You know, Mark, I don't know who thinks that an early start is safer, as I know from experience that the people we are up against are not ones for having a lie-in every day. Most are about at dawn and they are good soldiers, fighting for a justified cause, in their eyes. They also have a lot in their favour when it comes to a fight. Remember that they have lived in this difficult terrain all of their lives. This gives them a hell of an advantage over us. They also have the skills of 'smacking you' when you least suspect it, then 'legging it' out of sight only to come at you again from another position. Their favourite spot on the trip to Dhala camp was Dhala Pass. If you imagine a mountain with no greenery, only rocks and more rocks and leading into this mountain is a narrow winding unmade road, which gets little if any maintenance, then you have a rough picture."

Mark was still wide awake and seemed to be taking it in. I hope he is, maybe a little excitement is what he needs.

"Keep your eyes peeled, lads. The bastards usually have a go at us around here."

This came from Sergeant B, who was stood up in front of our truck. I turned to Willie, an old chum, and said,

"How come we are in the leading truck, they always 'smack' the front one."

No sooner had the words left my mouth than it happened.

'Crack, crack, crack' it was the sound of incoming fire as the bullets hit the ground around us.

Someone had fired three rounds at us, luckily with poor accuracy.

"De-bus," shouted Sergeant B.

He didn't need to repeat it, as most of us had already disembarked and were running for the nearest and biggest rock we could find. We returned fire at what we thought were the likeliest places where the enemy might be. After 15 minutes, we progressed up the road using our transport as cover. It wasn't all that hard to travel this way as all of our gear remained in the vehicle. It was, however, bad under foot, as the rocks were loose and unstable. Our Company Sergeant Major decided to join us for a quick briefing. He had legged it forward to our truck.

"Gather round, lads, and listen. We are going to go forward nice and slowly, one truck moving and the following truck prepared to give covering fire should the bastards have another go at us."

"Seems okay to me, Willie, a nice stroll in the country on a summer's day seems the order of the day. It's a pity it's so hot. I don't know about you but I'm sweating my nuts off already."

Willie nodded as if he agreed, then said:

"It's only 8.30 and that burning ball is up to full steam already."

He was wrong. It was cool compared with what it reached whilst we were making our way slowly up the pass. The sun gave you a 'double dose' due to the confines of the terrain. You get the direct heat and then the reflected heat as the rays bounce back at you off the rocks.

We were fired at another three times before we cleared the pass and, I am pleased to say, no-one was hit.

"Come on, lads, let's get aboard and get away from here," the Sergeant shouted.

He again was anticipated, as most of us were in the truck before his mouth closed.

"Carter, come up forward with me and mount the bren gun on the cab top. If you see anyone with a brown face wearing baggy pants, blow the bastard away."

"Anybody, Sergeant?" asked Carter.

"Yes, anybody. You lot make sure that we have all-round cover. I'm not letting these buggers have another go at me."

He then sat down behind the cab and fell asleep.

"He's a cool bastard that one, finds the best place on the wagon and has the fucking cheek to fall asleep," I said to Willie.

"Aye, but he has made sure is arse is covered by us lot first." Willie grunted.

"Mark, Mark, come on son, wake up, we are nearly at Dhala camp."

No such luck, he had slipped into a deep sleep.

As I drove home that night, my thoughts took me back to when I was a recruit. I recalled the pain I had had to endure during the very arduous training. The times you are stretched to the limit and totally exhausted, the cold and the dreadful weather on Dartmoor and the Brecon Fells, the discipline in the Commando Training Centre. All this hard work has one objective and that is to make you all work as a team and to 'mind over' your fellow Marines. It is uncanny how you instinctively work together and cover each other, regardless of the situation or the danger you might find yourselves in. A good feeling when you hit problems, knowing that your mates are by your side, a feeling you only experience when in a 'live or die' situation. To say that you and your mates work together as a team is very true, but I have also found that this training has made me a very self-disciplined person. It has also made me a bit of a 'British Bulldog'. By that, I mean that once I get to grips with something I refuse to let go until in my mind I have achieved what I set out to do. My determination often goes to the extreme, so much so that I know I can be a total 'arse hole' at times.

WEDNESDAY 13TH SEPTEMBER, 2000

Julie, on her morning visit, got herself upset because of the area around Mark's tracheotomy. The hole where the tube enters Mark's lower neck is very inflamed and looks as if it must be very sore. So the doctor was asked to take a look. He was in agreement with Julie, so started Mark on a course of antibiotics. He has also suggested that the 'trachea' be changed. He will speak to E.N.T. regarding this.

The following day, Thursday, saw Mark with a new 'trachea' and he has started on his course of antibiotics. By Thursday evening when I visited, he looked like a 'new man'. He was sat up in bed looking nice and alert. Fred, my brother, called to see Mark and he was very pleased to see him looking so well. We always let Fred take the stage when he comes to visit, as he loves to natter to Mark. Mum and I watched as Fred was telling Mark some tale or other, when suddenly Mark started to smile, move his arms and legs and made a couple of 'grunting' sounds. All three of us were astounded and, just to prove it wasn't a fluke, Mark did it again. That was his party piece for today, as two to three minutes later he fell fast asleep.

Physio is carried out daily; other than at weekends and, when it is possible, I take part in the action. The fact that you are actually involved in trying to get Markie back gives you mixed feelings such as compassion, frustration, impatience and, the worst one for me, great emotion. I am constantly urging Markie to try to do something or anything. When I do not get any reaction from him, I slip right down into the doldrums, often for long periods.

Sadly, you get it into your head that all of your efforts are a complete waste of time. Your thoughts and dreams of Markie making an amazing recovery are dashed. A bad time, believe me, a very bad time. Then suddenly you are given a massive uplift when Mark shows some response to your actions and requests. On one occasion, he sat bolt upright for a good 30 seconds. Something he has struggled to master, regardless of how many times you have got him relaxed on an exercise plinth. Then you move him to a sitting position, place his feet flat on the floor and get his arms to his side with his hands on the plinth. At this stage, two people, who are taking part in the session, flank Mark on either side. My constant encouragement is "Go for it, Markie, you need to go for it." Then when he does, regardless of for how long he sits there, his face full of determination and his body upright with no outside assistance, makes you want to cry and shout out "Yes, yes, yes, you have done it, Markie." Something I do quite often and I am never alone with these emotions, as all present are 'pushing and pulling' Markie in the same direction, and that is forward. These ups and downs are very difficult to describe and are something that you would not wish on your worst enemy.

People often say to you,

"I don't know how you can do it, Ollie?"

I now have a standard reply of,

"Put yourself in my position, then ask yourself the same question."

This often makes the person ponder in deep thought and the standard reply is usually,

"I can't, I seriously cannot imagine how I could cope, if I were in your shoes."

"I truly hope you never have to enter this world of pain and compassion, sometimes lifted high, only to be dashed to the ground again. Not easy, not a bit easy, but what can I do? I cannot walk away from Markie and leave him to waste, no way. Markie is going forward and I am going to be doing the pushing, even if it takes me the rest of my life."

The poor person who has made the statement suddenly appears to get the message of where I am coming from. Even with the finest of imaginations, they will never know how it feels and I sincerely hope they continue with life avoiding an experience such as this.

Funny routine really, as Mark has a shower each morning, then back to bed. When Physio time arrives, the bed is wheeled to the physio room, and is placed by a big plinth. This measures approximately 7 feet by 5 feet. It can be raised or lowered at the touch of a button. Bed and plinth are adjusted to the same height; the 6-ft long plastic board is laid on the bed and plinth to bridge the gap between them. Then Mark is slid from one to the other using the bottom sheet as a hammock. Sounds difficult, but it isn't and it is safe and effective, plus it creates little stress for the patient. That done, then the exercises commences. When the session is over, the transfer is reversed and the bed is taken back to either his bedroom or to the main room.

Physio on Friday was attended by Enty in lieu of myself. Enty is Mark's most loyal friend and has been for many years. I am sure he will be around to support Mark for as long as he can. He reported that Mark had had a good session, but when it was over, he was absolutely shattered, so back to his room to rest.

Brought my sister Norma in to see Mark that evening and she was delighted with his improvement over the past 2 weeks and it gave me a bit of a buzz to hear it. I took Norma home after half an hour, then went back to see Markie. I was so pleased to see he was awake and I decided to have our usual solo conversation.

THE HONEYMOON

"This one will make you laugh, Markie. Back in 1959/1960, I was serving with 40 Commando and we were based in Malta. Luckily we were allowed to go home for Christmas, not all of us, just a few as we were on stand-by to go to Cyprus."

I went on to explain how I 'palled' up with a Sergeant friend of mine called Chippy Carpenter. (No medals for guessing how he got called Chippy.) We sat together and were exchanging stories and reminiscing a bit on some of our more interesting experiences, when the Captain interrupted us.

"Sorry, fellows, but we have an engine problem, so we have to put down in Marseilles to have a 'look see'."

This problem was not to be a short one, so we were all moved off to a hotel for the night on arrival.

"Surprise, surprise," Chippy suggested.

"Come on, Ollie, let's have a few jars whilst they are waiting to check us in."

Several drinks and probably an hour later we moved off to find reception and check in.

"Sorry, but we have no beds left and the rest of your party have moved on to another hotel."

This came from a beautiful little blonde receptionist.

"Nay, come on lass, you'll have to find us somewhere to get our heads down. If you don't Chippy and I will have to sleep with you." I said, rather hoping she might take us up on my generous offer. With a look of shock on her face, she suggested that we go back to the bar whilst she tried to find us somewhere.

"Gentlemen, I have solved your little problem. If you have no objections to sleeping together, I can offer you the Bridal Suite."

This came from a cocky little chap, who turned out to be the manager. Chippy looked at me, nodded and winked, then turned to the manager and said:

"That will suit me, what about you sweetheart?"

"I can't wait, love, let's go." I skipped over to reception and the lovely blonde.

"You are welcome to join us, and you can be the meat in a bootneck sandwich."

She gave me a lovely smile, looked straight into my eyes and said,

"Pardon, a bootneck sandwich, what is this?"

"Sorry, forget I said that, it's me and my wishful thinking."

She continued to smile at me, as if considering the offer, my heart jumped as she leaned forward over the Reception Counter.

"Thank you, Sir, but no, I feel you gentlemen need your beauty sleep. Besides a sandwich with the filling that you suggest would only keep you awake all night."

She waved to us as the manager led us away to our room.

The room was fantastic. Big French windows opened onto a balcony leading to a terrific view. The crowning glory was a massive heart-shaped bed. We both looked at it, then Chippy said,

"Hardly one for a couple of hairy-arsed bootnecks."

"Come on Ollie, couple of shorts, quick check on revelry and then we can get our heads down", he paused, came up close to me, then said "sweetheart."

"I can't wait to get back to the unit to tell the lads in the mess that I slept in a Bridal Suite with Corporal Ollie."

"You'd better fucking not. We will get christened a pair of puffs."

Morning came and it was a gorgeous day.

"Fancy some breakfast, Ollie?"

"Yes, see if you can get the full English, I'm bloody starving."

I looked at Mark to see what sort of expression he might have on his face having heard his Dad had slept with another man. There wasn't one The little bugger had gone to sleep.

"Get you tomorrow with the rest of the tale, you will love it."

I chuckled most of the way home as I relived the event from my memory.

SATURDAY 16TH SEPTEMBER, 2000 (AFTERNOON)

Mark's trachea does not look good at all today. The area around the hole looks pretty nasty and there is a green grungy substance there. Wendy has had a go at cleaning it up; not a pleasant task, but it still looks very painful. Well, I assume it is sore, I just wish Markie could tell us. Perhaps, because of the injury to his brain, he cannot feel pain, I don't know. I wish I did, but then again if Mark was in pain and I knew it, what the hell could I do? Frustration is not the right word for the feelings I often get. Helplessness is probably the rightone, or anguish, or a mix of all three words. However you try to describe the feeling, it never does sound right. There is one thing I am sure of and that is that I hate feeling that way. The mental pain makes you feel useless and totally inept to do just anything for Markie. Not nice, not nice at all.

Kellie and Dannielle visited Mark today and Kellie has noted in the diary,

"Markie is looking handsome today and his skin and head look really good. In fact he looks better than he has done for years."

Dannielle has also made a note. It reads,

"I love you daddy from Dannielle."

It made me cry when I saw what she had written. I wonder what pain she is feeling and again I do not know how to counter it. I cannot love her any more than I do, that would be impossible. Again, I experience that useless feeling.

Back for my evening vigil to find Markie in bed and quite alert, so I took up my story about Chippy and me.

Chippy was very fluent in French and he went on and on trying to get a full English out of someone over the telephone. He managed it eventually and vanished off, naked, to the bathroom. I made a cup of coffee and got back into bed to wait my turn for a wash and brush up. Ten to fifteen minutes later, there was a gentle tapping on the door.

"Come in," I shouted.

The door opened and in came the waiter followed by the little blonde from reception. The waiter was pushing a large trolley and looked quite cocky.

"Bonjour, Monsieur."

"Good morning," I replied.

The little blonde had a grin on her face, which made her look even better. She made sure she kept behind the waiter and out of his sight. She looked at me and nodded her head towards the bathroom. I nodded back to confirm that

Chippy was in there. The waiter slowly set the table; he kept glancing at me and smiling.

"I trust Sir had a good night?"

"Sir had an excellent night, thank you."

"And Madame?"

"Yes I would say Madame had a very nice night."

The little blonde was still grinning. Then the penny dropped, she was setting the poor waiter up, why else would she be there? The waiter was now loitering, obviously waiting to see the beautiful bride. He didn't have long to wait. The bathroom door opened and out 'she' came, stark naked, not even a towel for modesty. The waiter froze as Chippy strode over to the table, lifted the metal cover off a serving plate.

"Ah! Good lad, that's a proper breakfast, just what a man needs after a hard night's work."

The waiter remained frozen to the spot, watching Chippy. The blonde started laughing, shortly followed by Chippy and I. Strangely enough, the waiter failed to see the funny side; he just shouted out loud something in French and fled the room. The little blonde, still in fits of laughter, pointed her little finger at Chippy and waved it about before she left too, still laughing. Chippy looked at me and, with a silly grin on his face, said,

"Silly frog wanker, never waited for his tip, and what was she trying to tell me, it's not that small, is it Ollie?"

I couldn't answer that for laughing, but when I had calmed down I said,

"I'm not the sort of guy who would question a lady's findings, but perhaps your cold shower made your 'dangling bit' look a little inverted. I can't wait to get back to the mess to tell the lads over this one, or are we going to have a truce?"

"Touché you bastard, touché," was Chippy's reply.

Markie had been listening to the tale as we made eye contact on several occasions. What did he hear? Was it just a sound, did he know it is his Dad making the noise? Did he know and understand the story. Who knows? God willing, we will know someday, but when?

MONDAY 18TH SEPTEMBER, 2000

Pam, my sister, called to see Markie, along with Chris, her husband. She has noted in the diary,

"It's been over a week since I last saw Mark and I do feel that he is more aware. Mark looked directly at me when we first came in, but he is now very sleepy. I noticed that his skin is looking a lot clearer which is another plus."

Thanks Pam, that is music to my ears, as it is so difficult to recognise change when you are with Mark every day. Pam has always been my 'minder' and she has looked out for me right from being a little lad. I told Mark that night, how protective she had been to me on one particular occasion.

I was about 6 or 7 and not a nice little boy. I was never bad in the true sense, nor was I vindictive. I was, however, somewhat of a mischievous sort of a boy. For some reason I had a fascination for worms. I would go down into Piccadilly Gardens, the tennis courts, and collect them. Not just one or two, more like 15 to 20. These I would transport home in my trouser pockets and put them into our garden in the backyard of 22 Piccadilly Road. When I say back garden, it sounds something leisurely, not so. It was a small strip of soil, about 12 feet long and 3 feet wide. It seemed pretty big to me and it was a perfect place to keep my collection of worms. Also, resident in my garden, was a toad. Tom, the toad, was my prize possession; I had acquired him from a river at the back of Hapton Valley Coal Mine. He was quite small when I first got him, but he had now grown to full size and was a magnificent creature. Loved by me and me alone, as the rest of the family used to give him a wide berth when coming and going by the backyard. Food for Tom was not a problem as he was pretty adept at catching flies. I would help him, of course, by trapping flies in jam jars. You only needed a little bit of jam in the bottom of the jar and the flies would come for miles to get at it. I never knew how or where they would sense that there was jam around but they did, to the delight of Tom and me. When I had captured perhaps six flies, I would get Tom to come from his 'den'. This was a big stone hollowed out underneath with enough room for Tom to have his home. I would place the jar on its side and Tom would wait for the flies to have their fill and fly out of the jar. He was amazing with his tongue, so fast that if you blinked, you missed the kill.

Mum had a friend called May, who used to call to see her on a daily basis. I didn't particularly like her, as she was what I call a 'user'. She would send me on errands and never give me a tip, not even a halfpenny. So I decided to set a trap for her. It took some time to 'set her up'. She was terrified of Tom and didn't even like worms. That's how strange she was. I used to think, how could you dislike toads and worms, they are brilliant? When she came round, she would open the backyard gate, just a little, and shout,

"Doris, it's me, May, is that bloody toad out and about?"

If my Mam didn't hear her, she would very cautiously open the gate and have a good look round to make sure that the coast was clear. She would then move up the backyard shouting,

"Doris, it's only me." She would shout really loud, hoping that Tom would stay in hiding.

It took about a week to get her. It was Sunday morning. I loitered at the top of the back street to watch for her coming. After perhaps half an hour, she appeared. You couldn't mistake her, as she was very short and very round. I dashed to set the trap. An empty box, a roll of black cotton and some old newspapers. I had rehearsed this over and over until it was perfect. The cotton was tied to the box and led to the outside toilet. Only one ingredient left, yes, Tom. I think he knew the plot as he readily got under the box with a little help from me. The plot was set. One last addition was about a dozen worms, which I threw under the box.

"Doris, it's me, May, is that bloody toad about?"

No reply from Mam, as she rarely heard her shouts.

She followed her pattern. The backyard gate opened slowly, and around it came her fat round face. From my hiding place in the toilet I could see it all.

"It's only me, Doris. Doris, it's only me," she was shouting.

One tug on the cotton and the box flew in the air. May froze, as there, 2 feet in front of her were Tom and the worms. She screamed out loud and lowered herself to the floor, not a faint but a look-alike. My Mam came running from the house, followed by Pam. Whilst Mam attended to May, Pam spotted me and put two and two together. She put up her hands to tell me to stay where I was, then she picked up the box and papers and stuffed them in the dustbin. Tom had vanished, but the tell-tale worms were still there. May quickly came round and Mam helped her to her feet and took her inside the house. I stayed in hiding, frightened to come out from the toilet. Again, Pam came to my rescue. She opened the back gate and waved to tell me that the coast was clear. Off I went as fast as my legs would carry me. I think I regretted what I had done, as, if my Mam found out, I would be in for a good telling off and maybe a taste of her dreaded 'picking strap', which hung on a nail behind the back door to the house. When I had plucked up enough courage to go home, I tried to act as if I didn't know what had happened, but there was no fooling my Mam. She was in the kitchen preparing a meal when I arrived. She stopped what she was doing and just stared at me, one of her famous ways of extracting information from just about anyone.

"Well what have you got to tell me?" she asked. As she stood staring at me. I could feel myself weakening. I couldn't tell lies to my Mam, as I knew she could tell if someone was lying.

"What do you mean, Mam?"

"You know what I mean. Don't deny that you and that sodding toad put the fear of God into May. You could have given her a heart attack. Come on, Peter, the whole set-up stinks of you. Who, other than you, would put a load of worms under a box with that bloody toad?"

I could feel a touch of guilt coming on. I knew I was not going to get away with it; I had no alternative but to confess.

"Well, Mam, I was playing with Tom and the worms. I wanted to see if he would eat worms if it was dark, so that's why they were under the box."

"Oh yeah! What about the cotton tied to the box? You must think I am stupid. I knew full well what you had done."

"No, Mam honest, I tied the cotton to the box as I thought Tom would hear me if I walked up to move it. I just wanted to catch him with a worm in his mouth."

"Good try, lad, but how do you explain why it all happened in front of May? You can hear her coming half a mile away."

"I didn't hear her coming, honest Mam."

"Did Pam have owt to do with this?"

"No Mam, it was all my idea, honest."

"So, you admit it then, you lying little bugger," with that she slapped me on the side of my head.

Pam to the rescue once more. She came running into the kitchen and stood between Mam and myself and shouted,

"Don't hit him, Mam, hit me instead, as I put him up to it. Our Peter only did what I asked him to do as I hate that fat old bitch."

So Mam did, but not in a vicious way.

"You should have more sense, our Pam, and I know you have. You can't go through life sticking up for that little bugger. Now get out of my sight before I give you both a good slapping."

We didn't need telling twice, so we legged it out of the house.

"Thanks, Pandy, you saved me that time." (Pandy was my pet name for Pam.)

She looked at me and gave me a big hug and said,

"Mam's right, you are a little bugger, but I love you for it." Then she burst out laughing. "You want to see your ear, it's massive and bright red."

"So is yours," I told her. With that we went off down the back street to see if we could find someone and tell him or her our tale of how we got fat May.

Mark was still awake at the end of my story. It must have been a good one, or am I kidding myself?

TUESDAY 19TH SEPTEMBER, 2000

It's assessment day for Mark today. Dr A, a Senior Nurse, Physio, Speech Therapist and anyone who has contact with Mark all get together to discuss what has been done, and decide what is going to be done up to the next assessment, which should be about 6 to 8 weeks away. It's funny to hear them talk about Mark as if he is just a job to them. When I say funny, I really mean sad. Well at least it is to us as a family. Mark to them is just another statistic. Probably only to be referred to as just another patient out of the many they have seen and will see during their time. Anyway, it went very well and thankfully a decision was made to keep Mark at Rakehead for a further period of rehabilitation.

WEDNESDAY 20TH SEPTEMBER, 2000

A very good physio session today. I think Markie is pleased that he is staying at Rakehead, so he has decided to reward them by showing some progression. G. (physio) actually got Mark into the standing position today. My feelings, seeing him standing up, were great. I had almost forgotten how tall he was. Mark is 6' 2" and a strapping lad, even if I say so. Standing, according to G, is good for head-injured people. Apparently, they tend to feel dizzy most of the time and they lose their sense of balance. If you can regain that balance, you are on the road to recovery, hence a lot of Mark's physio is aimed at the question of balance. Sitting on the corner of the plinth is a good exercise; Mark has to have someone at either side of him and another at his back. You then move him side to side, forward and backwards in a slow but positive way. On this day, Mark has done remarkably well.

"You deserve a good pat on the back, Markie." I told him at the end of the session.

THURSDAY 21ST SEPTEMBER, 2000

Mark got a nice surprise today as Claire has brought another young lady from our village in to see him. She is a great kid and I think, at one time, she may have fancied Mark. Claire has noted in the diary that, when Simone touched Markie's hand, he got hold of it and gave it a big squeeze. Then he kept hold of it for a while. Claire notes that she was really chuffed. The girls were with Mark when Mum and I arrived and Simone was quite excited with Mark's hand squeeze.

"He knew it was me you know. I could tell by the way he looked at me and he gave me a lovely long hand squeeze."

Mum and I were very pleased that Mark had acknowledged her or should I say appeared to have done so. The main point is the girls felt that he had shown them some attention and they left us feeling very happy and on a high. I turned to Marion when they had gone and I could tell that she felt 'choked up' as I did. I had to say something to stem my emotions.

"That is wonderful, those girls have gone well out of their way to play a part in Markie's recovery, let's hope all of their love, affection and concern pays off."

That night we called at our village pub, the 'Four Alls' for our evening meal. We were greeted with a bit of excitement as Claire and Simone had called in earlier to tell everyone about their visit to see Markie. It was so nice to feel that everyone was routing for Mark and feeling great concern for us also in our very trying time of this tragedy.

"That's the beauty of living in a small village. If someone gets a good kicking, everyone wants to limp," I said to Marion when we sat down.

Saturday 23rd September, 2000

Kellie has been in with Dannielle to see Markie tonight. I was very pleased to see them. I was sitting with Mark in his room when they arrived. Dannielle was clutching a 'Get Well Soon' card.

"I have bought this card for Daddy. Where shall I put it?"

"Give it to Daddy then," I urged.

She stood there for what seemed ages, then said, "Will you give it to Daddy, Grandad?"

"Of course I will, sweetheart."

With that I took the card and put it in Mark's better hand, his left one. He then took hold of the card between his fingers and thumb and to our surprise he waved it. Just a little wave but still something to give me a buzz. The look on Dannielle's face was the only thing that stopped me from bursting into tears.

"Does he know it's from me, Grandad?"

"Of course he does. See he is waving it to say 'Thank you, Baby'."

Tears again on my way home, so I stopped in the lay-by on Barden Lane until I could compose myself. It took some time, as I didn't really know why I was so upset. Was it for Dannielle, Kellie, Markie or myself?

SUNDAY 24TH SEPTEMBER, 2000

Mark had had a share of visitors during the day, but tonight it was my time. He was propped up by pillow and looking good. I noticed his eyes were almost aligned and very clear, a great improvement, as up to now his eyes seemed a little glazed over and he has developed a slight squint in his right eye.

"Mark, can you remember me telling you about travelling up Dhala Pass in Aden?"

No reply, but he was looking at me so I decided to carry on.

After our little bit of excitement, we finally reached the plateau and continued our journey to Dhala camp. This is to be our new home for some time to come. The camp is situated on the highest piece of land in the area of the plateau. This is for the obvious reason of not being looked down upon by our adversaries. The camp is remote, to say the least, and the terrain around it is very arid. If you can imagine a rocky desert, then you have got it. It's hot, very hot through the day, but at night, the temperature drops like a stone. Why anyone would want to fight for this place, I cannot imagine.

I suppose you can say you are living in the middle of no man's land, for that is where you are. The whole of the land called Radfan has various leaders and lots of different factions. The policing of these factions is very difficult to explain, as it is the local tribes controlled by their own separate leaders, who seem to police themselves. This, of course, is not very satisfactory, as if one Sheikh dislikes another, then the likelihood of a fight, should their tribesmen come across each other, is inevitable. This means that you are never too sure if they are friend or foe.

To the south of the camp is Aden, about 80 miles away. Ten miles short of Aden is Little Aden (the permanent base of 45 Commando). Then, about 10 miles to the north, lies the Yemen, which is not a very hospitable place. It seems to be full of people who are not too friendly towards Royal Marines of 45 Commando. Perhaps this is due to the Commandos paying uninvited visits into their territory. They do not understand that, if they can 'poke around' in the Aden Protectorate, then it is only right and fair that we should have the occasional 'look see' on their patch.

Anyway, Markie, that is all a little bit too deep for us and perhaps a little too serious. I just thought you might need an explanation of why we were in such a God forsaken hole. Dhala camp, as I said, secured the only major piece of high ground. It was hand built to be a natural defensive home. Its

91

perimeter was a very dense, barbed wire wall about 8 feet thick and all of the accommodation was tented. When I say tented, the tents were covering a hole in the ground. Actually, one felt quite secure when in your den."

Markie appeared quite interested and still looked to be 'taking it in', so I decide to carry on.

"Dhala camp had its own galley, dining tent (or the restaurant), as some of the clowns called it. Newcomers were given very little briefing about the no man's land, a stretch of sand about 20, 30 yards, along which spans the gap between the galley and the restaurant. My initiation was about to be lived. Some of the lads had been in the camp for a few weeks, but they had all had to encounter what I was about to experience. I got my meal plonked into my mess tins and set off into no man's land. Suddenly, there was a loud shout of 'look out'. Too late was the cry: I had fallen victim to the Kite Hawks. 'Whoosh, whoosh', two of them had attacked me for the food, leaving me flat on my arse clutching two empty mess tins. They were all part of the highlight that you get in such a place, a great source of entertainment for the observers that is.

The Kite Hawks (and that is their polite name) used to hover over no man's land awaiting any unsuspecting Marine to dare the crossing. I soon learnt the method of a safe trip, and that was to lean right over your food and run like hell over to the restaurant. Something that became second nature once they have had you."

Still awake but only just, so I changed the subject to try to retain Mark's attention. A bad move, as even before I had decided what to change to, Markie had fallen fast asleep.

MONDAY 25TH SEPTEMBER, 2000

Felt like we were not making much progress with our daily physio sessions, so I decided to ask G. if we could step it up a little.

"Peter, physio is not something you can rush. I know how impatient and helpless you must feel over Mark but believe me it is a slow, very slow progression However, we can try it, perhaps your bonding with him is telling us we must try. So, yes, let's go for it."

Go for, it we did. First on the plynth, G. on Mark's legs and me behind him with Mark leaning back with the aid of a wedge-shaped lump of foam rubber.

"I want you to stretch Mark's neck gently, put your hand on the side of his face, stretch his neck again gently, then slowly turn his head from side to side."

It felt really good to be taking an active part in Mark's treatment, a feeling of some achievement; let's hope all this effort on everyone's part pays off. I think it is paying off, as Julie has noted that Mark could only hold his head up by himself for 3 minutes last week and today he has managed 10 minutes, after the session on Tuesday and Wednesday. Physio followed a similar pattern but on Tuesday we attempted to get Mark standing. Not an easy task as it takes four people to do it safely. Nevertheless, we got him upright. We had attempted this some time ago but the results were so much better this time. I felt quite proud of Markie; you can see the high concentration and feel his determination radiating from him. If there was ever a trier, this lad must be the best. During the session on Wednesday, G. suggested that we 'cap off' Mark's tracheotomy. This was done, leaving him breathing via his nose and mouth. Exercises commenced with his legs first, then the neck and head, followed by attempting Mark to balance alone. We were into the session about 20 minutes, when Mark let out a massive cough. 'Bang' the cap flew off Markie's 'trachy' and hit the door some 20 feet away. Now that Markie had discovered a new weapon, we must be wary not to stand in front of him in his 'firing line'. Julie had taken Mark to E.N.T. for an examination on his ears, nose and throat. She reports that, other than a slight ear infection, the important goods news is that his vocal cords appear to be in perfect order. So, in time, speech could be restored. We, meaning Mum, Julie, Wendy and myself along with the senior nurses, Kat and Ali, think it would be good for Mark if we could get rid of the 'trachy' altogether. So, with that in mind, we decided to target longer periods on a day-to-day basis. Once Mark can manage with it capped off for a full

36 hours, then we can ask for it to be removed completely. A target we need to achieve, as whilst that tube is in place, Mark has bypassed his air filtration station called nose hairs. This in itself will render him more likely to pick up airborne germs.

Saturday 30th September, 2000

Got Markie to myself again tonight. He is wide awake, very observant but he is in training to fart for England. The sound and the smell are something to behold. If he can keep it up he would certainly achieve gold, silver and a bronze medal, as I am sure no one else would dare to compete with him.

Decided to go back to Aden and the camp at Dhala.

"Mark, when I say camp, it is more like a fortress or castle. Bren guns, set up on fixed lines by attaching them to a firm base, cover the whole of the outer perimeter. This base allows you to fire in a pre-set direction, regardless of whether you can see or not. So, the whole of our camp perimeter can be strafed with gunfire automatically in a 360° way. If attached, all you have to do is squeeze the trigger and move the gun through its pre-set arc of fire.

Still awake and looking at me, the only distraction was the rasping from his 'trachy' and the odd (now to be proud of) fart. So, on I went.

To complement the Bren gun cover we also have motors, again aimed at pre-arranged targets, i.e. all of the likely lines of enemy advance. In all, Markie, a very safe and secure place to be, that's if all things remain as they are. We often get the occasional film show, yes film show. During daylight, and with lookouts posted, we would erect our battle-torn screen. Then in the evening we would lie in a big hole in front of it. From here we would watch a film. Without failure during the show, the screen would come under fire, usually at the exciting bits. Crack, crack, incoming fire but on no occasion did the film stars get injured; however, our poor old screen took a pasting. The next day, again with cover, we would take it down, stick patches over the holes and stow it away until we got more films sent up.

TUESDAY 3RD OCTOBER, 2000

A brilliant performance from Mark in physio today. We had him sitting upright; to improve his posture we laid him on the plinth and exercised his arms and legs, and finally we had him standing. To get Markie standing is no mean feat, it takes a lot of hands on, something that is in great shortage in places of this nature. Today, however, we had enough: G. and Rob and Andy and Leanne and, of course, me, with Rob and Andy under each of Markie's arms, Leanne and I with a leg apiece to support his lower leg and knee, leaving G. in command and in the position of Mr Lifter.

Okay, on three we will go for it. "One, Two, Three." On that we all carried out our allocated task. G. to lift Markie up and forward. Andy and Rob to support him when upright and Leanne and I to ensure his lower legs do not fold or bend when he is upright. You do this by applying pressure to the knee pushing it backwards whilst ensuring his foot is kept flat on the floor.

"Bloody hell, Mark " croaked Robbo, "I didn't realise how tall you are, I feel like a little runt tucked under your arm."

Whilst standing, G. would do his best to get Markie into a perfect position, no mean task with a guy who has no sense of balance or co-ordination. Obviously, we try to maintain the stand as long as possible and even with massive determination you cannot maintain it very long, two, maybe three, minutes is a good one. The mental pressure you find yourself in is bad. You are willing Markie to stand there unaided. You are secretly and silently praying that he will do it. Something inside wants it to happen. Then suddenly crash and it is over, this crash comes when G. says,

"Enough for now, Mark, we are going to sit you back on the plinth."

Down Markie goes with all taking part ensuring that it is a safe descent, Leanne and I carefully letting his legs bend, Rob and Andy easing Mark down into the sitting position. Then finally he is down. During all this, someone has to keep a watchful eye on Mark's head, as it wants to slump forward, so if we can find another willing assistant that would be their task. Without the extra help, G. takes on the task, no mean feat as G. has 'enough on his plate', being in command. It is funny, well not funny in the sense that a person as fit as Mark can lose just about everything in just a simple accident. Not funny at all, in fact it is bloody tragic.

"Sorry we are late tonight, Markie, I have been performing some DIY chiropody to remove a corn from my little toe. Failed to achieve anything other than to make it a lot worse, so I will have to stick to plumbing and relent, and visit a chiropodist."

If Mark was listening to me, he was not concerned, as he showed no compassion for me. He sat there nodding off and totally expressionless.

The rest of the week followed a similar pattern; Wednesday saw a visit to E.N.T. where Markie was checked very carefully for any internal problems that may not be apparent. We came away feeling quite good, having been assured that Mark's vocal chords were intact, meaning he should be able to talk should he progress satisfactorily. His ears are fine, other than a slight inflammation to one of them. The other good news is that they changed Mark's trachy from a 7 to a 6, this means the size reduction makes Mark less reliant on air intake via the tube and he will have to work harder to breathe naturally. We started capping of the trachy during physio but, if Mark feels any stress, he coughs loudly; this in turn fires the cap off at a great rate of knots so I have had to warn people to beware of this new lethal weapon now in Markie's armoury.

Friday night

"I have been thinking of when I was a little lad again today, Mark."

We are alone and he is looking reasonably intent. I went on to tell him of my entrepreneurial skills when I was about 7. I was a proper little scrounger; I would go to any means to make a bit of brass or to ensure that my belly was always full.

"Don't get me wrong, Markie, my Mam always made sure we got enough to eat. It wasn't always what you fancied, but it always filled you up."

I told him of one of my Mam's sayings when you didn't fancy or like what she had given you. I remember on one occasion when I said,

" I don't want this, Mam, I don't like it."

Her reply was short and to the point.

"You will."

That same meal would be set aside and put in front of you at the next mealtime.

"There you go, lad, let's see if you like it now, I'm not throwing away good food just coz you say you don't like it, if you're 'ungry enough yu'll eat owt."

So invariably, I, or be it one of my brothers or sisters, bit the bullet and ate the meal.

On Friday mum would get a sheep head and boil it up to make a wholesome stock and a big pan of broth. The thought of eating a sheep's head was alien to me so I set about making other plans. There were lots of big, poor families around in those days but most in that position were kind caring people who would share and help each other. I targeted three families, by asking members of these families what they would get to eat on certain days. Sausage and mash was one of my favourites and I discovered that the Fitton family always had this on a Monday evening. The Town family on a Wednesday and the Bennetts on a Friday. So I hinted to the mothers of all three how much I loved sausage and mash. I remember saying to Mrs Fitton,

"Du you know, Mrs Fitton, I could live on sausage and mash, do you like it?"

"We like it that much, young Peter, that we have it every Monday tea time, I'll ask ye Mam when I see her if you can come round and eat with us on Mondays."

"It's okay, Mrs Fitton, I'll tell er."

I did and I also got a standing invitation from the Bennetts and the Towns.

Sometimes, my Mam would remind me what day it was and where I was eating that night.

"Why don't you ask Tommy Bennett or any other of your mates round when we have sheep's head broth?"

"I will, Mam, I'm sure they will love it!"

I didn't ask anyone, as I didn't want any of my mates to know that we were so poor that we had to eat sheep's heads.

Markie still wide awake so I went on to tell him of how I used to make a bit of money.

Burnley in those days was always under a cloud of smoke, as the mills all burnt fuel to operate the steam engines to drive the looms. All of the homes burnt solid fuel like coal but the poorer families burnt 'coke'. Coke is what is left over after extracting Town Gas from coal. In those days, natural gas had not been discovered.

"This is where I came in, Markie."

I told him of how I managed to acquire one of those large prams with strong springs and big wheels; just about all homes had one, as breeding children was the thing of the day when I was a lad.

Coal chaps used to deliver coal or coke via horse and cart, but I discovered that I could buy coke at the Gas Works and deliver it cheaper in my 'silver cross' pram.

I soon built up a lucrative business delivering coke to my area: Piccadilly Road, Albion Street, Every Street and Palatine Square (a posh square so I charged 2 pence more a sack). I had just one snag; I could only manage to push two bags at a time up Manchester Road, as it was quite steep in some places and uphill all the way. On occasions, men or even women would feel sorry for me.

"Dus ta want a push, cock?"

An offer I never refused, be it from a man or a women or in fact anyone who was willing to help. This always made the task so much easier, so I cashed in on it.

I got hold of two long lengths of washing line; this was plentiful as all homes hung their washing outside. Washday was Monday when the mills were not pumping out as much muck and soot due to the weekend shutdown. These lines I tied to the front of my pram. When I look back I can remember having at least four people pushing and pulling me up the road. It worked so well that I increased my loads from two to three bags and later I could manage four. This was as much as I could get on my pram. The secret of getting help is with guile; you have to look the part, always dress for the occasion. In this instance, torn and dirty clothes are essential, a mucky face and a tired, pained expression. The main ingredient, however, is the people who helped me. It was so normal in those days to help someone in need and help they did. It became quite regular for some people to loiter by the Leeds and Liverpool Canal Bridge if they saw me coming up Finsley Gate.

"Dus ta want a pull, cock?"

I noted that push had changed to pull due to the washing lines. I don't know how Markie listened to me all through that tale, perhaps I haven't told him that before. One thing is for certain; when I finished, he went out rather like switching off a light.

On my way home I had a nice warm feeling, due to looking back as to how life was as a little lad in the 1940s. Another of me Mam's sayings came to mind.

"If your belly's full and your 'appy, you'll want for nowt and that's good as there's nowt to get these days."

The thoughts of some of her comments seem to cheer me up and perhaps encourage me along the painful journey of Mark's recovery.

WEDNESDAY 4TH OCTOBER, 2000

Managed to cap off Mark's trachy for 1 hour 25 minutes, as someone notes this in the diary. I noted it when I got here for physio at 15 00 hours. Physio was another good performance on Mark's behalf. I sometimes wonder if Mark understands what is happening to him. Does he feel bewildered when four or five of us are manhandling him, up off the bench then back down, being laid back into someone's lap, then pushed up again? Four or more people pulling and persuading you to get into a standing position. Others clutching your ankles and feet to ensure they remain flat on the floor to enable a successful stand. Does he think,

"Why can I not do these natural things like standing, sitting, eating, talking and where am I? Is that voice my mum's and is the other one my dad's?"

"Oh Markie, I cannot answer any of your questions as I do not know if you are thinking this way, even if you could talk and ask me these questions. How could I tell you, you are still my Markie but you have had an accident and God has placed you in a locked box from where you can see and hear but you are comatose and you have no sense of the world around you."

I hate thinking like this. I hate Mark being away from us. I hate to think what our life will be like in the future. I hate to consider how little Danni must feel and Kellie and Wendy and Julie and all who have been damaged by Markie's accident. I hate feeling negative so I must pull up my socks and get on with life. From this day on, I have made myself a promise and that is to get Markie back with us. If I have to tread on a lot of toes on this journey, if people do not like me for fighting for Markie, then so be it. As from now, I am going to devote the rest of my life to my son Markie. I must, yes must, get him going forward, so keep out of my way if you do not want to help.

More physio for the rest of that week made me feel much closer to Mark. Had my negative vibes been replaced by my now more positive ones? I feel they have and I also feel that Markie feels the same way. I sincerely think we are now very much closer together and it makes me feel better.

SATURDAY NIGHT VISIT

"Been to see Uncle Fred in the hospital, Mark, he has been having some veins removed from his legs which have been a source of trouble for some time."

Mark just lay there, propped up, appearing to understand what I was saying.

"Markie, did I tell you about when we were attacked at Dhala Camp, Aden?."

Mark just continued to stare, not at me, more into space but it was interpreted by me that he wanted to hear the story.

At around 02 30 hrs one morning, I was manning one of the bren gun positions when I felt a tug on our communications line. To call it communications always 'tickled me', as all it was was a piece of string from one Sanger to another. We had a code of tugs to tell each other what was going on. Not sure if I can remember the codes but I think I have them right: 2 tugs was for sounds to the north of the camp, 4 for south, 6 for west and 8 for east. One I am certain of was 10 that meant I desperately needed the heads.

I got three tugs from the Sanger to my right, so I crawled over to see what they meant.

"What's with three fucking tugs?" I said.

"I needed to speak to you."

This came from one of the two who were manning the post.

"Sorry, Corporal, but this is all new to us, it's our first 'real posting'."

"Well what's your problem, lad?"

"We think we have seen movement over to our right but we cannot remember which way is North, South, East or West."

"Okay, cock, now where do you think you saw some movement?"

The lad was obviously a bit scared and was afraid of making a 'cock-up' by raising a false alarm.

"Out there corporal", he pointed in the direction where he thought he had seen movement.

"That's North, lad, keep observing and if you see anything or think you see anything raise the alarm, we can't afford to let any of these 'rag-headed wogs' in here, okay. He and his mate nodded a confirmation. No sooner had I crawled back to my Sanger than all shit was let loose.

"It's north, Ollie, straight to our front," said Sandie, my partner for the night.

102

"Go for it," I shouted.

Bang, bang, bang, and whoosh, whoosh, whoosh. It was the sound of our 2 motor as Sandie sent up three rocket flares in quick succession into the night sky. Seconds later more loud explosions as the rocket broke up and activated. The parachutes opened and the flares ignited and they started their descent to the ground, illuminating the whole area.

Slowly, your eyes become accustomed to the change from pitch dark to this artificial light and after a few seconds you can see.

Sure enough, someone was attacking us, as the beer cans tied to the perimeter barbed wire started clanging together right across the front of our position covering a length of perhaps 100 yards, I could now see shadowy figures trying to scale the protective wire barrier.

"They're fucking coming, open fire."

I heard myself shout. Bottom twitching, heart pounding and adrenaline running at its peak, I dived for the Bren gun and started firing with a sweeping motion into my arc of fire.

"Ammunition, Sandie, and get more flares up,"

Sandie reacted automatically, and he plonked five more full magazines of ammunition by my right hand.

"Do you want some H.E., Ollie?"

"Yeah do it and don't delay as I can see the bastards now."

Fear in a situation such as this is with you but training is paramount. You go onto autopilot and get on with the job. By now, high explosive mortar rounds were exploding all around the perimeter. Phosphorus flares were drifted down, throwing an eerie light over the camp; Bren guns were clattering away. I could clearly see the shapes of our assailants now as they valiantly tried to scale our defensive lines.

"There's a lot of 'em, Sandie, if they get over the wire we are fucking dead!"

Support came from every angle as fear mixed with duty drove men from their beds to join us in the fight to survive. The C.O. and his second in command joined us in our Sanger, and they positioned themselves to join in the firefight.

Suddenly out of the dark to our rear came our Sergeant Major.

"Sir," he shouted to the C.O. "cease fire, it's baboons Sir, baboons, look over there to your right."

As if by command, we all observed in the area indicated and sure enough you could plainly see that the old soldier was right. Our attackers were indeed baboons.

"There's been no incoming fire, Sir," shouted the Sergeant Major.

A point that none of us had realised. Had this been a genuine direct attack, the enemy would have most certainly put down a lot of covering fire to keep our 'heads down' during the assault.

"Cease fire, cease fire," you could hear the calls coming from various directions but only after the C.O. had given the first shout.

"Well done, Sergeant Major, all I could see was the whites of their eyes." This came from the C.O.

Then realising what he had just said, he burst out laughing, soon to be joined by everyone. I know, and I know everyone else knows, that the laughing was not just from the C.O's stupid statement but also from relief. I know mine was, anyway. It's funny but I felt no remorse for the baboons at that point in time. In fact I was mad at them for putting the fear of God into every man at Dhala that night. The feeling of no remorse was switched at first light to one of great shame and sorrow, as hanging from our defensive perimeter was the evidence of our actions. There were about 15 dead or dying baboons hanging from, or tangled up in, the thick defensive barbed wire fence.

"At least them poor buggers are no longer hungry," I said to myself.

Food was the motive of their assault. They had not come to kill but I felt they would have done had they got to grips with anyone. They are big, aggressive and very fearful; their big red bottoms and massive fangs are something I will always remember.

SUNDAY NIGHT

Markie has had a good day, with no setbacks and has been well rested. Out of four separate visitors who have been, three said he has been tired and sleepy.

Seems pretty much awake now and looking good, in fact a real 'smoothy'.

"Mark, did I tell you about the dog I had when I was a little lad?"

A wishful thought came to mind that Mark's answer would be,

" No, Dad, but I've a funny feeling you are going to enlighten me."

Rex was a black and white mongrel, of small to medium build, not too aggressive, except where cats were involved, and he was the best friend a little lad could have. We were inseparable. I well remember our camping expeditions. In summer, which always seemed better weather than we get now, Rex and I would often set off on a Saturday and trek off to various areas, and camp out for the night. I had a makeshift hand-me-down tent, a blanket and an old army backpack. I would cadge some food off me Mam and off we would go. We were never too fussy where, but one of our more popular places was to go right up Coal Clough Lane over Rossendale Road and down into the valley where there was a small, clear river constantly flowing. We often came here, as it was one of our favourite spots. It was about 50 feet from the footpath, in a slightly wooded area, and had a clear spot where I could pitch the tent and yet be out of sight. We would pass the day playing at floating sticks down the stream and sending Rex to recover them. On one occasion, some lads, bigger than me, came along the footpath by the stream.

"What av yu got there, cock?"

"Some frogs," I replied. I had caught three frogs and I had them in an old hole-ridden bucket that I had commandeered from a small tip along the way.

"Let's av. a luk, lad," he bent over and peered into the bucket.

"I don't like frogs, do you Andy?" With that he grabbed one of my frogs and threw it at Andy. He jumped back and let the poor frog fall to the ground.

"Cum on you wimp, pick it up and toss it back."

The lad called Andy backed off but the third lad joined in. He picked up the frog by one of its rear legs, spun it around and threw it at the first boy. The poor frog was tossed from one lad to the other for a few minutes. It was terrible to watch this cruel performance. I could not understand how throwing a frog about could get you excited, yet excited they were. I felt quite helpless, as those lads were far bigger than I was. I wouldn't stand a chance if I intervened. Rex and I just stood there and witnessed this sick event. The boy called Andy pleaded with them to stop but they continued throwing the poor creature, often missing to catch it, making it fall to the ground. One thing I could do was make sure they didn't get the other two frogs, so I moved to the bucket and threw its contents into the river.

"What the bloody hell do you think you are doing, I wanted them frogs," he shouted at me.

To say I was a bit scared would have been an understatement, so I slowly made my way across the river, even though the water came over the top of my wellies. Rex was already on that side of the river and he greeted me with a slight tail wag. I sensed that our Rex was aware of our plight, as he looked at the two culprits, he moved his head to one side and slowly walked to the water's edge, he then bared his teeth and started to growl at the enemy, as they had now become. The big one walked to the edge of the river and stared at Rex and tried to challenge him. He bent down, picked up a stone and threw it at him. Thankfully he missed. That was it; I have never known Rex to be aggressive, at least not like this. He was making a funny sound, half bark, half growl. The lad bent down for another stone but before he could pick one up Rex went for him; he rushed into the river and headed straight for him. Panic set in, Andy was the first to run and this triggered the second boy to follow. I thought the bully might stand his ground but all of a sudden he turned and ran. He was now showing what he was made of. Rex was going wild and I hate to think what he would do should he catch him, they vanished downstream with Rex in hot pursuit. I feared for my dog now so I dashed across the river and followed them. I hadn't got very far when Rex's barking stopped. Fear hit me, had they stoned him or caught him? All sorts of thoughts hit me as I tried to catch up. It was not easy as my wellies were still full of water. I kicked one off and, as I was struggling to get the second one off, I fell into the muddy path, wellies off and mindset to help Rex. I slipped and slid my way forward. Suddenly he was there in front of me licking my face. He was as large as life very proudly wagging his tail.

"Oh! Rex, oh Rex, you are bloody fearless, come 'ere lad, I love you."

With that he came forward a little faster, his tail was wagging as fast as his bottom would allow. I could not get over how Rex had done what he did for me. It was an amazing performance and I was so proud to have a dog like Rex. He was a dog who was a best pal, who had a heart full of love for me. He also had the temperament of a lion somewhere hidden in his little body. That night it rained and rained. I awoke to find Rex was not alongside me, wrapped up in the blanket as he always was. It was about 5.30 am when I crawled out of the soaking tent and blanket and went looking for him. "Rex, Rex, come on Rex, we can go home now." All my shouting was in vain as

Rex never appeared. With a broken heart, a very heavy pack and water in my wellies, I set off for home.

What am I going to tell my family? My Mam will kill me, as she dearly loved Rex too, I pondered. Had those lads come back and kidnapped him and maybe killed him? At 10 years old my imagination ran a little riot. I reached Albion Street and made my way down it towards Piccadilly Road when I suddenly noticed my Mam and our Fred coming towards me. To my surprise my Mam flung her arms around me and started crying.

"Where the bloody hell ave you been, I've been at me wit's end with worry since Rex woke me up with his barking at 6 o'clock." I too started crying, but not because my Mam and Fred were crying. It was because Rex was alive and safe. When we got home my sisters were all up and very upset at my absence but Rex never batted an eyelid, as he was fast asleep on the little mat in front of the fire.

"Mark are you still with me?"

No response other than noticing his eyes were moving rapidly under his closed lids – a sign of dreaming, I believe.

MONDAY 9TH AND TUESDAY 10TH OCTOBER, 2000

Mark's progress seems to be improving. He can sit out in his chair longer now and doesn't seem to tire as easy. He still has a lot of psoriasis about his head but that is improving, due to the tar-based shampoo prescribed for him. Surprise visit today from Billy and Pat Gott, along with their son or should I say Billy's son from a previous marriage, David. They have brought David in for further rehabilitation to enable him to 'fly the nest' of living with Billy and Pat and set up a home for himself. Some years ago, David and his uncle were racing around the fields on cross-country motorbikes down on the farm where they lived. Unfortunately they had a head-on collision; neither of them were wearing crash helmets. David's head impacted with his uncle's shoulder, causing him severe head injuries, which left David into a comatose state for a considerable time. Luckily his uncle only suffered a broken shoulder. They impacted at a combined speed of about 60 mph. I have been told that, if your head comes to an abrupt halt, the brain, being immersed in fluid, does not and it can thrash around in your skull causing all sorts of problems for the poor person. Now several years later David is okay, I can only say okay, as he, Bill and Pat know that he has not fully recovered but he has repaired sufficiently to 'go it alone'. Alone, well almost, as David will have to be under the watchful eye of mum and dad. With that in mind, he is hoping to find accommodation in Sabden, a small village by the foot of Pendle Hill. David has his dad to thank, as Billy got the bit between his teeth from day one and has fought for David's recovery ever since that nasty day. Pat also has been a martyr by taking David on and loving him as her own. I am so pleased to see David as he is now, almost free. Maybe Mark will follow in his footsteps. Let's hope and pray that he does.

Mid week, we had a family meeting and we have come to the conclusion that we are going to get rid of Mark's tracheotomy tube. So we have decided to have what I choose to call a tracheomarathon. Already, we have got Mark capped off for a maximum of 5½ hours. Alison, Mark's primary care nurse, is in agreement with this and she is going to suggest that we, all staff included, made a concerted effort to get rid of that trachea.

FRIDAY 13TH OCTOBER, 2000 AT 15 40 HRS

J., another care nurse, says that, when Marion arrived to visit, she was with Mark and said to him,

"Are you alright, Mark?" She says he replied,

"Alright."

"Is that a yes, Mark?"

"Yes."

"Your mum is here, Mark."

"Mum."

On hearing this Marion lost it for a few seconds and had to be sat down in shock. Upon recovery, she set about ringing everyone with the news.

I was in the warehouse at work when she rang me. I recall shouting,

"Mark has spoken. I'm going to see him."

I was so excited that I could not control my hysterical laughter on the way there. I arrived at Rakehead, closely followed by Wendy and Georgina then Kellie with Danni. We were all around Mark waiting for him to open his eyes and praying that he would wake up and say something. Sadly, he just slept on and we all went our separate ways with sunken hearts.

"Did he speak" or was J. being plagued with her imagination, who knows? Maybe tomorrow.

I went to bed that night early, as I wanted tomorrow to come soon. It did but Mark didn't speak when I visited him. What a bad day. I felt as low as I could all day, silent and deep in thought, knowing that Mark had probably not spoken. Poor J., she must feel really bad; my thoughts were with her.

Same Friday 13th October

Saturday evening visit

Marion and I arrived at 19 10 hrs, to find Mark's cap for his trachy at the foot of the bed.

"Mark must have blown it off," Marion said.

I put it back on but Markie sounded very chesty so I removed it again.

I took to thinking how we had progressed that week as we sat on our silent vigil. Physio had seen some good work. We had had enough hands to get Mark up into the standing position. When you are working on someone such as Mark you can tell how they feel. Little things like the eyes, hands and arms all seem to tell you something. There is no art to this. It comes instinctively, and you certainly could not write down what these signals are but they are there. Normally, when we are trying to stand Mark, he is tense and not very co-operative but other times he appears to understand what we want and he becomes much 'lighter'. Strange feeling when you know you have got a form of connection. Maybe I get it as I am his Dad but I am not too sure of that, as G. often comments on Mark's help, saying "Well done, Markie, that is great," and other words of encouragement. I am not sure that Mark would allow Mr G. to call him Markie but he does sometimes, especially when we have had a small achievement from Mark.

Still, looking back over the past weeks and I can see a big improvement on Mark's left hand and arm. They are quite active. When I say active, I really mean that Mark occasionally moves his arm by himself. The hand now occasionally returns your squeezes, but when it does it gives a very warm feeling inside but you also get the pain of knowing that Markie is in there and he is asking you to get him out. Oh God, if only I could.

Here I go, thinking negative again. I must stop doing that. It does not help anyone and I am still aware that Mark may pick up my vibes and get the message that I too am in great pain. The main and exciting progress is the tracheamarathon. It is not a week since we made our decision to get rid of it and already we, or should I say Mark, is going over 10 hours being capped off.

SUNDAY MORNING

Got here early, as I want to be with Mark whilst he is capped off, so the family are working in relays to encourage Mark to manage without his trachea. Allison, Mark's main mentor, has suggested that, as Mark could do with continuing having his nebuliser to loosen his chest, we could apply it via the face mask instead of via the tracheotomy. Good thinking, as if he can cope with that, then we will have another reason to remove the trachea altogether.

Three visits today 11 00 hrs, 14 00 hrs and back again at 18 00 hrs. We are all at it, as we now have the finishing line almost in sight.

Mark got his nebuliser again, firmly placed over his nose and mouth, and coping with it like a hero. I feel so proud of him, as I know he is fighting to get back to us. We will do it, son.

He was on his bed in his room, looking good and reasonably alert.

"Markie, I bet I haven't told you this one before. It's about my first encounter with a homosexual."

THE PANSY

Eastney Barracks at Southsea and we were almost out of training. It was a Saturday afternoon and I was going into town to have a wander around Portsmouth to see the sights. Caught the bus by the Barracks and went to sit upstairs for what would only be a 10-minute journey. Whilst sat watching the day go by, I got a funny feeling that I was being watched closely. "I'm sure you have felt that before haven't you, Mark." No reply, so I went on to tell him. I slowly moved my head to the side and there he was, a funny-looking chap, groomed to perfection and showing a hint of make-up; his cheeks were pinker than normal.

"Hello, Royal, how are you?"

I had to reply, so I attempted to lower my voice somewhat.

"Fine, pal, fine."

The only problem was it came out all wrong, I sounded just like a frightened little boy and I was.

The bus finally approached the station where I had decided to get off. I jumped from the platform at the rear of the bus before it stopped and set off at a jog down the road. I took an odd fleeting glance behind me to confirm that he wasn't following me. Assured that I was safe I decided to call into a café for a brew.

"Do you want the newspaper, sweetheart?" asked the lady who served me.

"Yes, thank you."

I got a stool and set out my stall, big mug of coffee, a doughnut and a chance to read what was going on in the big, outside world.

Then he or it pounced; suddenly his head came over my shoulder and his cheek pressed against mine. I locked up but not for long. I was off the stool in a flash; I could feel myself shaking. Should I smack him I thought or should I leg it?

"I've bloody told you before about coming in here and pestering my customers. Now 'piss off' before I come round there and sort you out, you queer bastard."

He didn't need a second telling; he turned and made a hasty exit. The lady glared at him as he left, then turned to me and said,

"First time you've met one of them, is it love?"

I nodded in confirmation.

"It won't be the last, so get used to 'em, love, but be careful, some of them can get quite nasty if you turn them down."

"Smack the bastards, they are a pain in the arse" This came from a well-worn sailor who was sitting by the door.

Ten minutes later, feeling composed and after thanking my advisors, I left the cafe feeling a little bit more worldly wise for the experience.

Markie was fast asleep by now but looking really at peace. I wondered if my nightly tales are of any benefit to him.

On the way home I had another little laugh when my thoughts took me back again to Portsmouth. The week before the incident I am about to relate I had been to a dance with my mates. Here I met a gorgeous young lady and convinced myself that she was the one for me. I pestered her that much that she agreed to go to the pictures with me. We had to go to an evening showing as not many girls would walk the street with a man in uniform for fear of being branded as being easy and cheap.

It was all arranged: Saturday night, at the railway station, I was to wait by the newspaper stand. Shining like a new pin I looked great; even the wiliest of sergeant majors could not have faulted me that evening. I caught the usual bus and off I went for the first real date for ages. I was excited to say the least. It would feel really good to hold her hand and maybe put my arm around her in the pictures.

Almost there, and again I positioned myself on the rear platform of the bus ready to do my early exit as the bus approached the station. I had misjudged the speed a little and almost lost my balance as I hit the pavement, still on my feet, thank God, but having to run like hell. Then the bottom fell out of my world, or to tell you in a better manner, the world, or what felt like it, fell out of my bottom. I clearly remember muttering,

"Oh shit", and I had so much that I could hardly ignore it. Again I had to compose myself as I hastily headed for the toilets, on the way I spotted my date but kept going. Once securely locked in the loo, I assessed the damage. "No date for you tonight, Ollie," was the conclusion as I was afraid that my discharge had been far from a solid one. I walked back to Barracks that night feeling very sorry for myself; I had to walk, as I could not have used a bus in my state.

The corporal stopped me at the gate to check my I.D. That done he stared at me and said,

"Where have you been, you smell like a shithouse."

A brief explanation made him burst into a fit of laughter and I must confess I had a good chuckle when I saw the funny side.

"Must tell Markie that one he'll love it."

TUESDAY 17TH OCTOBER, 2000

Allison is confident that Mark can do without his trachy, so she has arranged a trip to E.N.T. for tomorrow. Well done, everybody who has put all the time and effort to achieve this milestone. It means a lot to me, as it says that Mark is not relying on any equipment now other than the catheter and his peg, but that is another hurdle we will have to clear and we will.

Wednesday 18th October, 2000

Bye, tracheotomy tube, as it was removed earlier today. It certainly had no side effects on Mark as he looked good when I arrived for physio, sitting on the corner of the plinth with his feet flat on the floor was the order of the day. Forty per cent balance from Mark and the other 60% from whoever sat behind him.

Thursday there were the same exercises, but this time we had a visit from a speech therapist. G. and A. brought her up to speed with Mark's activities.

"Can Mark swallow?" she asked. G., A. and I all looked at each other for the answer.

I piped up, "Don't know really as Mark has been taking everything through his 'peg'."

(A 'peg' is a tube inserted through the wall of the stomach through which food, water and medicines can be administered.)

G. came back by suggesting that he could probably induce a swallow. A nod from the lady led G. to don a rubber glove and push a finger into Mark's mouth after asking him not to bite him. Apparently moving the finger around the mouth creates saliva, which has to go somewhere. We watched intently as the saliva built up, and then Mark swallowed, not good as it caused him to cough.

"Again?" asked G.

"Yes, please, as I feel he did a swallow and it wasn't a choking cough."

G. repeated his finger probing again, this made Mark move his mouth as the saliva built up. Once again, pensive faces stared at Mark then he swallowed, not once but twice and not a sign of coughing or choking.

"Mark, you are on the first rung of the eating ladder, well done." She then turned to me and said,

"Dad, I will meet you in Mark's room, as I want a chat with you."

I wondered why she wanted a chat as I took Mark back to his room. Good news? Bad news? Who knows, but I will soon find out.

114

"Now, Dad, it's up to you as to how soon Mark can get around to taking food orally. I know you spend a lot of time with Mark, so I want you to work on the inside of his mouth, stretch his cheeks and manipulate his jaw for at least 15 minutes daily. I'll show you how."

I then got a crash course on what she wanted me to 'take on'.

"Do you have any problems with that?"

"None at all," I replied.

She turned, bent over Mark, 'pecked' him on the cheek, patted him on the back and said,

"Well done, Mark, we will have you eating in no time, won't we Dad?" she said as she left the room.

"Did you hear that, Mark, it looks like we will be doing all the work and she will grab all the glory. Don't worry, Markie, we will show her and it will be sooner than she thinks."

FRIDAY 20TH OCTOBER, 2000

L. one of the male nurses gave Mark a 'down to the bone' haircut last night and I have to say that Markie looks superb. He really suits it and I am not on my own when I say that as everyone agrees how good he looks.

SATURDAY 21ST OCTOBER, 2000

"Mark, you know when I told you about the baboons, well the story goes on from there."

We were in Mark's room and he looked very alert so I went on to tell him how the baboons seemed to haunt the camp after the massacre. Wherever you looked during the day, there always seemed to be one, two or more of these fearful creatures watching you. I often wondered if they had vengeance in mind. I remember one day when we were doing a run to the rubbish tip. This was a big hole about half a mile from the camp. Obviously we were armed at all times and we were using Land Rovers and a 1-ton Land Rover to carry the rubbish. The rubbish tip was an obvious place for the baboons to congregate. Prior to the shootings, the baboons used to go about their business and ignore us. Not now, or at least as I saw it, they would loiter around our camp as if waiting for us to come out, something I had not noticed before. Then they would follow the convoy of two vehicles with armed marines on board and the 1-ton truck. They didn't have a problem keeping up with us, as in this terrain you can hardly speed anywhere. They would leap and bound in a very menacing way. At first I thought it was me being over diligent until I mentioned it to some of my colleagues. Apparently they were of the same mind but most shrugged it off, thinking as I had of being over-observant.

On occasions, we would come under fire from the odd dissident who would let off a few rounds at you and move on. You get quite used to this and treat it a bit like a game of hide and seek. However, with the baboons behaving like they were I felt a little more under pressure. I clearly recall one incident when we came under fire. The driver and I had gone to ground under the Land Rover as there was no other place to go. I spoke back to Dhala and asked for some heavy mortar fire (3" in those days) to be put down on a rocky outcrop about half a mile away, one often used by our enemy as it overlooked the tip. We were waiting silently for the rockets to fall on the position when suddenly shots rang out from the other Land Rover, they were firing at us or so it seemed. Not so, the driver and I had been so intent on watching for the rockets to fall on shot that we had forgotten completely about the baboons and their menacing behaviour.

Thankfully, the driver of the other Land Rover had observed that four baboons were stalking us. He had instinctively opened fire; killing two and making the other two run off. I hate to think how I could have coped with a hand-to-hand battle with one of those monsters.

On another occasion, I had to blast a large male, as it was hell bent on a full frontal attack on our vehicle. We were close to the tip when this beast leapt out of the ground and came straight at us. I crouched down in the front of the Land Rover and let loose a burst of fire, almost emptying an entire magazine of my S.M.G. (Sub-Machine Gun) Badly wounded, it turned tail and made off to the tip.

These baboons had changed their attitude towards us, there was no shadow of doubt about it. Could it be vengeance? I would say, yes.

Not far from Dhala was a short landing strip for fixed winged aircraft to bring us in essential supplies like mail, mail, and more mail. It was a highlight of your day when the plane arrived and you would try to act the hard man and look surprised when someone shouted out your name. You also had to act the hard man when you didn't get any mail and this somehow seemed a bit more difficult. The planes, twin pioneers, were great to watch, as they needed hardly any runway to land and take off. Prior to their arrival, we would place lookouts all around the camp in all of the likely approaches, as we didn't want our chums from the Yemen to claim a plane down.

The pilots were great. No fly past to see if the coast is clear, they approached low and fast and at the last few seconds they would just plonk the plane on the deck. Many hands, to grab the goodies on board, then a quick burst of the engines and it was gone.

As the Yemen border is only 8 miles from the camp, I always expected them to give us more attention than they did, as to get reinforcements from Aden would be no simple task as it is about 80 miles away to the south.

"Look out, Markie, there's a baboon coming," I said to him and he didn't flinch. I had got so carried away telling the tale, I had not noticed he had gone fast asleep.

MONDAY 23RD OCTOBER, 2000

Julie says that, when she was with Mark this morning, she asked him, "Mark, please speak to me."

"Where's Lauren?" she says he replied.

I refused to accept this. I wanted to but I did not want to build my hopes up, go dashing down there only to find that it was probably just wishful thinking or Julie being over-imaginative. I could not say she did not hear him speak, as the last thing I want to do is call her a liar. After the last time this happened with J., I made it my resolve to only believe what I personally see and hear.

Good physio today, a long sit, probably 60% Mark and 40% from the person supporting him. To make sure Mark doesn't fall over, someone has to be behind him all the time to catch him should he lose his balance.

Mark had not got a dressing over the hole in his neck where the trachea tube has been. It looked really strange. Apparently they just remove the tube and let the hole heal up in a natural way. I'm told this is normal, as some patients have to have the tube put back should the need arise. I suppose you can call it a 'cooling-off period'.

One of Mark's old mates visited today. Dave Gauger, he has been to see Mark before and noted in the diary that Mark has made a big improvement. He also left us a tape to play to Markie, so on our evening visit Marion and I played it to him. Don't think we got any reaction but who knows, it could have triggered something inside Markie.

TUESDAY

Mark was running a bit of a temperature so a nurse was keeping a watchful eye on him. She has also sent a sample of urine for testing as she suspects he may have a bladder problem.

Panic struck on our evening visit as a spider, said to be enormous, was in one of the corridors and all the staff were terrified. Off with her coat and off for the kill went Marion closely followed by three trembling nurses.

"Mark, your Mam is amazing, she just walked up to spider, looked it straight in the eye and picked it up, yes, just picked it up with her bare hands, then casually took it out into the garden and let it go."

This came from J., another of Mark's nurses. She told that story to just about everyone and, every time it was told, the spider got bigger and bigger. Marion was a true heroine in all of the eyes of this arachnophobia staff.

THURSDAY 26TH

Mark has got a urine infection so, rather than use more antibiotics, it has been decided to try to flush it clear with lots of water and cranberry juice. On our evening visit, little David Gott kept us company. When I told him of Mark's infection he promptly said,

"Don't worry about Mark at all, I promise you I will look after him."

"That's great, David, I'll jot my phone number down for you, if you are worried about Mark, tell the nurses and if they don't sort it out, ring me."

"I will, don't worry, your Mark will be alright with me." When I saw Billy and Pat that weekend they told me that David was well pleased with his new role of 'Mark's minder'.

FRIDAY 27TH OCTOBER, 2000

I got here for physio at 15 00 hrs to find they had already started. One of Mark's friends, Peter Greenwell, had been with Mark in the day room when L. from physio came to collect him.

"Would you like to join us in physio?" she asked.

"I would love to. I've always wondered what Mark got up to in there."

Mark performed like a hero, maybe showing Peter just how good he was. We put Mark on the edge of the plinth and I sat on a chair in front of him. L. then put Mark's hands onto my shoulders, and then, with A. kneeling behind, we rocked backwards and forwards. This was great; for the first time I felt that Mark and I had got positive eye contact. I could feel it and it was good. Such a strange feeling overcame me.

"You know it's me, don't you, Mark?" No sign from Mark but the connection was still there and it was wonderful.

"He knows it's you, I can feel it by his body language," said A. L. and Peter looked on; both had their eyes full of tears, not crying but both feeling very emotional.

"Thanks, Markie, that's wonderful."

I could not hold my feelings and I too filled up. We all just stayed there in silence trying to control our emotions, but managing to hold off our tears.

"Markie, have I told you about how I became a Royal Marine?"

No reply, so I went on to tell him.

I had three good pals in my teen years, John Bill Cowell, Barry 'Badger' Birks and Billy Pounder. John Bill, Barry and I worked down the coalmines at the time. At weekends we would meet up and enjoy a few drinks and swap stories on the past week's events.

In my early teens, I had been in the Army cadets along with my big brother Fred. I was a mere Lance Corporal but Fred was a sergeant and a bit 'power pissed' when he was in charge. I remember on one cadet night, when Fred talked about the wartime Commandos and The Cockel Shell Heroes. How he knew about them I don't know, but it got me a bit excited and hungry for more information.

"I would have loved to have been a Commando during the war, it must have been really exciting, I wish they were still going."

"They are, but they are no longer belong to the Army. The ones going now belong to the Royal Marines. To get into that mob you have to be something special and a bit of a hard man."

"Can anybody join them, Fred, could I join them?"

"Don't even think about trying to join them, our kid, they don't want lads like you, they only want hard men, men with a lot of guts and stamina, you know nowt about fighting or owt like that."

"Oh yeah, who says I know nowt about owt," I said.

"Let it drop, cock, just believe me, you have no chance of being a Commando, anyway me Mam wouldn't let you join."

That did it, "How does our Fred know that I couldn't be a Commando. He has never seen me fighting or doing owt really tough or brave, I'll show him you see," I remember thinking to myself.

At this time I was only 14, so I was far too young to even consider joining, but the seed had been sown and from that day I knew I wouldn't rest until I could become a Commando.

Some years later I was sat having a pint with my friends John Bill Cowell and Barry Birks in the Derby Pub when John Bill said,

"I'm getting close to having to do my National Service. If I weren't down Pit, I would have been 'called up' by now. I'll still have to do it when I'm 21, as everyone has to go in."

This triggered the Commando thoughts again.

"Why don't we leave the pit and join the Commandos, I reckon we could do it."

John Bill and Badger (a name Barry hated) just looked at me.

"Don't be stupid," said John Bill, "we wouldn't get in there."

"I bet we could. Anyway I'm going to the Dole Office on Finslay Gate tomorrow to see if they can tell me how to get in."

The following weekend saw us again in the Derby and I couldn't wait to unload my Commando information.

"I'm going to Manchester next Friday to the Recruiting Office for the Navy."

"I thought you were going to be a big hard Commando. Have you gone chicken or won't they have you?."

"Don't be stupid, John Bill, everybody knows that the Royal Marines are the Navy's soldiers, they have always been on Navy ships for hundreds of years. You must be a bit dim if you didn't know that."

I must confess that I had not known that until I had my visit to the Dole Office where a Navy Recruiting Petty Officer had given me the full story on how to join.

I had just finished educating John and Barry, when the heavy hand of the law was placed on my shoulder, in the shape of a Police Sergeant.

"Na then young man, you don't look old enough to be drinking, how old are ta?"

"I'm 18, sir."

121

"Well I find that hard to believe," with that, he took out his note book.

"I'll start with you," he said staring at me, "what's your name and address?."

I sat there speechless, all I could think was,

"Me Mam' ll. kill me if this copper turns up at our 'ouse."

"No I'm sorry, Sergeant, I'm sixteen and I've only had one mouthful of ale, please let me off."

"Oh! Yuv only had a mouthful 'ave yu lad, so that mex it your ale dunt it, now who bought for yu?"

I hadn't bought it, as I was afraid to ask for beer at the bar, for fear of being thrown out. I think it was John Bill who got them but if I told the copper he would have 'copped' him for buying it for me.

"A fella who was drunk gave it to me, coz he said he was pissed and he was going home." I lied and I think it was obvious.

"Good try lad, not good enough though, now let's get on wi' it, come on name and address before I lock you up."

I gave him my details and fell into the doldrums, "Boy am I in the shit," I thought.

SATURDAY 28TH OCTOBER, 2000

Mark inundated with visitors today. First Marion with Mark's Auntie Mary (Marion's sister) from Ashbourne, Derbyshire. Not a lot of reaction from Mark as he is a tired lad today. Next to arrive came Julie and Lauren, followed by Kelly with Dannielle, the two little ones have made notes in the diary.

Lauren's note: I LOVE YOU MARK, GET WELL SOON.

Then Dannielle's: I LOVE YOU LOTS AND LOTS, GET WELL SOON AS IT'S NEARLY CHRISTMAS X X X Dannielle.

At 14 30 hrs Wendy arrived. She cut Mark's finger nails, watched closely by Dannielle. At one point Danni spoke and Mark reacted by turning his head towards the direction of her voice. He stared for a brief period, then fell asleep.

Dad at 15 15 hrs.

Corrected his sitting position by lifting and pulling his bottom to the back of his seat, looks better but not for long, as he seems a very tired lad today. Mark put on his bed for a rest.

19 10 HRS MUM AND DAD

Back again, Mark, you are looking good propped up in bed, and responding to some hand squeezes on his left hand by squeezing back in reply. His arm is also very active; he now reaches over his body and grasps his right arm. I wonder if the right arm is giving him some pain and the left one is coming over to soothe it, I thought. It is what most people do, especially after banging their elbow on something.

SUNDAY 29TH OCTOBER, 2000

Very lazy day today, Mark slept for most of it, maybe getting as much rest as possible as physio and Giles are back tomorrow.

Mark's looking great this evening, so I decided to explain the origin of the Special Boat Service motto 'not by strength by guile'. The boatmen are not the only people who have this motto; there is someone else who deserves to use it, as this character is a born master of stealth and even better at guile.

Mark, back in 1966 I was sent along with 5 others to the Falkland Islands. We were sent there to carry out various tasks, but one which clearly sticks in my mind was this. Prior to our arrival, the Royal Marines on the island numbered about 30 and they lived about a mile out of Port Stanley in an old disused wireless station from World War II. They, as always, were a self-contained unit with their own chefs, drivers, officers, N.C.Os, etc. Unlike them, we were made up of: an officer and his aide (Batman or Lacky or whatever you choose to call him); a driver, who was nicknamed 'Topsy' as sadly he was not the fastest marine I have met but a good steady driver; Willey my mate, an amazing signalman and a wizard when it came to radios, aerials and anything to do with what is required to establish communications; a sergeant who Willey and I nicknamed 'The Old Lady' as his task was mainly to administer our needs; then, of course, me: my role was somewhat varied and complicated on many occasions.

Our accommodation was a bungalow on the top road in Port Stanley. The captain was billeted in the town close to Government House, as it was he who the governor would liaise with.

The old wireless station was now deserted but, because we had an underground cache out there, I had to make regular security visits, not that we had any thieves or vagabonds on the island but because, if the 'Argies' (Argentineans) got wind of what we had stored there, it would possibly encourage them to raid it. On my first visit I had a very strange feeling that someone was watching me. Had the Argies got to know that the place was now unmanned, who knows? That feeling never left me even after five, maybe six visits. I was so positive that I would approach the station from different directions. I even paddled out to it very early one morning in our inflatable boat in a sort of dawn attack manner. Alas, all to no avail. Whoever was watching me, was good, bloody good.

"Oh, Markie, stay awake, surely you want to know who it was?"

No deal, he had slipped into the land of nod once more.

MONDAY 30TH OCTOBER, 2000

Bad lad today, Mark didn't want to be put in his chair this morning. When the girls went to prepare him, Mark was as stiff as a plank, both legs and both arms sticking straight out. They had managed to get the body sling under him and connect it to the hoist but when they went to lift him he would not relax and let his body fold into the hammock-type sling. Luckily, G. came along and gave Mark some physio on his bed, this 'chilled' Mark out sufficiently to finally get him into his chair.

Physio later on was good. We had enough hands to get Mark to stand, as a new, smart-looking lad, fit and healthy, had arrived to join our ranks.

"Rob's the name, I've heard all about you and Mark, rest assured that I will give you my best."

"What a nice fella," were my thoughts.

"On three, one, two, three," said G. and up we took Mark into a great standing position. We held him for a good 5 minutes, and then sat him back onto the plinth.

"Let's go for another, seeing as we have enough of us. Everybody okay on three again, one, two, three."

Up went Markie again. We all thought the first one was good but this was a cracker. Legs straight, feet flat on the floor, head up and looking good. I would say, on the first stand Mark contributed perhaps 20%, however, on the second I would say 35% as he was so much easier.

Funny, when you get Mark into a stand, as at 6'2" he is in a position to tower over us all. It often comes as a shock to the staff if they have not seen him standing before.

"Well done, Markie, that was brilliant."

"And so say all of us," Rob shouted.

"Something about Rob that rings bells, can't put my finger on it, just something," I told Marion that evening.

TUESDAY

Good day for all today, as it seems that Mark is hell bent on giving us all a buzz.

Wendy 16 05 hrs, Mark was in occupational therapy when I arrived, neither Dad nor I could get him to wake up; we decided that the heat may be an underlying factor. Thinking about it, if we knew times, maybe we could take him outside for fresh air and a stroll before sessions, weather permitting. After his treatment, he was wide awake and kept squeezing my hand. I kept giving his hand three squeezes for I Love You. You may think I'm losing the plot but I'm sure he did it back. Maybe all of us can do the same with him. He had a really good grip on my mobile phone and moved his arm up, down and right across the front of his body whilst holding it. I called Jane over to watch him moving it. When she came over and spoke he turned his head immediately to face her, and she was really chuffed. I even had him holding a pen in-between two fingers. God! My brother's a star today. I even made it so he could give me a hug, I cuddled up to him and put his left arm around me, he gave me a squeeze, and it was wonderful. After all that he zonked back off at 10 past 5.

DAD @ 15 00HRS FOR MARK'S PHYSIO

Present were A., L., the speech therapist D. and G., but only for a short period as he had a pre-arranged appointment. D. was brought up to speed by G. and A., regarding Marks past and present performances. Mark did very well again. He was sitting upright, holding his head up, his hands were placed onto my shoulders and we just sat there face to face trying to form a bonding or some sort of connection between us. We held this position for a good 5 minutes in silence, all of us watching and waiting for something to connect but alas nothing, other than a strange feeling within me that we were almost there.

After physio, Mark was taken by S. for occupational therapy. Unfortunately he was very tired, so we failed to get much action. Wendy took over from me and it seems that he came alive and very active for her.

DAD AND MUM AT 19 00 HRS

Mark on his bed and partly awake. Marion decided to adopt Wendy's cuddling method. She wrapped her arms around him and placed his arm and hand onto her back (left arm). He stroked and gripped his mum's back. Then said 'mum' twice. Marion was overcome but is sure he spoke. More please, Mark, we need it.

Sadly, I had gone for a brew so I didn't hear him speak. If I had I would have probably fallen on the deck.

WEDNESDAY 1ST NOVEMBER 15 00 HRS

Arrived at physio just as Mr G. was about to start. He explained that probably the most important area of the body for a head-injured person is the trunk. Obviously, everything else is of high priority but in his opinion the area around the middle is top of the list. So today's exercises were aimed at getting Mark to relax his stomach muscles. Mark was laid on the plinth after transferring him straight from his bed using a 'man size' board made of plastic. The board's full name is a patient slide but everyone calls it a pat slide, obviously an abbreviation.

"Right, Mark, we are going to exercise your tummy area as it feels as tight as a drum." With that said, G. took Mark from laying to sitting, bit stiff at first but by the time Mark had sat up five or six times he had got the hang of it. G. commented that Mark was supplying most of the power in the sit-ups, which was excellent for Markie's first attempt at this.

Whilst the exercises were going on, my eyes were drawn to the area of Mark's throat where his 'trachy' had been. It looked really angry so, after physio, I sought out Alison, Mark's principal nurse and she kindly put a dressing on it.

"Mark, your hole has just about healed up, you must have good healing flesh, don't worry if it is a little sore, they always are for a few days after removal."

That was probably the last treatment she will give Mark, as sadly she is leaving tomorrow to have some rest as her baby is due in a couple of weeks. I wonder how she felt when she opened Mark's thank you card.

Thursday 2nd November, 2000

Mark not a good lad at physio today; he just refused to keep awake. Tried all sorts of things from back tickling (which he used to love) to whispering 'sweet nothings' in his ears, lifting up his arms then letting them drop to the plinth but, alas, all in vain, he was shattered. So, out came the pat slide to bridge the gap between plinth and bed and over he goes with a little pushing and pulling from those performing the transfer. Even that didn't wake him up. I pushed the bed back to his room, feeling a bit downhearted, as Mark was unusually tired.

"I hope to God he has not picked up a bug or something, that's the last thing our Markie needs."

That night I got a pleasant surprise when I visited, he was in his bed, propped up and looking quite alert.

Mark, can you remember me telling you about the baboons and how they attacked our camp in Aden? Well, something else came back to me today, whilst I was out seeing customers.

When the excitement of the fire fight, well not really a fire fight, had died down, the horror of it all started to hit me, the bulk of the lads had gone back to their beds and the remainder of us were left on duty.

As the light got progressively better, it gave us a much better view of the carnage we had created. I didn't feel sorry for the death of the baboons, as I am sure that if they had got to us they would have been virtually un-fightable and, if they had managed to sink their massive fangs into us, God knows what the outcome would be.

When you get better, Markie, I will take you to a zoo and let you form your own opinion.

The noises coming from these animals was eerie to say the least. It was a sort of grunting, not loud but quite strange to listen to. Daylight had now dawned and we all watched the animals in silence.

I suddenly realised that they were removing their dead and wounded from the wires and the strange grunting sound was due to this sad and arduous task. Now I felt sorrow, so much so that I felt sick. Don't get me wrong, Markie, I hadn't cracked up but the scene was enough to turn the stomach of even the hardest of hard men. Looking around the lads, I knew that the feelings I had were replicated by all that watched, a very humbling experience for us all.

The old sergeant major walked up close to the wire and surveyed the carnage, he 'cupped' his hands to his mouth, then shouted out loud,

"What a fucking mess, and all for fuck all."

I suppose that summed up what we all felt.

Mark's eyes were almost closed, so I lowered the back of the bed down, made him comfortable and left him to sleep.

FRIDAY 3RD NOVEMBER, 2000

Julie, first visitor today, she appears from her notes to be a little concerned.

"Mark was awake but not dressed when I arrived. He does not look quite right, his right eye looks puffed up and the bridge of his nose looks swollen. I have asked the duty nurse to keep an eye on it. See what you think at physio today."

On arrival for physio, I viewed Julie's notes and had to agree with her finding, I requested that the doctor be alerted just to be on the safe side.

Physio, just Giles and me today, so very much limited on what we can get up to.

"Mark, I want to concentrate on your middle region today." With that he manoeuvred Mark across the plinth and, with me behind Mark, we got him sitting on the edge of it with Mr G. facing him.

"Now, Mark, your dad and I are going to move forward and backwards to try to let you find your point of balance. It is important that you attain this as the speed of your recovery depends a lot on you having the ability to balance." G. went on to tell us that most head injured people feel dazed all the time and dizzy most of the time.

"I have learnt from past patients who have recovered enough to explain their experience that they have a constant feeling of losing their balance and felt that they were about to fall all of the time."

Well, coming from G., a man with a wealth of experience, I have to accept that what he has told us is correct.

"I hope you have been listening, Markie, do you feel we should make balancing our next goal?" No reply from Mark but I had a strange feeling inside me that he understood as I could feel the vibes coming from him.

Wendy on her visit has noted that the dentist called to see Mark to check him out. She had a good look into Mark's mouth and reported that he needed some work doing in there. Treatment is to start next week, then continue it over a period of time, as she did not want to put Mark to any stress by trying to do too much in one session.

Night visit with Marion was as normal, other than Bill and Pat calling in on us. They are here to collect David and take him home as he has completed his stay here, learning to rehabilitate himself, to allow him to have a place of his own. David made us a present of his pre-packed chocolate drink cups.

"You can have these, as I know how to make a proper brew now."

"Thanks from us, Dave, keep in touch, won't you?" Marion said.

131

Saturday 4th November, 2000

No physio today, as Mark is shattered. No apparent reason but, if Mark decides he wants to sleep, then Mark has a sleep.

Mark wide-awake when I got here for my evening visit so I decided it was time for a touch of my history.

Rag Bone Donkey Stone

I don't think I have told you this tale before, Markie. You know how I told you about delivering coke. Well, that part of my income was taken from me. The real 'Coal Men' managed to get the gas yard where I got it from, in order to 'Black Ball' me, and they stopped supplying me. I went on to tell Mark about my next venture to make money.

I told Mark how, along with the help of a horse and cart, I would seek my fortune being a rag and bone man. Now, a rag and bone man is one who tours the back streets looking out for, and asking for, anything of resaleable value, including scrap metal, clean rags, old furniture, in fact, anything that could be turned into cash. In lieu of payment, you would offer your customers a donkey stone for the goods. Knowing Mark would have no clues as to what a donkey stone was, I continued with an explanation.

In the areas where I was growing up, there was little money but lots of pride, especially in the appearance of both the home you live in and personal presentation.

Once again, Mother's rules came to the forefront.

"We might not have a lot of brass, our Peter, but that's not an excuse to be scruffy. It's not important that your pants are patched and repaired just as long as you're clean in yourself."

Back to the donkey stones. These were little blocks of soft stone, usually white or bright yellow. Their usage was to highlight the edge of the steps to your house. It may have started in the days of the wartime blackouts to assist you in getting up and down your steps safely when it was pitch dark. Each neighbour was never prouder than when her doorstep gleamed brighter than any of the others.

To get started on my new bid to be wealthy, I needed the raw material on which to barter with, yes, donkey stones. My mum had plenty as, when our clothes became beyond repair, she would pass them over to the rage and bone man in return for some stones.

132

Even though we donkey stoned our steps (a chore carried out in rotation by all in the family) on a weekly basis we always seemed to have more stones than we would ever use. So my Mam was quite happy to let me have some, but not before she had had her inquisition.

"I know tha's up to somat Peter, come on, lad, let us know," Mam asked me as we sat at our long wooden kitchen table having tea.

"I'm not up to owt honest, well I'm not up to owt that's dishonest anyway."

"If that's the case, lad, why do you want a load of donkey stones?"

Seated at the table was Fred, Pam, Norma and me Mam.

"E's up to somat, Mam, I can tell when e's planning sommat," said Fred.

"Come on, Peter, tell us," said Pam.

As Pam was always 'my minder', I decided to reveal what I was going to do but only after I had sworn them to secrecy.

"I don't know if you know John Bill Cowell's dad, Barnie?"

"Course we do," said Norma.

"Well e's got 'imself in a bit of trouble over sommat and 'e's bin sent to jail."

"So, what's that gotta do wi you," this time Norma acted that 'need to know part'.

"Well I 'ave asked John Bill's Mam if I can borrow Barnie's 'orse and cart cos he was a rag chap before cops got 'im, and she has said that, if I make any brass, I will have to give her some for 'thors's feed.'"

"My lad a rag chap, over my dead body, ur Dad'll be turning in his grave if he 'as one."

"No Mam honest! John Bill's Mam and his brothers are as skint as we are and she can't get rid of th'orse as Barnie would kill her when he gets out of jail."

Support came from Fred and Pam. They suggested that if I didn't go around our area and stuck to Lane Head and Stoneyholme, it would be okay with them.

"What do you think, our Norma?" Mam asked.

"If it's alrete wi them then it's alrete wi me, but don't bring it round here, Peter. I don't want folk shouting out at work, eh! look there's Norma, her brother's a rag and bone chap."

"Well, Mam, is it okay?"

"Aye, go on then, I've just one question and that's how do you know how to handle a horse and cart?"

"That's easy, I have been going around with Barnie a few times now an he told me how to do it."

"You little bugger, you planned this a long time ago didn't you. I 'ope you have nowt to do wi Barnie goin to jail so you cud get your hands on his 'orse and cart."

"Give o'er, Mam, I wouldn't do owt like that."

"Think on, Peter, don't do owt to bring shame on us or u'll be in for it."

The following day was to be my debut but it was torrential rain and it did not seem a good idea trying out my new career in that sort of weather.

The next day was better, still raining but not as bad, so I called at John Bill's house to get him to come with me and help me get the tools for my new trade.

"You should have seen me, Mark, I had on an old raincoat, some old pants and a pair of 'wellies' which were probably two sizes too big for me."

Horse and cart at the ready, so I thanked John Bill and off I went on my new venture but, before getting down to some serious work, I sneaked home to collect my donkey stones. That done I set off.

Down Manchester Road where I got my first fright as, when I got to the canal bridge, I applied the brakes on the cart. Well, I say I applied them but they were virtually none functional. I jumped off the cart and tried to help the horse hold the cart back. Thankfully for the horse and me, some firemen were changing shifts at the fire station on the corner of Finslay Gate and Manchester Road. Seeing our plight, four firemen rushed over and grabbed the cart, two were at the front, backs to the cart and leaning on it. It did the trick. We slowed down enough to guide the horse onto Finslay Gate, where we stopped by the dole office.

"Thanks, cock," said one of the firemen, "that's first bit of excitement we 'ave' ad for a few shifts."

They went on their way, laughing and cracking horse jokes, and I can remember one of them shouting, 'neigh neigh'.

By now I had calmed down and the horse seemed to be no worse for the experience so we got on our way. Just down from the dole office was a bakery. It was housed in part of the old mill on the right going up Finsley Gate, a bakery I knew well from my coke-round days as I used to call there to see if I could scrounge something to eat.

I banged on the open bake-house door and thankfully a familiar face came. It was John, a very kind man as he always gave me something.

"Hi, John, I'm starving 'ave u any burnt pies?" I asked.

"Bloody hell, young Peter, 'uve cum up int world, 'ave u swapped ur pram for that 'orse an cart."

"No, I've borrowed it I'm gonna 'ave a go at being a rag chap."

"Y'ur a little bugger, tha'l mek it some day, but I can't see u making a fortune out of being a rag chap. Hang on an a'll go an see if I can find owt for you and th'orse."

He returned after only about a minute.

"Sorry, cock, I've no burnt pies at all."

My heart sank a little as already I was hungry and I had a long day ahead of me. I let my head slump forward and moved to go back to the cart.

"'Ang on, young Peter, just give me 5 minutes, al just go an burn yu some pies."

True to his word he came back with a flour bag with six meat and potato pies in it.

"There u go and gud luck."

"Thanks, John, I'll remember you when I'm rich."

He watched as the horse and cart and I made our way up Finsley Gate.

I opened the bag and took out a pie as I was starving. When I got pies in the past I used to break off the burnt bit on the bottom and throw it away. No need to do that today, for all the pies were perfect. I turned and waved at John. He returned the wave then went back into the bakery. I found it a bit difficult to eat the pie as John's kindness had made me feel sad and I had a big lump in my throat.

By now, Mark had either got bored to sleep or he had had to give in to my endless story telling.

"Sorry, Markie, I'll try to finish that tale tomorrow night if I can remember where I left off. Oh, I remember, I had just got some pies from John. No reaction from Mark as he was well out of it. The following night, Saturday, was an uneventful trip as Markie was fast asleep when I arrived, even though lots of fireworks were going off outside. On reading his notes, he has had a pretty lazy day. On the way home, my thoughts went to one of my Mam's favourite sayings. She had several ways of coming out with this message, one I remember well is,

"If you're not rete, cock, go to bed and sleep, it's best cure in't world."

I took her advice that night, as I was feeling a bit down, as seeing our lad laying there in his hopeless state and knowing that you have nothing else to offer that can help him. I have searched my armoury and I have no ammunition in there that can help him or any of us on this occasion. Time is the answer but I have a horrible fear of running out of that.

5TH NOVEMBER (AT LAST)

Maybe the fireworks will stop after tonight; as for the last month we have had a bombardment of these money-wasting pyrotechnics every night. It is taking a long time for the novelty to wear off for some of the people who now live in Burnley and surrounding areas. Marion first on the scene today and, thankfully, she has found him in a more co-operative mood. Julie next and she too is pleased with Markie's turn around. She reports that his mouth is looking very dry, so she got one of his pink swabs (rather like a sponge lollipop), soaked it in water and wiped out his mouth. Her words are,

"Mark has his mouth open a lot, so I put some water on one of his pink sponge mouth swabs. He sucked all the water off because his mouth and throat were very dry. We got some wonderful swallows, well done, Sparkie."

When I read these comments, I was smacked with a touch of adrenalin, 'some wonderful swallows' is what hit me as I had a terrible fear that Mark would never eat or drink again, then here we are with him giving us 'some wonderful swallows'. I decided not to make a big play on this but it certainly gave me a 'feel good' sense.

Linda Bloomfield came to see Mark today. She is an old family friend, and her husband John had been a good personal chum of mine. We used to spend hours together swapping tales of our past. John had been a member of a Special Force in the South African Army and some of his stories were quite frightening. Not my kind of fighting as it was far too racist but, then again, I was not in his shoes. Sadly, due to being badly injured by a fanatic on a motorbike, he was repatriated back here. He and Linda ran a successful haulage business for many years but, alas, as a result of his injuries, he finally passed away. A very sad day for me and all of his chums.

Linda's observations were encouraging to us. She mentions that she felt conscious of Mark's awareness of her presence, not all the time but some of the time. She also talks of eye contact, again not all the time, but certainly some of it. On the whole, she is quite pleased with Mark.

Marion and I got here at 18 15 to find Linda still with Markie. I felt a little sorry for Mark as Linda is a journalist and has a reputation of being something of a great orator. I know how my Mam would have described her.

"That bloody Linda cud talk th'ind legs off a donkey."

A statement most people would have gone along with. Having said that, Linda's heart is a big one and one she would share with all of her many friends. A very wise and caring lady and she and Mark had a special bonding and it shows.

I found out from one of the nurses that Mark's nightly drip feed is to be supplemented with an energy-creating drink to be administered by his PEG. Let's watch out for results.

Alison, Mark's primary nurse, left to have a rest before her baby arrives. Mark's card reads,

"Thanks, Alison, for all of your T.L.C. I promise I will keep trying to get myself well. Love, Markie."

Monday 6th November, 2000

Markie is a tired lad again today. Regardless of a visit from two of his old friends, Peter and Shamus, he refused to wake up.

I missed physio today but Enty stood in for me and he reports that Markie almost balanced on the end of the plinth. I wondered how near 'almost' was.

"Hi ya, Markie, are you ready for the rest of my ventures as a new 'rag chap'? No reply, so I decided he was going to get an update, ready or not.

After leaving John, the pie man, I continued towards Burnley Wood, but not before I had called at the homes of the Cheetham family. This was a big, big family. My Mam once said to me,

"If all Mrs Cheetham's babies had survived, she would have had enough players for two football teams."

A tale I never investigated but there were a lot, so much so that they had knocked through two or maybe three houses at the top of Finsley Gate to accommodate them all. Everybody could boast of having a Cheetham for a friend as they were spread over two decades.

Burnley Wood was a big area of terraced rows, as was most of Burnley. This area like most, was full of people fighting to survive in a very poor climate. There was work but there were a lot of workers, so not all could find a job.

My trusty horse and I travelled up and down the back streets trying to scrounge what we could.

"Rag bone, donkey stone" was my practised cry, copied from all the other rag chaps. I did that much shouting and that much walking that I was getting 'hoarse' and certainly very wet. I pulled my pants over the top of my 'wellies' in an effort to stop the water getting in, to prevent me getting sore legs. I had done it too late, as I could feel and hear my feet 'squelching' in the wellies. Apart from a few rags off the Cheethams, and the odd bit of junk given to me, I was having a pretty poor start to my new career. Stoneyholme was worse than Burnley Wood, nothing, and again nothing in the Barden Lane area.

As the day was going on and my throat was sore, my feet wet and the wellies wearing away at my legs and creating a bright red ring around them, I decided on one last try, this time, on my own territory, Trafalgar Street. I decided not to target the homes as I would have been recognised and possibly put my family up for ridicule. So, my last target was the weaving shed at the bottom of Albion Street.

We made our way along Trafalgar Street, past the Lord Nelson and the Malecov Pubs and the bus depot to the Trafalgar Pub at the bottom of Albion Street. Knowing I was in familiar territory, I was walking close to the horse and using it for cover. I didn't feel too conspicuous as there were a lot of rag and bone men in those days.

Sharp right and down into the yard of the mill. Again, using the horse for cover, I sought out someone to talk to. Standing by the door of the boiler house was a man in an overcoat and flat cap. He was sheltering under the canopy over the boiler house entrance. Assuming he was in charge, I approached him.

"Wot are you after, cock?"

"I'm after any old scrap iron that you don't want, Mr." I tried to look really down and poor, a role which was easy to play, as I was.

"I can't pay you as I 'ave nowt."

"'Elp 'urself to that lot, cock," he was pointing to the corner of the yard bounded by a high wall. The Leeds and Liverpool canal ran behind the mill, as it did in all of the mills. In the past the canal serviced the mills, mainly with coal for the boilers.

I looked at the pile and suddenly felt good. It was massive, so much so that I could be very selective on what I was going to load. I didn't know anything about scrap iron but I did remember words of advice, again from my Mam.

"Just coz it glitters, cock, it doesn't mean it's gold."

With this in mind I went for the dull, heavy pieces of metal, cast iron. My labours went on uninterrupted for some time; the load on the cart got higher and higher. The cart was hardly the Rolls Royce of carts but it did have springs for suspension. By now they were looking a little bit inverted, as they were bending down from the axle. In my mind I was trying to work out which scrapyard I would head for. Little or no brakes meant that I would have to stay on the flat. I had to dismiss going to the ones I knew down in Burnley under the arches of the railway, as it meant I would have to go downhill regardless of which route I took. To go down by the Waterloo pub, past Watt's Clock would be out of the question as, when you get over the canal bridge, it gets really steep. I could go to the far end of Trafalgar to the Mitre pub and turn right down Westgate. It was not as steep that way, but it was still downhill and with no brakes another big 'no no'.

"Got it. If I headed towards the Waterloo and turned left up Sandygate, I could go up past Coal Clough Lane and the Empress Picture House onto the junction of Accrington Road, and the Barracks Road, the one with the General Havelock Pub on the corner. Somewhere along Barracks Road was another scrapyard called Critchleys. Just where it was I couldn't remember but I was sure there was no downhill bit.

My thoughts were broken by a loud male voice.

"An where do you think your going wi' that lot?" This came from a short, fat, dirty-looking chap. He was wearing a flat cap and a big belt and a pair of braces held up his pants. For a few seconds, something from my Mam went through my mind.

"Don't tek any risks in life, cock, before setting off on owt. Alus put on your belt and braces, it's alus safer that way as you won't let the side down."

Wise advice, as I have discovered over my life.

By now, this bigger than ever man was close to me, more round than tall, but certainly big.

"Am going tut scrapyard we it."

"You're not goin' anywhere lad, come 'ere an see."

With that he led me to the front of the cart.

"Look ya daft little bugger, go on look, that poor bloody horse is not going anywhere."

I took one look and with shock and horror I could see that the poor horse was dangling from the shafts of the cart with is harness tight around its neck and its feet clear of the ground.

"Yud better chuck that lot off yer cart before that poor 'orse pegs out."

With that I started to discharge my precious cargo. What a let-down I thought, all this possible scrap and no way of turning it into money. The horse was coming down now, so I continued to throw stuff off until all the horse's feet were firmly on the ground.

"Is that okay now, can I go?"

"I told you, cock, you're not going nowhere. Who said you could av the scrap anyway?"

"That chap who works with you, he was here by the door when I asked him and he said I cud 'elp me sell."

"What bloody chap, I don't have a mate and I don't bloody need one."

"Honest, Mr, this chap was 'ere and I wouldn't dare tell you a lie, as me Mam wud kill me."

I was getting a feeling of fear, as me Mam would go up the wall if I got caught stealing.

The man had removed his hat and was looking at me and the cart in a funny manner.

"That's Barnie's 'orse and cart, where as ta got that from?"

"I've borrowed it off Mrs Cowell and John Bill Cowell as 'is dad 'as been taken off to jail for doin somat wrong."

"You're rete on that, lad, as I know Barnie well. 'E usually gets my scrap, and I believe your story on that chap who were 'ere. He were after a job but I know him from old, not a nice chap at all, in fact he is well known round 'ere for being a thieving sod. Steer clear of 'im, cock, if you want my advice."

"A will, Mr, a will, can I go now?"

"Not yet, cock, cum we me a minute."

He took me into the boiler house and over to the door of the boiler. He knocked the door open and said to me,

"Yu stan in front of that, cock, for 10 minutes and dry tha sel out, yer bloody wet through."

I did but not before I had ran outside to retrieve the last two of my pies.

"Do you want a pie, Mr?"

"Aye, I'll 'ave a pie wi' you, cock, I haven't eaten since six this morning."

He took the pies from me, placed them on a very shiny shovel, then he knocked open the boiler door.

Carefully, he moved the shovel into the fire opening, held it there for a few minutes then slowly pulled it back out.

"Na then, cock, sit thee sen down an let's enjoy a nice warm pie together, tha don't want ta be eightin cold soggy pies on a day like this."

We sat down together on a low bench in front of the boiler and set about enjoying our pies. "Are you legs sore, cock, I've noticed you've been limping a bit."

"Ye' me wellies 'ave been rubbing me legs all day an' they're killin' me."

"Jus sit there, cock, an' give us yu'r wellies, I'll dry 'em a bit."

I took off the wellies and handed them to him.

"Thae ar bloody soaking, no wonder yur legs a sore, I'll dry 'em out a bit fo yu. Na let's av a luk at tha legs.

He carefully looked at my legs, then said,

"Soon sort them out, cock."

He walked over to a tub, reached in and dipped his hands in. He pulled his hands out and I could see they were covered in grease, walking over to me, he said,

"Gee us them legs, lad, an let's rub suma this on em, it'll sort 'em out."

It did, and after 15 minutes or so, I was dressed up, wellies on, feeling much better and ready for off. He took me out to the horse and cart and said,

"Remember, cock, steer clear of dodgy buggers like 'im you met today, tek a leaf out of my book, alus ask before ya tek, an if ur not sure it's rete, don't tek owt or ask somebody else if it's rete tu ave it. That's wot I av alus dun. I call it belt and braces, cock."

With that, he hooked his thumbs into his braces and went back into the boiler house.

"That's funny, I thought, I wonder if he knows my Mam. He must do or 'e wouldn't have sed I call it belt an braces."

I took the horse back to his stable off Healy Wood Road, made him comfortable, fed him and set off home.

"Not learnt a lot today, I thought. Yes I have, axle grease is good for stinging wellie marks and alus check things out before you tek owt. I'll call it belt and braces."

TUESDAY 7TH NOVEMBER, 2000

Not a lot going on with Markie today. When I say not a lot, I mean from our observations during our visit. Sarah went to check the notes on Mark's activity through last night. The duty nurses had noted,

"Mark very vocal through the night, he kept shouting 'mum'."

Sorry, will have to take that with a 'pinch of salt'. I will have to hear it clearly and positively myself before I can even think about getting excited. Funny smell in Mark's room and, according to Julie and Wendy, it has smelt a bit foul all day. On making enquiries, it seems that Mark's urine bag burst through the night and completely saturated his carpet. Arrangements have been made to clean it tomorrow.

WEDNESDAY 8TH NOVEMBER, 2000

Julie has noted that Mark has developed a nasty cough today and that he is very vocal. So much so that she took him back to his room during the lunch break as he was alarming the other patients. Something not quite right with Mark, she notes. Nothing to be too concerned about. It was only that someone had put his slippers on the wrong feet. Julie, like us all, is constantly on the look out for change, more in hope of seeing improvement. So, the fact that his slippers were on the wrong feet had been observed was significant but not classed as very important. Wendy has written,

"Here at 16 10 hrs, Mark in his chair in the dayroom. I took Mark's hand and gave him three squeezes saying with them I-LOVE-YOU and Markie squeezed back three times then he went off to sleep. Doesn't matter, I got my squeezes and it was wonderful."

Interesting physio today. L, Mr G, Andy and I putting Mark through his paces. About half way through physio, Debbie, the speech therapist, joined us. She observed Mark for quite some time then said she would like to see physio around his mouth, neck, cheeks and throat. She asked if I would meet with her the following day after physio in Mark's room, when she would teach me what needed to be done to exercise this area.

Thursday's meeting with Debbie was very informative. She spent a lot of time teaching and demonstrating just what she wanted me to do with Mark. I had no idea what an important role the mouth and surrounding area plays in everyday life, such as speech, drinking, talking, the most important of these swallowing. It was agreed we should concentrate on the swallowing,

143

as Mark, on occasions, gets excessive secretion building up in his mouth on which he often chokes, causing him to cough it out rather than swallowing the excessive saliva.

"Think about how many times you swallow even when not eating or drinking. Go on try it now," she said. I did and I was quite alarmed as to how many times you swallow. I now got her point and I was so proud that she had given me this task, a task I would enjoy (if that is the word).

I would carry out the mouth and facial exercises on a daily basis, along with all of the other tasks I had taken on, perhaps a better name would be 'labours of love'.

I now have two main priorities. First, I must get Mark to balance, second, to swallow.

I felt rather like a dog with a big bone.

"It's my bone and there is no way that I am letting go of it," I thought.

Now I am determined to get on with the job in hand, so, completely out of character for me, I may consider sharing the bone with someone. However, to consider sharing my precious bone, I must be certain that this will increase the possibility of quicker and more positive results for my Markie.

At 16 10 hrs an ambulance appeared and Mark was whisked away for a chest X-ray. This came completely out of the blue for me, as I had not been told anything about it. I was grateful that a necessary procedure was being done. I just wish someone had told me, as it came as a bit of a shock.

Pam, my big sister, called to see Markie today. Friday 10th November and her notes read,

"Called early this time as I was determined to catch him awake. I do see an improvement in Mark. He looks directly at me all the time that I am talking to him. Wonderful. He has not gone to lie down before his dad comes to torture him again."

Pam still with Mark when Julie arrived and they had a good chinwag by the sounds of things.

"Mark has developed a boil on the top of his nose and it looks really angry, have a look at it dad and see what you think." She has noted.

Probed into Mark's mouth after physio today and carried out everything I had been taught by Debbie. It seems very alien to be stretching his cheeks, massaging his gums, stimulating his tongue and generally making as much activity in the mouth as you can. I am amazed how patient Mark is with me. He sits in his chair and looks at me intently, as I talk incessantly in an effort to convince I am doing it for his own good. Not an easy task, believe me. Now I know the true meaning of the saying 'a labour of love'.

After the mouth training, I took Mark to the dayroom, scrounged a brew, then took a good look at the boil on his nose. It looked painful, so I asked

Nurse K to see what could be done. Being a very experienced and a caring person, I am sure she will do what is right.

Mark very tired on our evening visit and he did not wake at all. Marion and I just stood over him for about half an hour, deep, very deep in our own thoughts.

Quite uneventful Saturday and Sunday, with the exception of our visit on Sunday evening. First we entered Mark's room, no Mark, then theday room, no Mark, the corridors, no Mark. As a last resort, I called at the nurses' restroom, and knocked on the door.

"Come in, Peter, we know it's you, Mark has joined us for supper," and he had as he was sat in his chair, bolt upright observing the girls. Well, at least it looked that way.

Sarah took me from the room to say,

"We think Mark's catheter is blocked as urine is bypassing and soaking him. I have put a pad on him but we are going to have it checked out tomorrow. Don't worry, it is not unusual."

She went on to explain,

"When a well person goes into hospital, it is normal practice to have a catheter fitted. They can then pass water when they wish in a normal manner. However, in cases such as Mark's he will pass water at any time and with no real force behind it. With the lack of force or pressure, sediment can build up in the bladder and cause a blockage. I feel this is the root cause of the problem."

"I understand you fully on that one, Sarah, thanks for that, what's the cure?"

"A new catheter needs to be inserted. So I am making the necessary arrangements to have this done."

"Fine, what happens in the meantime?"

Once the catheter is removed, we will try a sheath. Not the sort of sheath as you probably know. These sheaths have a nozzle on the end which connects to a urine bag via a tube."

" Is it the same sort of bag that Mark has fastened to his leg now?"

"Yes, exactly the same."

The blockage of the catheter was confirmed the next day as, when we got Mark onto the plinth we discovered that he was wet through again. Mr G. set the other staff about other tasks and he and I had a close examination of Mark's 'plumbing'. His bag had some urine in it but very little, so G. asked me to sit it out with Mark and confirm that he is bypassing. As if he understood what was required, Mark decided to prove his point and tried to pass water. He was certainly bypassing, as most of his 'wee' came out of his 'Willie' down the side of the pipe, and very little passed down the pipe to his leg bag.

TUESDAY 14TH NOVEMBER, 2000

Sarah had to remove Mark's catheter this morning due to the blockage and discomfort. This had caused him to feel unwell and he is running a temperature. She told me when I arrived that Markie's penis appeared very sore, so she has sent a swab away for analysis. Poor old Markie also has the 'runs' so a faeces sample has also been sent off.

When physio was due, Mr G. decided that we should go for it.

"What about Mark's waterworks" I asked G.

"No time like the present, let's get Mark fitted with a sheath and have a trial run."

That done it was off to the physio on his bed. I have had a lot of practice. The 'patslide' was used to transfer Mark onto the plinth, all in a clockwork manner. With a little grunting, pushing, lifting and coercion, we got Mark onto G's knee, as we were planning on standing Mark. Things ground to a halt when G. announced that he could feel 'warm water' running into his lap. I made a swift examination of Mark's plumbing and sure enough the sheath had come off Mark's 'dangly bit'.

"Sorry, but the plumber has made a close examination and I have to say that a fitting has come off a pipe."

No one argued with me as they knew I was a trained plumber.

"Sorry, Markie, but it's back to your cell and you will have to wait until the plumber gets some different fittings."

We had a little chuckle about that but in my mind I felt so sorry for Mark. Instead of smiling, I really wanted to cry for him. To be subject to such a personal happening and have your body exposed to everyone and then to make a joke about it all is sad, so very sad. I vowed there and then not to do this again to Markie and I have stuck to my vow.

The following day, Mark went the whole physio session wearing a sheath and it was still in place when I checked him out before leaving him for the night. As I was leaving Markie, I could see something in his right hand, it was Wendy's tin that she keeps her manicure gear in. I tried to take it from Mark, but no way was he going to part with it. It made me feel good, such a simple thing, but it is something new and it was his right hand. Yes! It made me feel good.

"It's okay, Markie, I won't steal your bone, come on let's have a cuddle."

I put my arms around him and pulled him to me and held him in a strong cuddle.

146

"Hang on in there, son, you are not on your own, we are all fighting to get you back, honest."

I hung to him as I was feeling quite emotional. Suddenly, Mark gave a loud moan and he shrugged me off. It was too much for us both of us. When I looked into his face, I could see tears in both eyes. "Too much, just too much for me," I said and I burst into tears.

It took a good 10 minutes to get over that moment. Not that I wanted to, I just could not leave him until we were both composed.

FRIDAY 17TH NOVEMBER, 2000

New catheter fitted today. Also had a visit from a lovely Catholic nun, a lovely lady according to Julie. Dentist also called and worked on Mark whilst on the plinth. He has had four fillings on his front teeth and one to his rear lower left. No physio as no time left with all that Mark has been up to so, after dental, I left him sleeping on his bed.

Got Markie to myself Friday evening, he is bright eyed and bushy tailed, so what can I tell you tonight, son?

THE PREDATOR

Mark, can you remember me telling you about when I was in the Falklands and how I knew someone was observing me on my every visit to the old wireless station to check out our arms cache.

I constantly got that feeling and I thought I needed to sort it out once and for all. So, one Friday I went out there with enough gear to last me the weekend. To get there on this occasion, I took a very round-about route and approached the station very cautiously from a direction I had not used before. It was quite dark when I had set out my stall. I had 'made camp' in the corner of the big room where the transmitter had been housed. I selected the corner so as not to be in a position where I could be compromised from behind.

I settled in quite well, my rifle pointing to the open doorway, torch ready to illuminate anyone who chose to visit me, food and water to hand, and my heavy-duty sleeping bag should I get cold.

After about an hour, nothing, and I started to feel a little uncomfortable about being alone. When I had set ambushes in the past, I had never ever been alone. In these situations you are always covered by at least two other members of your ambush team. I don't think I was frightened; just unsafe was what I felt. No danger of me falling asleep on this one but then I have never done that in an ambush situation. Well I have, but only when it was my turn to sleep. My mind was wandering as I lay there in the dark thinking about home, my wife Marion, and my precious baby Julie. I was wondering how Julie would look now, as she was only 4 months old when I had to leave them.

"What's that?" I jerked back to reality.

"There it is again."

Someone was on the move out there. Slowly, I moved position to get behind my rifle. I pressed my body hard down onto the floor, located my torch, then waited. Someone was definitely moving and he was coming towards me. I cocked my S.L.R. as silently as it would allow.

"Come on," I thought, "just try me you bastard, I have known you've been after me for months now, come on, come on, try me."

Adrenalin running high, finger on the trigger.

"What if it is 'Willy' my mate," I thought, "No, he couldn't have pulled this one off."

Other thoughts were going through my head as the sound got slightly louder, someone was moving towards the door. Whoever it was, he was very cautious and carefully slow.

"Wait whilst he gets into the room, Ollie, and don't fucking miss or you're dead."

The fact that I was alone was hitting me hard now, "What if I did miss and this bastard takes me out or if he lobs a grenade in here. God, I hope it's not a white phosphate grenade, I'll be fucking toast in minutes."

"Almost here now, get a grip, Ollie, if you miss you're as good as out of it."

For a moment I wished I had brought my sub-machine gun. Why did I bring a self-loading rifle? I knew I was going to be inside and a sub-machine gun is shorter and far more suitable for close quarter battles.

"Too late now to think what I should have done, as whoever is coming to get me is close, very close."

I was ready, body tensed, eyes focused on the doorway and adrenaline pumping into my mind and body. Again, I felt that twitch in my bottom.

I raised the rifle to ensure I would hit him square on, and waited.

Suddenly, there he was in the full glare of my torchlight. He was frozen to the spot, and he was glaring into the light. He knew I had him.

"You bastard."

I heard myself shout. There was a wild scurrying of feet as my mentor turned and fled.

Fear and the surprise of being compromised had taken him over and all he could do was run for his life. I wanted to give chase but the relief of the encounter, and fact that I, and I alone, had stood my ground froze me to the spot.

"Come back you bastard, come back and fight."

The reality of the encounter hit me then. I dropped to my knees and burst into fits of laughter, so much so that I was completely out of control. Was it relief that caused me to 'crack'? Or, was it the fact that the person who had been haunting and stalking me for all this time, was not an 'Argie', nor was he capable of putting up a fight?

He was most certainly not the sort of person who would be interested in our arms cache, as he would not have known one end of a rifle from the other.

The clothing would hardly have been his goal, as this guy spent all of his time streaking about naked.

I decided to track him down, as is automatic to a Marine. I picked up my rifle and checked that it was on safety, then went in search of him. I searched everywhere but failed to locate him. He had gone to ground somewhere and he was staying there for the time being. Suddenly I was taken over by a feeling of great relief. At last I had traced my unseen mentor. No more would I be looking over my shoulder for a sign of him. I didn't have to alter my lines of approach when I was coming to the camp.

The whole experience was behind me now and I felt good. I just wandered around with a stupid grin on my face and I kept bursting out with fits of laughter.

Back at the Land Rover I climbed up on the bonnet, had a good look round, then shouted out on the top of my voice.

"You weren't wrong, Ollie, you knew someone was around and you finally tracked the bastard down. Well done, lad, all that hard training and the 'blood, sweat and tears finally proved worthwhile. Can you see me, Mam? I did it. I got the bastard, even if it was only a fucking Rooster."

Tears were rolling down my face and I was still laughing as I climbed down off the bonnet and went to collect my 'gear'.

Loaded up and ready to head back to Stanley, I took my last look around to see if I could see my friend but, alas, he was nowhere to be seen. He was there somewhere as I could feel that those beady little eyes were watching me. It was the same feeling I had felt in the past. However, the feeling I was getting now was different. It had changed from a hint of fear to one of great relief and happiness.

"Mr Rooster, I'll be back and when I do you're as good as in the pot," I shouted as I crossed the stream onto the track.

I didn't mean that as, if I ever caught the rascal, I would certainly not have killed him as already I had grown very fond of my little friend. After all, we have been acquaintances and had our eyes on each other for some time. Correction, I should say my friend the rooster had had his eyes on me for some time.

I wondered how I would tell the lads of my daring ambush, and how I had, single handedly, stalked and compromised my mysterious enemy. One thing was sure and that was that the whole of Falkland Island's people would soon know and I would not be allowed to live this one down in a hurry.

After that encounter I made even more regular visits to Moody Brook, not just to check the 'cache' but to feed my newly found chum.

"Eh! Markie, wake up, don't you want to know more about my new mate?"

No reaction, he had slipped into a deep sleep, either that or Markie is one hell of a good actor.

Saturday and Sunday 18th/19th November, 2000

Not a good weekend for Markie as he is unable to wake up for any length of time. He is also as 'stiff as a plank', so much so that the girls are having difficulties in getting him into his chair to sit him out. Must be something 'bugging him', but what? All one can do in a situation like this is observe, look for signs that could cause discomfort. Are his trousers too tight? Is the sheath hurting him? Has he got a stinker of a headache? If only he could communicate in some way. I have tried all ways to connect with him. A nod of the head, the squeeze of the hand, anything would do, but regardless of my endless questions I fire at him, nothing, absolutely nothing. Funny, but you seem to acquire a sixth sense in a situation like this. We are all of the same mind that all is not right with Markie.

MONDAY 20TH NOVEMBER, 2000

Catriona, Mark's principal nurse, a very loving and caring person, must have been checking our diaries and she has received our vibes. She told Julie that Mark probably needed a bowel movement so she had given him something to help earlier in the morning. As another precaution, she had also taken a urethral swab and sent it to the 'path lab' for it to be cultured to see if there could be any infection 'down below'. The result is due back any time today.

Wendy reported that Mark managed a bowel movement just before going to physio at 14 00 hrs and says that he felt brilliant and that he sat bolt upright on the edge of the plinth for a good 10 minutes. She also says that Catriona must be a mind reader.

19 00 HRS

Marion and I were greeted at the entrance by Margaret, another senior nurse, when we arrived.

"Not good news, I'm afraid, Mark has got M.R.S.A."

"What is M.R.S.A?" was our joint reply.

"It is an infection prevalent in almost all hospitals and certainly rife in Burnley General. It is a germ that can spread like 'wild fire'. It goes mainly for open wounds or it can spread to other openings like the ears, nose and any other orifice into the body."

She went to great lengths to tell us the strict routine we must adopt when on a visit. We must wear gloves if we intend touching Mark. If you do touch his hands avoid, touching any other part of the body for fear of spreading it. The danger area for Mark is his peg as, if that gets infected, we are going to have serious problems as the peg is an open passage into Markie's body.

She led the way to Mark's room and explained what precautions everyone must take. On the handrail in the passage were three boxes of gloves, small, medium and large. Plus a big box had been fitted to the wall. This dispensed plastic pinafores. These are a one-off use if you are going to handle Mark. They must be discarded on completion of your visit and placed in the bright yellow bag for disposal later. She demonstrated how we should 'scrub up' before we leave Mark's room, first with a pink wash called 'Hibiscrub', then finish off by rubbing an alcohol gel firmly into the hands.

With that, she left us with Mark, surprisingly he looked great, I don't know what I expected him to look like but it came as a shock to see him looking as 'cool as a cucumber'.

"What next," I heard Marion say.

"I don't know, love, but someone is putting us to the test and without any doubt he or she is doing a bloody good job."

We stood there silent for a good 10 minutes just looking at Markie, afraid to go near him or to touch him.

"Bollocks to this," I heard myself say; it came completely out of the blue, just a spontaneous reaction.

"I'm going to 'pinny' up and get some gloves on. Stand by, Markie, you're in for one hell of a cuddle."

Suitably dressed, I did just that and as usual I got Mark's normal reaction. He fought to shrug me off but he still got his cuddle.

I felt good after I had discarded my gloves and pinny, then a good scrub up with the pink soap rounded off with the alcohol gel. Yes! I felt good. No way could I have left without his customary loving cuddle, even if he doesn't like it.

TUESDAY 21ST NOVEMBER, 2000

Mark not very co-operative today. Understandable if he is not feeling well, just would not relax at all. Plenty of leg extending which causes him to slide forward when in his chair.

WEDNESDAY

Same as Tuesday, so Andy has recommended that we do not recline his chair but keep it more upright. He demonstrated what he meant. Whilst in physio, he sat me on the plinth, then tipped me backwards. Sure enough, out went my legs to counterbalance myself.

Julie's birthday today and she is a bit down. I think she was expecting Mark to sing to her but no such luck. Some day, jewels, some day.

THURSDAY

Julie met the dentist lady today, she wanted to teach a member of the family how to clean Markie's teeth and Julie kindly volunteered.

Physio was very good that afternoon, as we tried a new way of standing Mark. Mark seated on the plinth, two people seated facing Mark but to each side. Giles standing in front of, and close to, Mark, and Andy behind Mark on the plinth.

On the count of three from Giles, Andy slowly raised the plinth. The two seated people, Leanne and I, supported Mark's legs at the knee as he was raised. Giles in overall charge as he pulled Mark forward and up. 'Bingo', after a lot of grunting, pushing, pulling and persuading, we finally got him standing.

Actions reversed and Mark back to sitting.

"Let's go again, on three, one, two, three."

Andy raised the plinth once again and once again we got Markie standing, we held him there for about 2 minutes, then eased him down back into his sitting position.

"Well done, Markie," said Giles. That came as a bit of a surprise to me as Giles has always called him Mark. Maybe Giles was feeling closer to him now.

FRIDAY 24TH NOVEMBER, 2000

A first for Marion today. She came to watch Mark in physio. Giles took her step by step as to what we were doing with Mark and he skilfully explained the reasons why. I feel he made her feel better but I don't think she had the urge to watch on a regular basis. I could see the pain in her face and I knew what she was feeling now. That's a stupid saying, how could I possibly know what she was feeling. I am being as daft as the other people I know, when they inadvertently say,

"I know just how you feel," or

"Don't worry it will be alright."

I don't let such statements get through to me now, as I know when people say such things that they mean well and are trying to reassure me and make it seem easier to accept.

That night I had Markie to myself again, sat up well and eager to hear more tales from my past.

"Markie, have I told you how we worked out of Dhala camp?."

No answer so I must assume I hadn't.

I went on to tell him how we would go out to meet any road transport coming from Little Aden Camp to Fort Dhala, called a fort but not one you would recognise. I preferred to call it Camp Dhala.

We would be briefed the day before as to what and who was coming and the proposed timings. This was all important as we needed to be in position before first light on the day. Dhala Pass was the favourite place to 'smack' us' and this was where we would be on the proposed day of the convoy coming up the pass.

It was essential that we had control of all of the high ground as, in such a position, we should be able to observe the whole of the pass and hopefully prevent the convoy coming under attack. That was the theory, in practice it was somewhat different.

The enemy, affectionately named 'rag heads' were good, exceptionally good, both at moving covertly and in the accuracy of their fire. When up against these people, we treated them with respect as they are born and bred in the environment and have known nothing else all of their lives. Our old sergeant major used to say:

"Watch the bastards. They are good, bloody good. Never try to anticipate what they will do, as the craft sods will do the opposite. Think on lads. If you

157

are down to two of you, make sure one of you is watching your back as these buggers are experts at encircling their prey."

Good advice and something that stuck in all of our minds.

Up early in the morning, rationed, ammunition packed up and off for a day's work. The routine was never copied, as on each occasion there was a chance that the rag heads had spotted our line of approach.

On my first patrol, I remember being issued with three Shemages. All three had different colours.

"What do I want these for?" I wondered. I was not for asking as I didn't want to appear ignorant but I was soon to learn.

Vehicles dumped and camouflaged out we set off to yomp to our destination, leaving behind five lads to act as minders of the wheels, a job I hated.

Working in close proximity to each other, and every man aware of where we were going and what bearings we were using. Just in case we got separated, we would move as cautiously as possible on such a bad terrain. To be quiet was almost impossible, as every stone seems to be loose under foot as we stumble along. You hope for a reasonable moonlight sometimes but I was always thankful for the dark, as if you can see a rag head he most certainly can see you.

Funny, going in on any mission can take hours. You travel slowly with great caution, stop often to listen, everyone perfectly quiet. You even breathe as quietly as you can but most of all you listen and listen. Any sounds in this sort of terrain can travel miles and if heard you can guarantee you will be 'smacked'.

Safely arriving at our planned location, we set about picking our holes for the day. Six men working in pairs. All must think alike and, thanks to the arduous training, you do. Your position must not be such that you break any of the basic rules: shape, shadow, silhouette, the wearing of anything shiny and, probably the most important of the S's, sudden movement. A difficult one this, especially when you have flies buzzing around you. The urge to swot them gets quite unbearable on occasions.

This is where I learned the answer to why we had the shemages. You use them mainly to protect you from flies, sand, dust, etc. but why three? So, I had to ask. My mate that day was 'Robo', a seasoned lad who was on the ball.

"Robo, which shemage are you going to wear when we get settled in our O.P. (Observation post)?"

"Don't know yet, Ollie, it's up to the rag heads."

"What do you mean it's up to the rag heads?"

"Come on, Ollie, think about it. If Iqbal is wearing the red and white one, then Robo and Ollie wear a red and white one. Then if Iqbal eyeballs you, he might be confused into thinking you are his best mate. It's called confuse the bastards if you can."

I felt such a 'dork'. How come I had not thought of the obvious.

Positions sorted out well before first light and in such a way that we could observe each other. Communication lines run out and all we have to do is wait, which is the hard bit.

Cat napping, one at a time, to try to conserve energy is difficult, as this is for real and already your pulse rate is starting to increase.

Its not like training in the Brecon Beacons where you are tired, hungry and wet through, overseen by some instructor who is treating you as if you are the worst bastard he has ever known. He is driving you on to make you crack. No it's not like that, as in my mind I always knew I would never crack and, as bad as it got, I never even felt close to it. I must admit I often had the urge to hit out at the instructors but, if you do, he has won. Always, somehow I managed to maintain my sense of humour. Keeping that was my saviour, much to the annoyance of my mentors who often said,

"I'll knock that fucking grin off your face, Holroyd."

A threat they issued on lots of occasions but one which they never carried out. My theory was, if he is trying to 'waste' you and make you give in, make it hard for him, and a good grin when times were trying worked, much to the annoyance of the instructors.

Secure in our make shift 'sangas' we continued our wait. First light came, and all on our toes watching and listening, afraid to move or make a sound. As dawn breaks and the sun starts its rapid ascent, long shadows are cast from the rocks. If you lack concentration, you can mistake the shadows for someone on the move. You almost will someone to appear so you can observe them as they set out their stall to ambush the impending convoy.

Two sharp tugs on our communications line startled me into the present, as I was so intent on looking down into the valley that I was out of normal contact. I looked over to the sanga the message had come from and saw Benson making our well-practised signal, simple but effective, first three fingers then two then five, meaning 325° on the compass. I gave him the same signal back and got a nod of confirmation. I dug the compass from my pouch, flipped up the lid and looked at the bearing I had been given. Bingo, 'rag heads', six in total making their way down the rocks at the other side of the pass.

"That's probably all of them, Ollie," Robbo whispered to me.

"You can get dressed for the ball now, Cinders," he said as he removed his green and black shemage from his pack and placed it over his head and shoulders. I was pleased it was the green one as I honestly don't think I would wear the red and white one whilst in the O.P. I felt it would be like waving a flag at them. When they were about to reach the road, they stopped, closed ranks then split up into three teams of two. One pair crossed the road and started to construct a low defensive wall. Another pair set themselves up across the road opposite the first pair in the middle of the two positions.

"I think they have been reading the same fucking training manual as we have, that's a perfect cross-fire ambush," Robo whispered. I nodded in agreement.

"What's the other pair up to, Robbo?"

"Don't know but they are not crouched round that pack for nowt. Oh! Shit, they are priming anti-personnel mines, look."

The small mines are about the size of a rear light that you have on a push bike. They are shallow buried with three prongs just below the surface. These mines are designed to inflict injuries rather than kill. Stand on one and bang off goes your leg. You are now a great liability as it is going to take another two men out of the 'ball park' to carry you out of it.

They moved around, placing about ten of them just forward of each defensive position.

"They've definitely been reading up and they must know that it's bootnecks that are coming."

I knew where he was coming from as the Royal Marines are trained to charge straight at the enemy in an ambush situation. In this instance some poor bastards are going to lose their legs if we don't prevent the rag heads performing their 'party piece'.

I looked around at the rest of the lads. We were all aware of what was unfolding in front of our eyes. Strange feeling watching someone set the trap, especially when the trap is your mate's.

Four tugs on the line, the signal for heads together. Robbo and I very carefully crawled our way to our central sanga. Ten minutes later we were all huddled around Corporal Steve (Dusty) Rhodes, our leader today.

"All we can do is try to contact Dhala camp and find out what frequency the convoy will be working on," said Steve.

"Won't have much joy from this position. I will have to get back up to the top of the ridge if we hope to reach Dhala." This came from Paddy our signals boffin.

"Ollie, Biff, check our position and that of the rag heads, both co-ordinates, and don't put your heads together as we need to get them spot on or some poor fucker is going to be limping the rest of their lives." Dusty was right. We had to get it right. Biff Blyth, a chubby lad with a strong Geordie accent but an exceptionally hard man, said,

"I'll go right, Ollie."

"Then I'll go left."

First job when taking a fix on a position is to work out exactly where you are. I had already done this when we first set up our O.P. My findings compared well with Robbo's so I was happy that I knew just where I was. I moved three times and noted the bearings of the ambush site on my map. Confident that it was the exact position, I crawled back and did a comparison with Biff. Thankfully we were almost dead on the spot.

The only problem was the quality of the accuracy of the maps. They were, to say the least, not up to Ordinance Survey quality. The consolation was that poor as the maps which we were all using were, they are the same ones, so if our position, or should I say the ambush co-ordinates, are put onto the convoy commander's map then it should be the right place.

"Paddy, here is the info I need you to get back to Dhala, stress to them that we need the working frequency of the convoy. Ensure that they understand the map reference and ask them to confirm the position, colour code and number. They should come back with yellow 47." Dusty turned and looked at me.

"Is that right, Ollie. Yellow 47?"

"It certainly is, boss."

"Ollie, get your spare battery for the radio and look after Paddy. Biff you tail them and keep them covered."

We mustered our gear and carefully made our way out of the valley. Once confident that we were out of sight of our 'friends', we legged it away at a steady jog.

Time was of the essence now and it was of paramount importance that we alert the convoy. After about 10 minutes Paddy said that we were probably okay to try a contact.

"Grandma, Grandma, this is Hawkeye. Hawkeye, how do you read me, over?"

Paddy had his mouth within the cup-shaped microphone and his head set firmly in place. He looked at me and gave me a negative shake of the head. Nothing, so Paddy repeated his message. Another negative.

"Come on, let's get to another site. Don't like it but I would prefer it if we headed for that rocky mound up ahead, it's more elevated than here."

With that he was up and on his way.

I glanced back to check if Biff was keeping tabs on us. He was, as he gave me a brief wave, then vanished from sight. Good feeling knowing you have a guy like Biff covering your arse. It fills you with a bit of pride to know your minder is such a perfectionist and professional to the extreme.

At the rocky outcrop Paddy went to ground and quickly set about calling Grandma again.

"Roger, Grandma, this is Hawkeye, I am hearing you loud and clear. I have priority communications for you, over."

Listening to Paddy was like listening to a news reader, he had changed from his Irish brogue to perfect and very precise Queen's English. This one-sided conversation went on for about 5 minutes. I could only hear Paddy's side and what he said was spot on, exactly as we had been briefed by 'Dusty'.

"Grandma, this is Hawkeye, I read back to confirm Yellow 47, I repeat Yellow 47, over."

"Roger, grandma, I say again yellow 47, I need to establish communications with Orient Express, this is Hawkeye, listening and out."

Suddenly he was Irish again.

"Won't be long now, Ollie, they are going to come back with more info soon." He sat back, headphones on, handset at the ready and a look on his face that reminded me of the old saying. He looks like the cat that's caught the canary.

Suddenly, Paddy's face changed and he started to write on his note pad. I moved over and had a peep. He had written down the frequency that Orient Express was using.

"Roger, Grandma, I will listen out on this channel awaiting their call for further 10 minutes, Hawkeye listening out."

By now, Biff had moved up to us but he had not relaxed at all, his head was forever on the move, watching, waiting, a bit like the familiar cat stalking the canary.

"What's the score, Paddy?"

Paddy took off his earphones and started to gives us the whole scenario.

"Grandma is talking back to Little Aden, Little Aden will talk to Sunray on the Orient Express, Sunray of Orient Express will call us on our frequency along with a link to the 'Ferrets' who are escorting the convoy. If all that falls through, then we can call Orient Express on their frequency, all everyday stuff really."

"Paddy, if all that works I'll show the Padre my arse," I said.

"I wouldn't," said Biff, "Don't trust any bugger who wears his collar back to front."

The earphones crackled and Paddy whipped them over his ears.

"Orient Express, Orient Express, this is Hawkeye, this is Hawkeye, you are loud and clear, loud and clear, Hawkeye listening out."

"Looks like the Padre is in for a treat then, Ollie, this I must see."

Biff had a grin on his face from ear to ear.

We yomped back to where the rest of our team was as quickly and cautiously as we could.

"Well done lads, a job well done. Now let's settle down and watch the fireworks."

"I'm bloody starving," Robbo said when I joined him in our O.P.

"Why have you not eaten, you prick?"

"I was missing you, darling, and besides I hate eating alone."

With that, we set about our ration packs. Even they taste good when you are famished.

"Markie! Markie! I hope you have been listening. I am sorry I got a bit carried away, but it all floods back to me once I get my brain into auto memory. I'll finish that tale another time."

On the way home I had a good laugh to myself and was still chuckling as I drove into the drive.

"What has tickled you tonight? You are having a laugh at something?" enquired Marion.

"Nothing really, I just remembered on my way home that I forgot to show the Padre my arse."

"What are you on about, show which Padre your arse?"

"Oh, it's nowt, cock, I'll explain it someday, honest I will."

SATURDAY 25TH NOVEMBER, 2000

Marion, Mark's first visitor of the day, has noted that he is sat out in his chair in the day room but he was very tired. She has written,

"Markie seems very tired today, so I just sat with him, holding his hand. For the last two hours he has drifted in and out of sleep so at 14 15 hrs I asked if he could go back on his bed. That done, I left him fast asleep."

Julie and Lauren arrived at 15 00 hrs to find Markie awake but only just.

"Markie woke up when he heard Lauren's voice so I took advantage of his awareness and gave his teeth a good clean. He was doing a bit of moaning but stopped when dad appeared at 15 25 hrs. Dad gave Markie a big cuddle. This, I am sure brought a smile to Mark's face. Excellent!"

Wendy was next in line,

Julie, Dad and Lauren about to leave when I got here, so I settled with Mark, who was fast asleep. Mark has got a massive boil on the side of his nose, it really looks tender. Before I leave, I will mention it to the nurse on duty and ask if Mark can have some antibiotics as I am sure he is suffering with some sort of blood infection.

DAD AT 18 30 HRS

"Saw Markie this afternoon, gave him his customary cuddle and got back the groans and moans that I usually get. Julie has noted that he smiled when I cuddled him. I couldn't see his face so I can't argue with that. All I can say is that he sounded like a man not too happy, perhaps he was saying,

"Get off Dad, I'm 31 years old. I don't want bloody cuddles." Who knows?

I have to agree with Wendy regarding the boil on his nose. She didn't mention if she'd caught anyone, so I will double check when I leave.

Sunday 26th November, 2000

Mark looking great when I got here at 11 00 hrs, not dressed but about to be as Michelle and Lee were 'seeing to' him today. Lee told me our concerns over Mark's infections had been entered into the main diary and a note had been put on Mark's records.

The boil on his nose has receded a little but this was due to Michelle having taken a swab from it and sent it to the 'path lab' for testing.

Julie at 10 00 hrs

Dad and Mark waiting for me in the dayroom when I arrived. Markie is looking good, so I took him to his room to give his teeth a good cleaning. He was brilliant, he kept his mouth wide open and not once did he bite the brush as he usually does.

"Thanks, Markie, but I missed having the usual fight."

Mum with Mark for about an hour as she took over from Julie at 14 30 hrs.

Mum and Dad at 18 00 hrs

Markie was having his feed in the dayroom when we got here, seems funny seeing him in his chair with his feed bottle on the stand and the long pipe leading to his peg via a pump assembly.

Markie was very tired and we had to support him in an upright position. So at 19 10 I asked Bob to put Markie to bed and he kindly did so.

MONDAY 27TH NOVEMBER, 2000

Doctor called today, had a look at Mark and prescribed a course of antibiotics. Kathy B. also called to see Mark and she is an old school chum of Julie's who has taken up nursing as a career and is doing a good job of it from all accounts.

Giles told Wendy and Entie that Mark had been very active with his left hand during the session, something that he seemed quite pleased about.

That evening when Marion and I called, Mark was trying to have a bowel movement. I know it is hardly a spectator sport but I felt so sorry for him as he was getting so upset. His face was strained and his forehead furrowed, not with trying to have a movement, more with total frustration and perhaps embarrassment. Here he is, a strong, fit young man, felled down in his prime, which has left him in this impossible situation.

Marion and I stood there speechless, knowing that we were totally and utterly helpless.

"How can I help?" I thought, but nothing, absolutely nothing came to mind.

I know Marion was in as much pain as I was. The look on her face said it all.

"That's my best mate laying there, Marion, and I can do fuck all to help him." This came out spontaneously. I didn't intend for it to come out loud and I certainly did not intend to swear.

"I know, Peter, I know he is your best mate and I know how helpless you feel. He is my best mate as well, but first of all he is my fucking baby."

For Marion to actually use a swear word came as a shock to me, as she very rarely swears especially the F word.

This brought her feelings home to me and I could feel her pain joining us together.

On the way home I thought about what had happened. Why am I sad? I should feel joyous as, if Markie was upset by the fact that he was lowered to having to have a bowel movement in bed, then surely that must be a good sign. It is alien to him to be doing this so that tells me something very, very positive. If he knows it is alien and it is making him so upset then surely this means he is aware that it is wrong. Could this be a glimmer of light in the dark, dark tunnel of Markie's mind?

"God, I hope this is the case", I thought, "I sincerely hope it is."

TUESDAY 28TH NOVEMBER, 2000

Case Conference day today.

The case conference, as they call it, was interesting. I always thought that a conference was a body of people sat around a big table, discussing a topic, then making a decision.

As this is our second case conference since Mark was admitted to Rakehead, I had had about 6 weeks to evaluate what had happened at the last hearing. At that one we talked about Mark's progress since he arrived and it was agreed that Mark would be 'kept on' for a further 6 weeks. However, this decision was not arrived at by discussion amongst us all but was made prior to Marion and I being summoned into the meeting in our absence. Somehow, I had the horrible feeling that all present had been given a firm briefing as to what to say when it comes to question time when we are present. Each actor in turn, when asked for their input as to why Mark should stay or go, was too 'glib'; a point I had kept to myself over the past 6 weeks as to disclose my feelings after just one assessment would have been irresponsible on my part.

Now, at this conference I was more prepared to form a judgement as I felt that I needed to know that any decisions made from each person's comments were, in fact, fair and democratic.

The meeting began, or should I say the stage was set, at least an hour before Marion and I were informed by Andy,

"Peter, Marion, the meeting is about to commence, would you care to join us?"

Dr P was in the chair for this assessment not Dr A as he was away. As expected, however, the actors were all the same. There were representatives from Physiotherapy, Occupational Therapy, Speech Therapy and Mark's principal nurse who would report on his medical condition. Last but not least was a man from Social Services, a very quiet man, who was a bit like a ship in the night, now you see him, now you don't.

Physiotherapy was great and truthful, I can say that with confidence as I have been present for most sessions and it was agreed that, as Mark was making some progress, we should continue. That's one, for us only five more to go. Medical now, again another one for us as it was said that, regardless of Mark's setbacks, he was still progressing. Speech Therapy gave a true report but did not have a lot to say other than to explain that, with the help of the family working on Mark's mouth and throat, we could consider giving Mark something orally or a swallow test as she referred to it, that's another one on our side. Occupational Therapy was next. This young lady was definitely one seeking promotion as she lied when she said she had had several sessions with Mark but could not see any noticeable progress.

"Should I intervene and blow the whistle on this one?" I thought, as I knew she had only briefly seen Mark once and on that occasion she spent 10 minutes with him as I was with him. In my mind I had to agree that she could not see any results from her session, but 10 minutes, no way, she was a liar, not a 'miracle maker'.

I had made the decision to follow my wise Mam's way of life. In my mind I could hear her saying,

"Don't rock the boat, cock, especially when you are winning," so I took her advice and kept my mouth shut. I didn't say anything as I was so mad with what had been said that it would have all come out wrong.

"Don't put your gob into gear until the brain is running perfectly." Sound advice again from my Mam, wise recommendations which, much to my regret, I have often ignored.

Now the Social Worker,

"It is my opinion that Mark will soon reach a level plateau and once there he will progress no further. What thoughts have you both got as to where you will place him once this happens? Have you looked into nursing homes?"

Silence fell on the meeting and eyes turned to focus on Marion and me. You could have cut the atmosphere with a knife.

"Excuse me, Mr Social Worker, but what fucking medical qualifications have you got to come out with a statement like that? My lad is going forward and everyone here is saying so. I suggest you stick to being a Social Worker and stop making stupid comments on something you know fuck all about."

Silence again, all I could hear was my dear mother turning in her grave. It seemed ages before someone broke the ice. It was the doctor.

"Peter, if I may call you by your first name, please don't get stressed over what has been said by the Social Worker. His comments were both untimely and inappropriate at this point in time. His question may have to be answered some day but today is not that occasion." He turned to the Social Worker and said, "Perhaps a meeting with Peter at a later date, but may I say not just now, as the fire is still raging and no one can see for the smoke."

Silence again and an empty silence, broken only by me.

"Thanks Doc., thanks, I promise I won't rip his head off, well at least not in front of you lot."

Peace returned to me when the wise doctor closed the meeting saying,

"I feel we need to keep young Mark for at least a further 6 weeks and then let's get our heads together again. Sorry may I suggest that that statement is not taken literally." The wise old sod was looking at me when he said that.

FRIDAY 1ST DECEMBER, 2000

Great physio today, considering we were short in numbers, just Andy, Leanne, Bob, the male nurse and me. My role today is bed driver. To make life easier, we take Mark to physio whilst he is on his bed. Not a simple task, as hospital beds are a bit like supermarket trolleys, they go anyway bar the way you want them to go. Once the corridors and corners are taken, the bed is placed alongside the plinth, both adjusted to the same height, then Mark is transferred over using a plastic slide to bridge the gap. I then take the bed back and return to physio with Mark's wheelchair.

Physic is not pre-planned. Whoever is in charge assesses Mark's demeanour and then decides what actions should be taken during the session. Andy weighed Markie up before saying,

"Mark, I feel that you are ready for a stand today, are you going to come along with us?."

I find it very professional the way the whole staff talk to Mark and explain things to him. I am glad they do that as I am sure, in fact I am positive, that Mark knows what is going on, not all of the time but certainly some of the time.

"Right, let's go for it."

With that, he positioned himself behind Mark, who was seated on the edge of the plinth. Andy sat behind Mark with his legs either side of Mark. Leanne and Bob were on the floor taking a leg each, their job is to ensure that Mark keeps his feet on the floor, plus they brace the lower leg by pushing back on the knee and shin.

"Right, Peter, let's go for it."

With that, I slowly raised the plinth until Mark was fully upright. Some slight correction to Mark's posture and then Andy said,

"You're on your own, Markie, go for it! Yes, yes, you are there, that is brilliant, Mark, well done."

We all watched in silence as Mark towered above us. There he was, 6 feet 2 inches of a big lad.

I could feel myself filling up with emotion as I looked at my lad. I was so very proud of him, his face had a strange blank stare as if he was concentrating everything he had on that stand. Seven minutes went by before Andy broke the silence.

"Right, Markie, that's enough. Okay, Peter, lower away, let's get this lad back down."

With that I lowered the plinth until Mark was once again in his sitting position.

I took one look at Leanne and her expression said it all, a tear ran down her cheek and she didn't attempt to hide what she felt. That did it for me. Here was a total stranger to Mark feeling great emotion for his achievement and not afraid to show it. The lump in my throat felt like an egg and I too felt tears trickling down my cheek.

"Mark, you little sod, or should I say big sod, you have done so well that you have reduced us to tears," croaked Andy as his words came out slowly and intermittently, as you do when full of emotion.

"Come on, Markie, lie back lad, you deserve a chill out after that." Andy tipped Mark backwards as Bob swung Mark's legs onto the plinth. Mark turned to 'jelly' then he totally relaxed, head on pillow, both arms by his side.

SATURDAY 2ND DECEMBER, 2000

I arrived to find the lounge area had been trimmed up for Christmas. This came as a bit of a shock as I hadn't realised that Christmas was almost upon us.

Mark has had a very lazy day today according to the entries in the diary, hope he is not coming down with something. Wide-awake for me, however, so I decided to tell about an occasion when I was about ten. It was a really nice summer's day and I had set off for school. I don't know what possessed me but, as I got off the bus at Rosehill, I decided that I would play truant, so I crossed the road and made my way towards the park. The route was familiar to me as I had taken it many times since I was chased by the geese years earlier. Since that event, I had learnt to stand my ground whenever the geese decided to have a go at me. I have even had enough courage to chase them off sometimes. After crossing over the bridge into the park, I sat on a bench to consider what I could do with my new-found freedom for a day.

"I know, I'll go and help the barge men down at Gannow Tunnel."

I took off my jacket and hid it in some bushes along with my school bag. I made my way to Gannow Tunnel via St Matthews St, Coal Clough Lane, past the Empress Picture House and up Barracks Road to Gannow Top. I remember stopping for a while at Walton's Fireplace Shop as the day was so nice that the fireplace slabbers were working outside.

"Can I watch ow yer make e'm, mister?"

"Aye, corse yer can, cock, sit thi sen down on them boxes an watch, am just about to slab one up now."

I was fascinated with the technique as he carefully placed the tiles in a pre-formed template, he explained his every move and I enjoyed every minute.

"I bet u didn't know that there were different tiles did you, cock. This one 'ere is a R1X, that means it's rounded off on one edge and this one is a corner tile and it is rounded on two edges R2X. He went on and on explaining what he was doing as he carefully filled the mould with tiles of varying shapes and sizes until the whole template was full.

"How du u know what it will look like, all the tiles ar't wrong way up?"

"No lad, they're rete way up, just watch and u'll see."

With that, he started to shovel concrete from a wheelbarrow that another man had mixed. As it got about half full, he put a long length of metal into the concrete.

"That'll stop it breaking in two when you are moving it, cock," he explained as he topped up the mould.

"Na then," he said, "now u know how to mek a fireplace, lad, we don't say we mek em, we say we have slabbed up a fireplace. Come on wi me an al show u sum finished un's."

I followed him into the showroom and was so surprised to see the finished article. They were great, all shapes and sizes and lots of different colours.

"When you finish school, cock, come an see me an al get u a job mekin the templates as that is where the real skill lays. U don't want to be a slabber like me, any fool can du that, think on lad u want to be the fella as has the skills, an I'm the chap as can 'elp u."

"Thanks, Mr Walton, I'll remember wot u said, honest, and thanks for showing me how to mek, oh sorry, how to slab a fireplace."

With that I made my way down Gannow Lane and climbed the wall onto the canal bank by the Leeds and Liverpool pub. Within 10 minutes along came a barge being pulled by a giant of a horse.

"Can I help u wit 'thorse', mister?" I asked the Bargie.

"U can that, cock, as ta dun it before?"

"Corse I ave, ave dun it loads a times."

"Gud, u tek thorse an al elp leg this bloody thing through tunnel."

"Oh God, I thought, why have I lied, ave never dun it before, ave elpt wi thorses but never dun it on me own."

He released the horse from the long tow rope and handed me the reins.

"There u ar, cock, al see thee at tother end ut tunnel."

I looked up at this gigantic horse and it looked down at me, its nostrils snorted and then plodded off up Boat Horse Lane. I just did my best to look as if I was in charge and to make sure this beast didn't stand on me. I remember thinking,

"I'm as gud as dead if he stands on me foot."

Up and over Gannow Top and down the well trodden track, past the cinema and finally arrived back on the canal bank at the mouth of the tunnel. Five minutes later the barge appeared along with three very sweaty bargies.

"Am getting too old fer this job, them bloody barges get evier and evier an them bloody tunnels get longa and longa every time I cum through 'er. 'Ere u are, cock, there's a tanner an thanks fert lift, ye never know lad ye might be a Bargie yoursen one day."

I scrounged a lift on the barge and left it at the canal bridge on Manchester Road and set off to spend my well-earned tanner.

"Eh, young 'olroyd, what are you doing off school." It came from our local copper, he was standing across the road from me, hands on hips and he was looking straight at me.

Not knowing a good answer to the question, I decided to leave the scene. I ran off as fast as I could. Past the Red Lion pub and the Grande Cinema heading towards the Odeon Cinema, lots of streets ran off to my right so I dashed down Croft St. or I think it was Croft St. as I was going so fast I was not too sure just where I was. The copper was still in pursuit but losing ground.

"I can't run forever and ever," I thought, "I will have to go to ground and hide, but where?" Round a gable end and into another back street, now out of sight of the copper, I climbed a backyard wall and hid behind the air raid shelter. Then I heard it, a low growl. I turned to face a dog, a big dog. It was stood in the doorway of the shelter, growling and snarling. I put both hands up and lowered myself onto my knees and clamped my mouth shut. I did this on the worldly advice from my Mam.

"Never smile at a strange dog, cock, he'll think you are baring your teeth at 'im an he'll attack you."

How that came into my mind I will never know but in a situation like this your whole life flashes before you. By now, the dog had taken a step towards me.

"I hope that copper comes quick an rescues me," I thought, "should I shout for him?"

I didn't need to as the copper was coming down the back street.

"I know ur in one of these yards, u can't 'ave got down the back street that quick."

He was slowly coming my way. I could picture him looking over the walls trying to get me. He was getting closer and closer.

What do I do, face the copper or get eaten by a wild dog?

I was frozen to the spot. Suddenly he was at my yard, he couldn't see me as I was around the corner of the shelter. He rattled the gate and he must have reached over to un-bar it. Then it happened. I heard the bolt slip back and I knew he was coming in but so did the dog. Suddenly, I was history to the dog, he had a new enemy in the form of a policeman. Off went the dog barking and snarling and off went the copper at high speed down the back street with Fido in pursuit. I nipped out to watch the race and I couldn't help but laugh. An old chap was standing by his back gate. He had a bright coloured pullover on and smoke belched from his pipe. He was rocking with laughter as he watched the dog chase the policeman. He turned, looked at me, then shook his head from side to side.

"Tha's lucky to be alive lad, that soddin dog ell kill somebody one day."

"I know, I really thought I was a gonner when it looked at me and growled."

I made my way up the back street and climbed up the banking and got back onto the canal towpath; after coming off near the footbridge leading to Albion Street, I went and recovered my school bag and jacket.

"Time to go home now as school has just finished," I thought as I made my way back down Albion Street. I went down the back street and into my backyard, said hello to my pet toad and went in.

"Is that you, Peter?"

"Yes, Mam."

"Come 'ere, cock, ave got someone who wants to meet u."

I hung my coat up at the cellar top and entered into the middle room and froze on the spot. He was sat there with a steaming mug of tea in his hand, his helmet on the table.

"I've been telling your Mam about our little game today an how you set a raving mad dog on me. It's lucky for you it didn't get me or you would have been up to your neck in it. Tell your Mam how big it was. I don't think she believes me."

"It wer massive, Mam, 'onest."

"Am not bothered how big the bloody dog was, it's you playing truant that I want to talk about."

In bed that night, hungry, as me Mam didn't give me any tea as a punishment. I thought about my day, I could now slab a fireplace, have my own barge and train big dogs to chase policemen.

"Not a bad day, not a bad day at all but I'm bloody hungry," I thought as I waited for sleep to come.

I think Mark has listened to the whole tale as he was still awake and did I notice a slight smile on his face? Yes, I think I did.

"Night, night and God bless you son, I will see you tomorrow."

Tuesday 5th December, 2000

Markie has moved rooms today. No longer is he 'on the doorstep' of the nurses, room, these rooms are reserved for the high-dependency patients. Wonder if they think Mark has made enough progress to go to a quieter area of Rakehead. It's a nice room with a nice outlook. In front of his window is a little tree. Julie has noted that, after picking Danielle and Lauren up, she will get a bird feeder and get the girls to hang it out. It should attract young birds and maybe catch Mark's attention.

On our evening visit, both Marion and I were convinced that he said 'mum', or at least a sound that sounded like mum. Whatever he said is not too important. It's the fact that he made a deliberate noise that gave Marion and me a buzz.

WEDNESDAY 6TH DECEMBER, 2000

Not a very good physio today. We put it down to Markie wanting a bowel movement and we were right, as no sooner had we got him back to his bed than he began, so it was a quick strip job, pad under his bottom and a quick exit to allow him as much privacy as possible.

His task over, we got him dressed and in his chair. He was wide awake so I decided to give him some oral hygiene. He was brilliant, opening his mouth nice and wide and allowing me to stretch his cheeks and stroke his throat. Mark is starting to make saliva, as on each occasion when I exercise the cheeks he appears to be making more. This pleases me as this is what we are aiming for. Next on the agenda will be getting him to swallow and we will, I am confident of that.

Wheelchair playing up again today, so I rang Preston to find out where his new chair was. I got nowhere; it is as if they don't want him to have a good chair. Decided to postpone calling a little longer before I throw something in the fan and have one of my now famous 'wobblers'. That night was a very emotional one for Marion and me as, when we were about to leave, Mark put on a strange face and started to make funny sounds. We were convinced he was trying to talk to us but the noises coming from Mark were not words, just sounds. His eyes were full and the odd tear ran down his cheeks. I felt very sad but also elated as, if Mark can get emotional and upset enough to have a cry, we are making progress. Sad I know and so difficult to deal with you, just want to hold him and reassure him that all will be okay some day and that is exactly what Marion did.

We stayed late that night as we couldn't leave him in that state. Eventually he calmed down and fell asleep and he looked at peace when we finally left him.

THURSDAY, FRIDAY, SATURDAY AND SUNDAY

Mark has been laid up the past 4 days so there is not a lot to report as each day followed a similar pattern, sleep, sleep and more sleep. Swabs have been taken from various parts of Mark's body, along with samples of his urine. These are now in the Pathology Department being cultured and tested.

MONDAY 11TH DECEMBER, 2000

Mark's a better man today, temperature is back to normal and physically he looks a lot better. Physio was great on this occasion we; had two lovely female assistants in the shape of Vicky and Janine. They helped us to get Mark standing and, when we finally got him upright, it was a great treat to see their faces as they looked up at Mark.

"I'm gob smacked as to how tall he is," said Vicky. Janine just nodded to confirm her feelings.

Another first today. Instead of putting Mark back on the plinth and using a sling and hoist to put him in the chair, Andy decided that we would take him from standing and encourage Markie to sit straight back into his chair

With good preparation and precise instructions from Andy we gathered around Mark. No need for a lot of 'hands on' as Mark did a perfect 'sit down' straight into his chair when Andy

asked him to sit, he did and he was in control all the way.

Occupational therapy actually surfaced today after a long time wandering around with a file under her arm, trying to look as if on a mission. She actually sought me out to tell me she had had a session with Mark. She had been doing 'switching'. She went on to explain that switching is a box fitted with an on or off switch. On this occasion, she connected a radio to the box and asked Mark to switch it on and off. Apparently, Mark did switch the radio on and off but not when asked to do so. He did it randomly and when he wanted to do it.

Her assessment was one of 'not too good, Markie' we will have to try again another day.

GO TO JAIL

"Markie, did I ever tell you how and when I was sent to jail. It's true, son, your dad is an ex-con."

I was sent to jail back in 1959. In fact it was bonfire night, or should I say bonfire day.

I told you the tale about how I had fallen madly in love with a girl called Lucy in Portsmouth and how I had to 'stand her up' due to a slight accident. Slight accident! It was a complete disaster. It was when I jumped off the bus on my way to meet her, can you remember? My body came to an abrupt halt but my bowel didn't, what a mess. Anyway, I got told by one of my mates that every Saturday night she went to a dance hall in Southsea. Can't remember its name but I went to see if I could apologise for standing her up. If the worst comes to the worst, I will have to tell her what happened. I don't know how I can put it but I'll face that should the occasion arise.

It was early October 1959, Saturday night, and I was being allowed ashore. Not that I was on a ship, as going ashore, even when you live in a Barracks, means going out.

Anyway, I was going ashore in civvies. There I go again trying to confuse you. I mean civilian clothes, and not a uniform. Funny how you are so excited at being allowed out, not in uniform. As soon as you are told that you can wear civvies, you dash ashore and buy yourself a black blazer and grey trousers and get the tailor to sew the badge of the Royal Marines on the breast pocket. That is what I called my civilian uniform when I got more seasoned and wiser.

All dressed up and feeling well pleased with myself, I set off for the ball. I wasn't a drinker then, I didn't need to have beer to chat up the girls. I was just cheeky and a bit brass necked in those days.

Suddenly, there she was over in the corner of the ballroom with two of her mates. She looked more gorgeous than I recalled, she there, quite tall, her long blonde hair was glistening and flowing. The frock she was wearing had lots of petticoats under it, giving it the appearance of a bell. I remember thinking how nice she looked in that dress. Ye' it looked just like a bell with two lovely legs hanging out of it.

Plucking up the courage, I edged my way towards her. She glanced at me a couple of times as if to say,

"Am I supposed to know you?"

Her comment came as a surprise, but I then realised that she had not seen me out of uniform. Her facial expression suddenly changed. I felt that the penny dropped. As she walked directly towards me, she stopped facing me, glaring straight into my eyes. I suddenly felt a little dizzy and I came over a bit strange. Here was a virtual stranger, very beautiful with piercing bright blue eyes looking me straight in my face.

"Well," she said, "I waited over an hour for you, so your story had better be good."

Still I found it difficult to find an excuse. I just stared back into those eyes.

"I can't tell her anything other that the truth. She will know I'm lying," I thought.

"Will you sit with me and I'll explain."

"No, tell me now, you're not going anywhere until you tell me."

"I had an accident and I had to go back to the Barracks."

"An accident, what sort of accident? Were you hurt or something?"

"No."

"Come on, Peter, if you are not prepared to tell me the true reason, then you might as well get lost now."

I prepared myself to tell her but I still found it difficult to find how. I went on to say,

"Okay, when I jumped off the bus I had an accident."

"Oh! One of these clever sods who can't wait for the bus to stop, are you? I suppose you fell over?"

"No, it's not that, well it could have been the cause of it, but to tell you the honest truth,"

I stopped, closed my eyes and prepared myself to tell her what happened with no holds barred.

"I shit myself."

Silence, complete silence, she just stood there looking straight into my face.

"Yes! I shit myself, the impact of jumping from the bus made me shit myself ."

Again, silence and again that stare it seemed like an eternity.

She was looking me straight in the eyes looking for something, if I had lied, this would be the point when she would have seen through me.

Suddenly, a smile appeared on her face, then a big grin followed by laughter. The next moment I was in heaven, she put her arms around me, gave me a big cuddle and laughed and laughed. I got quite excited and joined in the laughter. It was so funny and infectious that her two friends started to laugh.

"It must have been a bloody good excuse," said one of her friends.

"It was no excuse, I know it must be true. No-one would ever use that reason as an excuse."

"Come on, let us know what happened," enquired her other friend.

"I can't, I don't want to embarrass Peter."

"It's okay, tell them. They will only dog you to death until they find out."

"I may tell you some day but this is not the time or the place. I just can't tell you."

I was overcome by her comment. She really did feel for me and she had made her first commitment to me. I felt great.

"Sorry, it's a state secret, maybe some day" she said to her disappointed pals.

"One thing I will say and that's that my Peter is sound, 'as sound as a pound' as my dad often says. Oh! By the way, I didn't tell you my dad's an ex-Royal Marine, did I, Peter?"

"No you didn't, but as he is an ex-bootneck you can tell him why I didn't keep the date, he will appreciate that."

"Oh can I? Honest can I? He will love it."

"Be my guest."

We had a great time together that night; we sat down and I told her the whole story of having to walk all the way back to Eastney Barracks and what the Corporal of the guard said. She laughed all the way through the story and looked at me as if I was a little puppy. A wonderful warm feeling was radiating from her and I was soaking it all up. I walked back to the Barracks that night, chest sticking out and head held high, I thought what my Mam would have said to me had she seen me.

"Tha's strutting away like a pouter pigeon lad, wats ta bin up to."

Our courtship blossomed over the next few Saturday nights; we were so compatible and very happy. Then came the fatal night.

I met her at seven and we went for a nice stroll before going to the dance hall. We met up with her friends and the new boyfriends that they had acquired. A good time was being had by all until a matelot in uniform decided that my girlfriend was his.

He kept excusing us on the dance floor and hanging around us. He was being a complete arsehole.

"Can't you tell him to get lost," I said to Lucy.

"What do I say? I don't want to be rude to him. Let's just ignore him, he will get fed up and go away."

No such luck. In fact, he got more persistent and I was getting more and more annoyed. When he came to excuse us again, I decided I'd had enough.

"Look Jack, the lady is with me, she wants to be with me, ask her."

He didn't. He just glared at me in a threatening manner.

"I'll dance with who I want, Royal, and an arsehole like you cannot stop me."

"Come on, Peter, leave him," said Lucy

I turned to walk away but couldn't as the matelot had grabbed the back of my collar.

"Come on, Royal, what sort of man are you?."

My better senses told me to bite the bullet and try to shrug him off but he was spoiling for a fight.

"Look, Jack, just calm it and leave us alone."

I turned again, but this time he grabbed my collar and pulled me backwards onto the dance floor. I caught the edge of the wooden floor with my heel and down I went. As soon as I hit the deck he dived on me, raining punches. One of the lads pulled him off and I got up, ripped off my jacket and shouted.

"Come on, you bastard, you need sorting out."

I went for him big style, beating and punching him as hard as I could. I can remember holding him by the lanyard which he wore around his neck and thinking that I should strangle him with it, but before I could go any further I was grasped by both arms by two of the biggest sailors you could wish to meet. They were the Naval Shore Patrol, big, strong and as thick as 'workhouse butties'.

I was bundled down the stairs and thrown into their patrol vehicle. No mess, no fuss, I was completely overpowered.

"Are you at Eastney Barracks?"

I nodded. "Yes."

"Well let's take you home. Get on the deck, Royal," he pointed to the floor of the van.

"Why, I'm not going to do anything, just let me explain what happened."

It fell on deaf ears. The van, a Bedford Dormobile, started up and moved off. The two shore patrol men sat there glaring at me. The Killick (same status as a corporal) was in charge and once again he said,

"Get on the deck, Royal."

"What's the point, I'm coming peacefully."

"If you don't get on the deck, I'll fucking put you on it."

I sat there just looking at them, trying to understand why they were insisting that I got onto the floor of the van. I just didn't understand why, so I made my mind up there and then that I was not going to do it.

They were sitting on the long bench seats that ran either side of the back of the van facing each other. I was on the one behind the driver. They stood and came towards me, swaying from side to side due to the motion of the van. The grabbed an arm apiece and started to pull me down and back to get me onto the floor. At that point I knew I was onto a loser, no way could I win or resist their brute strength. So I relaxed. They were taken completely off balance, as I don't think they expected me to give in. They were pulling that hard that, when I ceased to resist, all three of us shot towards the back of the van, they crashed into the back doors which burst open and out they went. Thankfully, they had released their grip on me in an attempt to stop their unexpected exit.

I can still see them to this day, literally bouncing down the road. I dashed to the front of the van and banged on the bulkhead and shouted to the driver.

"Your mates have fallen out."

Within seconds, we ground to a halt and the driver was running back towards the two bodies lying in the road.

"Oh shit," I remember shouting out.

"I'm up for the bloody cup now."

I put my head in my hands and slumped down on the bench.

"What's me Mam going to think about this one,." I thought.

I re-capped my position. They have no idea who I am. They know I am a Royal Marine from Eastney Barracks, I had told them that. Would they bother to look for me or would they put it down to the one that got away? What if they were badly injured or even dead? Just about every option went through my head, even the thought of going to jail. Should I go back and help them or should I stay here and await my fate? It seemed like an eternity as I sat there and looked back to where they were. Both men were still on the ground. I could see one of them moving about a little but the other was dead still, dead still, could that be possible? Dead still.

I don't know what possessed me to make the decision to run but run I did. I leapt out of the van and ran as fast as I could away from the scene.

"I must get back to Barracks before the alarm is raised, as they will start checking everyone coming back," I said to myself.

As I approached the big gates of Eastney Barracks, I slowed to a casual stroll and composed myself. I got a cursory glance from the corporal on duty as I checked in, but that was all.

I stripped off and made my way to the shower room, an unusual move as the water was always cold after 10 o'clock. That didn't worry me. In fact, I would have probably had a cold shower anyway. I had to get my mind into gear and try to put the incident behind me and try to forget it.

No chance, I relived the entire event over and over all night. Sleep evaded me. All I could do was lay there in total fear of what my fate would be.

The next day came and went without even a mention from anyone of what had happened, but why should they? Incidents like mine happen several times every night. I have seen Marines pushed into the Guard Room when I have been on guard duty. They are usually let loose after the patrol has gone and they have been given a good bollocking by the sergeant on guard duty.

Monday was a good day, as canoeing over to the Isle of Wight and back used up most of it. My partner that day was a guy called Derby Slater, not his real name. The Royal Marines had christened him that. As he was from Derby, it seemed Marine logic to call him that.

"Ollie, can you slow down a bit?" said Derby, "You're paddling like a man possessed and I'm getting knackered."

I must confess I was pushing myself to the limit, my arms were killing me but I pressed on and on, forcing myself to the limit.

"Why the hell are you taking it out on your mate?" I thought.

"Okay, Derby, you set the pace but, if the tide turns, I'll be kicking arse."

"Markie, Markie, I hope you have been listening as I'll be asking questions tomorrow night."

He was sound asleep, so I gave him his customary cuddle and left him at peace.

TUESDAY 12TH DECEMBER, 2000

Got a new patient at Rakehead today and his appearance came as a heck of a shock. Julie has noted that he frightened her when she saw him. His poor body is badly contorted thus making it impossible to do anything for himself. The biggest tragedy for this poor soul is that, unlike Mark, he is compos mentis. So he understands all that is going on. Again, he can, unlike Mark, understand, communicate and talk. His voice is quite distorted but his mother was having a conversation with him, so perhaps in time I too will understand him.

Physio was brilliant today, we had Mark in the standing position three times and each stand was longer than his last one. After the last one, we asked Mark to sit back into his wheelchair and he willingly obliged. I took Mark off to the dayroom, found a quiet corner and set to work on his mouth. He was a hero, not trying to bite me, as he has done in the past. No struggling, just a very good lad, it was as if it was normal to have someone poking and pulling at your cheeks and tongue. It seems strange but it gives me a buzz when Mark accepts what is going on and he lets you get on with it. It's as if he knows that it has to be done for his own survival or hopefully for his recovery.

Mark has developed a mark in his left eye, so Giles had recorded it and requested that the doctor have a look. On the evening visit, we found Mark dressed and lying on his bed, which had been transported to the dayroom. This I thought was a good, productive move as he was amongst people with the television on, and life was going on around him. Perhaps it was good for him as he was thrashing his left arm about more than he has ever done before.

WEDNESDAY

Mark not too co-operative today. He seems a little off colour. Physio not as good as yesterday, even with the presence of Jayne, an auxiliary nurse who is as mad as a brush. (Mad as a brush, where does that originate?)

THURSDAY 14TH DECEMBER, 2000

Found out why Mark was a little lethargic yesterday. He has been having some problems with his catheter. Apparently it keeps blocking up and bypassing the tube when he wants to pee. So it was decided to remove it. Poor Markie. Just the thought of having a tube pushed down your Willie into the bladder makes me feel pain for him. Then to have it pulled out again. Poor sod, I honestly could cry for him.

Mark got a big surprise today: a visit from Pauline and her daughter Simone. They are from our village and frequent our local pub. I have a particular liking for Simone, mainly due to her sense of humour. Our banter when in the pub is great. She insists that I call her 'mummy' and she calls me her 'naughty little boy'. Good, and a great distraction from our real life of the dreadful trauma created since Mark's accident. Simone is in her late teens but going on 40 to listen to her. She is a very compassionate girl, who is always to hand if any of her pals get upset over one thing or another. At the moment she is looking after a 4-year-old boy who has Down's Syndrome. This little chap has made Mark a Christmas stocking with help and encouragement from Simone. Hence her visit. She has brought the stocking in for Mark and fixed it to his wall. Pauline kindly came with her, as Simone felt a little insecure at visiting Mark alone. They were still with Mark when I arrived and both gave me a comforting cuddle.

How wonderful to have such lovely caring people around you in your time of great pain. Thanks girls, from all of us, I have noted in Mark's Diary.

Friday 15th December, 2000

Doctor called and fitted Mark with a new catheter today, so little wonder he is not on top form, who would be? Mark, being the man he is, did not use this as an excuse to miss physio. He showed us what he has been made of by doing two first-class stands. Up to present, Mark has been standing on the balls of his feet but today his feet are flat on the floor, a considerable achievement according to Giles.

The Reckoning

I arrived at 18 30 hrs to find Mark in his room prepared for the night but looking very much alert. I wondered what he would like to hear from me tonight.

"Mark, you know last week when I told you about my encounter with the shore patrol?"

I went on to tell Mark what happened to me.

Derby and I returned safely back from our arduous trip to the Isle of Wight, we stored the big heavy inflatable rubber boat in the boat-house and made our way to the NAAFI for a brew and something to eat, as we had missed our evening meal.

"If you had not been such a wimp, Derby, we would have got a proper meal tonight."

"Shush, Ollie, I'm trying to 'earwig' what the lads on the next table are on about."

We sat there listening when one of them said,

"Ye. Some crazy bastard threw two naval patrol guys out of the back of their 'meat wagon' on Saturday night, so because of that all shore leave is cancelled tonight and every man Jack has to be on the Parade Ground at 08 00 sharp."

"Are you okay, Ollie, you've gone as white as a sheet," he looked at me very intently.

"It was you, weren't it. I knew there was something wrong, you haven't been the Ollie I know all fucking day." He looked me straight in the eye as he waited for my response.

"It was you, wasn't it?"

"Derby, it was a accident honest."

I went on to tell him the whole story of how the Patrolmen fell from the van.

"I believe you, Ollie, but I bet I am on my own. Why did you run, you daft bastard?"

"Cos if I had stayed put and another naval patrol had turned up, I would be fucking dead meat now."

"You'll be dead meat anyway, Ollie, if they find you. Come on, let's have a couple of pints, they may be your last ones for a long, long time."

"Cheers, Derby, that's really cheered me up."

Almost everybody stood on parade the next morning. A few had been excused to continue the running of the Barracks, as they all had not been ashore on the Saturday night.

The Regimental Sergeant Major called the parade to attention and explained why all had been summoned. He frightened me a little as he made me out like some sort of lunatic or raving mad man. I had a horrible feeling that only the very worst could happen to me now.

"It has to be jail and then a dismissal from the corp. How could I go home in such disgrace? What would me Mam say?"

We were stood at ease and stood easy and waited and waited.

"Parade," shouted the R.S.M.

"Parade shun!"

As we all 'banged' to attention, the R.S.M. handed over to the C.O.

"If the perpetrator is on Parade, you must step forward now. Or if anyone knows this man, you must let us know, as we cannot tolerate this sort of behaviour in the Royal Marines. Shortly the two injured Patrol Men will pass amongst you. They are confident that they will recognise you. So think and think hard about your future and step forward."

"I'm in deep shit now so I am going to see it through. If I step forward, it won't alter my position, I'm still up for the cup."

Mind made up, I decided to run the gauntlet. After all everybody looks the same when in uniform. Slowly, they passed amongst the ranks. There must have been a thousand men in the Barracks, what hope have they got of picking me out.

I could only see their heads and shoulders as they moved amongst us, they towered above everyone, both of them were massive, and looked even higher than I remembered them.

Then I got a full view of them, one was on crutches, left leg in plaster and the other had his left arm in a sling, also in plaster.

It seemed like hours as we stood and waited, they were being very thorough. They even got some of them to speak to them and turn so they got a side view.

Closer and closer, would they or would they not recognise me?

As they started along my line I could feel the blood draining from my face and I started to feel dizzy. Suddenly, he was there staring at me, it was the Killick.

"Turn to your right, lad."

"Now your left."

Only now did I realise that he was speaking with an accent not unlike mine, Blackburn or Accrington perhaps, or even Burnley.

He turned to his colleague and summoned him to look at me. He did, as he hobbled on his broken leg as he was not very adept on his crutches yet.

He looked and looked but his face was expressionless as he weighed me up and down.

"Ask him," he said.

The Killick said to me,

"I want you to say, what's the point, I am coming peacefully."

"What's the point I'm coming peacefully," I said in a low voice.

"Say it again, lad, an in a rete sort a way."

"Wot's the point, I'm coming peacefully."

"Yur from Burnley aren't you. I'm a Burnley lad so you can't fool me, it wer yu who chucked us out'et van weren't it."

"Ye it wer me, " I croaked in my best Burnley accent.

In seconds I was marched away at a very fast pace escorted by no less than six Royal Marine Police. Bang! The cell door slammed shut as I was incarcerated in the guardroom to await my fate.

I sat there, head in hands, feeling as low as I have ever been. My thoughts suddenly went to Lucy. I was supposed to meet her parents tomorrow night and we were going to a bonfire. Oh! What a mess, she will never give me another chance. This certainly made me feel worse.

"If I only hadn't run away or even gone to their assistance, I'm sure I couldn't be deeper in the shit than I am now."

Numerous thoughts raced through my head. The future certainly looked bleak.

At about eight that night I was visited by Derby. He wasn't here as my buddy he was here to bring me some gear to clean up ready to go in front of the Commanding Officer the next day.

"I've said before and I say again, justice in the Royal Marines can be somewhat 'lop-sided', it is never in the favour of the accused or it hadn't been to me from past experience.

"Remember my spud-bashing days, Mark, well that was nothing to what I was about to face."

At six in the morning I was taken to see the R.S.M. A long-service man and one I respected a great deal.

"You have some serious charges against you, Holroyd, very serious charges. So serious that a young officer has been appointed to represent you. He will be here in about half an hour, so meanwhile tell me how a scrawny little sod like you managed to throw two fucking giants out of their van. Sit down, lad, I want the full story."

I sat down and told him the whole truth from start to finish and he took it all in without any interruption.

"Sometimes, lad, you have to do things you don't want to do and this was one of those occasions, when Mr Giant says get on the deck, Royal, you should have got on the deck. I would have done, if them two big bastards were stood over me."

"Yes sir, I know what you are saying but strangely enough they didn't frighten me. I just thought it was a bit of an insult to force me, a Royal Marine, down on the deck with no better reason other than to belittle me."

"I'll say something, lad, you've a fair set of bollocks but fuck all sense."

A young Second Lieutenant arrived and was shown into the R.S.M.'s office.

We both stood to attention and the R.S.M. saluted him. He replied with his salute and asked us to stand easy.

"This, Sir, is the way we are going to play it. I have known Marine Holroyd for a long time. He is a reputed marksman and both he and I have represented the Corps in shooting competition. His actions on Saturday were completely out of character for this man."

He went on to tell the whole story but this time his version was a little glossed up. He made the shore patrol men appear to be the guilty party and me an innocent bystander.

Then came torrents of 'bull shit'. He went on about the way all Royal Marines should defend the good name of the corps at all times. As he rambled, on my mind went back to when I was a recruit and I remembered that I had known him from those days he was the Colour Sergeant who ran the corps shooting team. I just didn't recognise him, so it was all bull shit.

I was snapped back to awareness when the R.S.M. said,

"I have had a good chat to Marine Holroyd and I, for one, don't think Portsmouth is big enough for Holroyd and the Royal Navy. So I want you to suggest to the C.O. that Holroyd gets a week's jankers here in Eastney Barracks Prison then, on release, he takes a Pier End Jump."

"A what, R.S.M.?"

"Sorry, Sir, Pier End Jump means a quick, well, very quick, overseas posting."

This was all news to me; we had not even touched what my future was to be. I certainly didn't agree to any pier end jump. Then, again, 7 days in the Barracks jail was okay by me. It was better than anything I had been imagining.

"I honestly do not want Holroyd being sent to the Portsmouth Dockyard Prison. It is a notorious hard home for those who work there, let alone those who get time there. Can you imagine what sort of time Holroyd would get in there? I know, and know well, the Chief Petty Officer who runs the prison. He is an animal known as 'Tiny'. Holroyd would be 'dead meat' if 'Tiny' got his hands on him. I must stress that Portsmouth Naval Prison is not a suitable place to send a Royal Marine who has had an accident due to the ill-fitting doors on a shore patrol vehicle. I agree, Sir, that Holroyd has done wrong. He should have done as he was told and got on the deck of the van. But, because he is a very proud Royal Marine, he thought it was wrong for a corp member to be treated in this way and the silly lad stood his ground."

The young officer was busy writing away on a note pad and all three of us sat in silence whilst he continued to write.

"Well, R.S.M. I will give it a whirl but I can't see the C.O. going along with any of it. Why a Pier End Jump? How would this be significant in getting Holroyd off with this incident?"

"That's the point you need to play on, Sir. Let's assume Holroyd gets time in Portsmouth Naval Prison. That place will wreck him and the Royal Marines would lose a good, very good, man. Portsmouth is not the place where Holroyd would be safe. So let's do our utmost to keep him here in Eastney Barracks, then pack him off overseas."

"Okay. R.S.M., I'll do my very best. You will be a lucky man, Holroyd, if this goes the R.S.M's way."

With that, he stood to leave and the R.S.M. and I jumped to attention.

I turned and looked at Mark but he was almost asleep, his eyes kept opening and closing. He was on the edge of sleep, so cuddles, grunts and pushes and I left him to enjoy his sleep.

Friday 15th December, 2000

Marion first on the scene today as Mark is being fitted with a new catheter today. My thoughts are with you, Markie. She has noted that Mark's fan and radio have gone walk abouts, can't find them anywhere.

Catheter fitted at 12 15 hrs much to Mark's displeasure, so to get his own back he is refusing to co-operate with the nurses when they attempted to get him in his chair. There were three of them at one time but still a big No, No from Mark. At 15 00 hrs I wheeled Mark, still on his bed, off to physio. What a show, two of the best stands he has done to date. Perhaps it was due to another new face being present. Vicky, a physio lady who usually works on people in their own homes, for some reason made herself available to us to work on Mark.

Wendy arrived at 16 10 hrs to find Mark in his chair, sitting out in the dayroom. She notes that he is not a happy chappy as he has a very sad face on. Perhaps it is due to having the catheter fitted this morning, so she has asked the staff to put him on his bed.

I found him quite alert that night so I decided to bring him up to speed with my prison career.

Back from my meeting with the R.S.M. and the lieutenant and locked back in my cell. Breakfast was served. I remember thinking, "This is a bit of alright, breakfast in my own private room," but I was soon brought back down to earth by the Sergeant of the Guard.

"Enjoy it, Holroyd, you'll be on porridge after the C.O. has done with you."

Breakfast over, I set about cleaning my gear. Best blues, white belt, hat also white. Buttons and buckles gleaming and boots highly polished, so much so you could see your reflection in them.

09 30 hrs. Only half an hour to go. I felt like I was on death row and about to be led to the gas chamber or whatever form of execution they use.

"Clunk, clunk, clunk," it sounded like an army was coming for me. My escort consisted of four N.C.O.s all in best blues like me.

"I bet they love me to bits," I thought, as they will have had an early start to 'bull' up their gear for the show.

The Sergeant of the Guard lined us up outside the Guardroom.

"At the double, double march," he screamed out and off we went.

"Left, right, left, right, left right," he shouted. We progressed to the block where I would learn my fate.

191

"Prisoner and escort, halt."

Prisoner and escort, the prisoner is me. I never realised up till then that I was a prisoner. Well, I suppose if you are deprived of your freedom, you are a prisoner. One thing for sure was that I was 'banged up' in jail.

The R.S.M. took over now and he briefed the escort and me of what was to be the 'routine' as he called it.

The R.S.M. knocked on the C.O.'s door and went in after someone shouted 'enter'.

Minutes ticked by, I was feeling more and more nervous again. That sinking feeling and the strange one of knowing you are turning white as the blood seems to stop flowing to the brain. You feel like you are losing the reality of the situation.

Suddenly, I shot to earth, the door opened quickly and the R.S.M. was there staring at me.

"Prisoner and escort, shun," he bellowed out.

"Left turn." There was a loud bang of boots all in unison.

"Quick march, left, right, left, right," he shouted out until we were in front of a long table.

"Prisoner and escort, halt."

Prisoner and escort, right turn."

There they were in front of me. The Commanding Officer, the Adjutant and the Padre.

"Why him, why the Padre? Is he here to read the last rights before I go down?" That thought flashed through my mind. A Naval lieutenant was sat at the end of the table and opposite him at the other end was my defence man in the shape of the young R.M. Lieutenant.

The escort, which was down to two men, and me were still stood to attention. It seemed ages as I stood there knowing I was being studied from head to toe as if you were waiting for someone to say,

"He looks quite normal, to say he is a raving lunatic and potential killer."

No one did of course but it felt like that.

"Stand the prisoner and escort at ease." This came from the C.O. The R.S.M. sprang into action.

"Prisoner and escort, stand-at-ease."

The words were deliberate and spread out, a particular trait of the R.S.M.

The naval officer was the first to report. He had a dull and boring voice and barely lifted up his head as he read from his notes. His version of events were true up to where they dragged me from the dance hall and put me in the shore patrol van. It was then said that I refused to stop fighting so they tried to restrain me by forcing me onto the floor of the van. During the skirmish, I am said to have rushed at them and physically knocked them out of the van.

"The bastards, the lying bastards," I thought. How the hell could anyone believe that? I am 11 stone, wet through, and these two beasts must have weighed in at least 18 to 20 stone each."

When the naval officer had finished his tale, it became my officer's turn to tell our version of events. It was strange to hear him telling the tale, it was as if the words were coming from the R.S.M., as he came over so well especially when it came to how good a Marine I am. It was embarrassing to hear it coming out. I could not imagine whom he was referring to. One thing was sure, it certainly was not me. My only claim to fame was my uncanny ability to be a good shot with the old MK3 Lee Enfield 303, a bolt action rifle. It was a gem to use, due to its accuracy.

He told them how the R.S.M. had selected me for the Corp shooting team and how we had travelled to lots of competitions and had come away victorious.

"Lots of competitions, bull shit," I thought as I could only remember two. But who am I to argue? It certainly painted a good image of me.

When it came to the Pier Head Jump bit, I was again left in shock.

"Holroyd, Sir, fully regrets what he has done and is sorry if it has thrown the Corps into bad light with our colleagues in the Royal Navy. If he receives a custodial sentence this day, he has volunteered himself for immediate posting abroad upon his release. He cares not where he goes and his spirit to request a posting shows one of Holroyd's fine qualities of his Royal Marine training.

"What a bloody set-up."

The C.O. after hearing all the bull shit turned to the Naval Officer and asked him if he had met the two Naval Patrolmen.

"Of course I have, sir, I took my notes from my interviews with the men."

"Did you interview them separately?"

"No sir, together."

"Do you think there could be some collusion between the two of them?"

"No sir, why should they?"

"Come on, Lieutenant, you have seen Holroyd this day and you know the two ratings on your own admission. Do you honestly think that they could be being a little economical with the truth when it comes to the part where Holroyd threw them from the van?"

The Lieutenant started to show signs of embarrassment but the C.O. did not stop there.

I was on the Parade Ground on the day of their visit and I was amazed at the size of them, perfect for the task they perform and I am sure they are excellent at carrying out their duties.

"Now we come to Holroyd. Do you honestly think he could physically throw your two men anywhere? I very much doubt that he could throw one of them anywhere let alone both of them at the same time."

"No, Sir, I cannot accept that it would be completely physically impossible."

The naval officer sat there trying to compose himself, but the C.O. had not finished.

"This hearing is to see if there is a case of wilful assault by Holroyd on your Naval Ratings. I think there is not. I also think it was a silly sequence of events that led up to the Ratings' untimely exit from the van. Perhaps the van doors were suspect, who knows?" He paused, staring at the Naval Officer, then continued,

"I propose that you accept my findings before the whole incident is blown out of all proportion." The Commanding Officer then turned to look at me.

"Holroyd, you are not forced to accept my judgement but if you want to honour yourself and the Royal Marines, I would suggest that you accept my decision. Are you prepared to have the matter dealt with by me here and now?"

His eyes were fixed on me. They were blue and very piercing, and I felt he was compelling me to accept his decision. I risked a glance at the R.S.M. and he too was saying 'yes', take it.

I thought then that this was my chance to end the matter and get it behind me.

The C.O. turned again to the naval officer.

"If Marine Holroyd accepts my findings and my decisions, will you go along with that? Then this whole nasty incident can be concluded here and now."

The Officer stood up and said,

"Yes, Sir, I would accept that."

"Well, it all rests on you, Holroyd."

Silence and tension rose almost to the point where you could cut it with a knife.

"Well, Holroyd?"

I could feel the whole assembly was willing me to accept.

"Yes, Sir, I accept ."

I don't to this day know what made me say that but when I did it felt like someone had cut the straps on a fully laden back-pack, letting it fall to the floor. Still silence.

"What now?" I thought.

"Prisoner and escort, shun."

"Turn to the right, right turn."

"Quick march, left, right, left, right."

When we cleared the room, the R.S.M. brought us to a halt and stood us at ease. I risked a look at him and he replied with a very slight nod of the head.

Moments later the door was opened by the Royal Marine Lieutenant.

"Bring the prisoner back in, please, R.S.M."

We went through the whole march-in procedure again and ended up in our position facing the officers.

The C.O. looked me straight in the face and said,

"You know the errors of your ways, Holroyd, and you know that I cannot let you off without some form of punishment. I therefore sentence you to 14 days' imprisonment. Take him away, R.S.M."

"Prisoner and escort, shun."

"Turn to the right, right turn."

"Quick march."

Again clear of the room, we were stood at ease.

"Keep there, Holroyd, I need a word with the boss."

He went and knocked on the office door and got the invite to enter from a simple "come." The R.S.M. went in and shut the door behind him.

After a good 15 minutes he appeared, a grin on his face from ear to ear. He suddenly looked at me in a serious manner.

"Fourteen days, Holroyd, and you will be serving them here in Eastney Barracks. There is just one very sad Naval Officer in there as he wanted you to go to 'Pompie' Dockyard, but the C.O. said that, as you were going straight abroad at the end of your sentence, it made sense to keep you here."

"Prisoner and escort, shun."

"Move to the right, right turn."

"Quick march."

Back to the guardroom to collect my gear. Then I was taken to my Barrack room where I was told to pack everything. Out came my sea bag, a massive kitbag so big I could get everything into it, and I did, under the watchful eye of the Sergeant and my escort.

"Say bye, Holroyd, you won't be coming back here," said the sergeant.

I carefully took down the photograph of Lucy that I had stuck on the inside of my locker door.

"Pack her away, Holroyd, you won't be allowed anything like that in your cell. By the time you see her again, she'll be wed with half a dozen kids."

"You bastard," I thought. That sort of comment was totally uncalled for.

I will have to get used to having the 'Mickey' extracted as I am not going on holiday to Billy Butlins', I am going to jail.

I was marched at the double from the accommodation block, which is no mean feat when you are carrying all your gear. We went down the main road, heading for my 'new home'.

The prison was an old Victorian structure, built more or less in the middle of the area taken up by Eastney Barracks. It was out of sight to all outside, as a 20-foot high wall surrounded it, topped with barbed wire.

"Prisoner and escort, halt," screamed the Sergeant as we got to the gated entrance to the prison. The gates were massive, wide enough to get a bus through. I remember wondering why they were so big. My thoughts were disturbed by the sound of bolts being drawn on the small door fixed within one of the big doors. A Corporal appeared, a very stern-looking man, or was it a scowl. My thoughts went back to my Mam.

"Wot's up wi u ya miserable sod, ya look like yuv swallowed a bee?"

That's what she would say to anyone if they were miserable or sulking.

Whilst the corporal and Sergeant were exchanging paperwork, one of the big doors slowly opened. I can remember how thick the doors were. They must have been at least a foot thick. Two marines appeared dressed in working clothes, obviously my fellow inmates. They were pulling a large cart about 7 feet long by 4 feet wide. It had a single long shaft with a bar through it at the end. They rested the cart down onto the shaft and, after a nod from the Corporal, they ran back inside.

"Your transport has arrived, Holroyd, get your kit loaded onto the cart."

"Better than carrying it," I thought, or was it? What was the point in providing a cart now, I was at the prison already.

"Come on, Holroyd, jump to it."

I loaded all my kit onto the cart as fast as I could.

"Grab the shaft, lad, and let's get on our way to your new home," I told myself as I picked up the shaft and gripped the bar, which went through it, turned the cart around and headed for the open gate.

The prison was impressive to say the least. There was no mistaking it for anything else. It reminded me instantly of the prison in the film, Papillon. That prison had been on an island in the Mediterranean but this one was here in Eastney Barracks, Southsea, England. It just looked completely out of place. I headed for the only entrance I could see to the building and stopped in front of yet another remarkable piece of woodworking skills.

"Where do you think you are going, Holroyd, you're not there yet. It's normal here to let new prisoners take the scenic route, the trip is somewhat longer but the sights are well worth seeing."

I heard the big doors close and turned to watch as two uniformed Marines slid the big bolts closed and secured them with two big padlocks.

"Come on, Holroyd, grip the cart and let's get on our way."

He walked ahead of me slowly increasing the pace. We went right around the building and continued on a second circuit, by now I was almost running and the cart was clattering behind me, its metal-edged spoked wheels were bouncing on the well-worn flagged surface. The corporal closed up to my side and said,

"Now you know the way, Holroyd, I'll drop off after the next circuit, it's time for tea. He was looking straight at me. Don't even think of slowing down, as I know every bump and joint in this courtyard and I can read your speed from them. As we got to the entrance to the prison, he went inside and left me to it. The two marine guards took turns at watching me go round and round. From just one point in the courtyard, you could see the clock in the tower by the main entrance to Eastney Barracks.

Two twenty-five when I first noticed the clock and I reckoned I have been going round for a good half an hour. Determined not to crack, I pushed on and on but the cart was getting heavier and heavier. By four forty-five I thought I would have to stop but I couldn't, I had to fight my way through the pain barrier. More or less on the hour the Corporal would join me but only for two circuits, but all the time he was there he stared at me.

"He's looking for signs of me giving in, that's what the bastard's up to. Well, you're going to have a fucking long wait, pal, yes a fucking long wait," I said to myself.

It was eight-fifteen when the corporal stood in my path and stopped me.

"Have you had enough, Holroyd?"

"Yes, Corporal."

"Pity, as you're not half way yet, come on get cracking you lazy sod."

I suddenly had the terrible urge to beg him to let me stop. I was dead tired, my legs felt like lumps of uncontrollable flesh, my arms were numb, my hands had been gripping the bar that long that I was sure I could never open them to let go.

Without more ado, I decided to go on, without a word from me, and a surge of energy from somewhere, I set off at a vigorous pace. As I came past the door, the Corporal emerged with a bucket of water, which he threw over me. It came as a shock as it was stone cold but it invigorated me and it gave me the opportunity to drink from my sodden tunic top. I sucked and sucked, it was great. I wondered why he had done that but was thankful for it. Two more laps and it was over. The two marines stopped me and the Corporal shouted.

"Right, Holroyd, get your gear in here at the double."

I lowered the cart and tried to get my hands to let go of the bar but I couldn't open them. Try as I may I had not the strength to open them, my hands were completely ignoring me and would not respond. The Marines had obviously seen this performance before. They took a hand apiece and forced them open, then continued to pull at my hands until all my fingers were straight. By now I was on my knees.

"Put your hands flat on the floor and put some weight on them or your fingers will curl up again," whispered one of the Marines.

The Corporal seemed to be enjoying himself as he stood in the doorway gloating over how he had wasted me.

"The bastard," I thought but that was all I could do, think.

"Get him inside and stick him in the shower."

The guards took an arm apiece and I stumbled along with their assistance as my legs were as my hands had been, they had gone deaf to the commands from my brain.

Straight into the shower, clothes still on but without my boots as the whispering Marine had removed them for me. It took me a good 20 minutes under the cold water before I had the strength enough to remove my clothes. As time went on, I heated up the shower and by 30 minutes I found the strength to wash my clothes.

"Come on, Holroyd, it's lights out in half an hour and your kit is still in the cart." Naked and with my clothes draped over my arm I emerged from the washroom.

"Excuse me, Corporal, do we have a drying room?"

"Fucking drying room, where the fuck do you think you are?" He was staring at me in his own special way, a stare of a strange man.

"Of course we have, sir, follow me."

We went up a metal staircase onto a metal walkway from which the cells led off.

"This cell is specially set aside as a drying room. As you can see it has two ropes running its length. You can dry your clothes from them if you wish or if you could afford me a big favour, you could fucking hang yourself with one."

Again, that stare, the evil one.

"This bastard is bad news. I think he would take great pleasure from someone hanging themselves in his care. He is the sort of bastard who would probably swing on your legs to speed up your demise," I thought.

I was taken to the cart to get my kit, which I moved to my cell; I had to make three trips as I was completely 'shot at'.

Saturday 16th December, 2000

Marion, first visitor of the day and she found Mark up, dressed and sitting at one of the big tables in the dayroom. She has noted that it seemed strange to see him sitting there with all the others. It was as if there was nothing wrong with him. But she soon came down to earth when she settled in the chair next to him.

The distorted man I mentioned earlier whose name was Tom was actually playing dominoes. When I say he was playing, he was telling one of the nurses which domino he wanted to play. This was really a process of elimination. The nurse would point to the dominoes one at a time and Tom would make a sound when she pointed at the one he wanted to use.

Norma, one of my sisters, called to see Markie. Her notes in the diary read,

Called to see Markie, fast asleep, tried singing to him but he wouldn't wake up. That tells me something. I always thought I was a good singer, oh well. He is looking very good and comfortable and I love him, my super lad.

Wendy after Norma and she says in her note,

God I am glad I missed the 'Auntie Norma Opera'.

When Marion and I arrived, we found Markie in his chair in the dayroom. Catriona his principal nurse was with him, and she was holding his hand and talking to him. Not stage set as she had her back to us and she did not see us approaching. It's so good to see something like that. It puts your heart and mind at peace. Some actually radiate their feelings for Mark. You can feel the strange 'vibes' on occasions. We sat around and chattered to Catriona until Mark decided he needed his bed. Catriona and Jayne took him away. After 10 minutes Jayne said he was done and dusted and by the time we got to his room, which was probably a minute away, he was fast asleep and looking very much at peace.

SUNDAY 17TH DECEMBER, 2000

I was first in today as I was up early and needed to have a walk, so I yomped in to see Markie via the scenic route, a route I regretted as it took me over the fields. It was hard going and very muddy but it did me good, I think.

I found Markie in the dayroom; an auxiliary nurse accompanied him, a nice girl called Anne. Mark was sitting up well; left arm quite active, head upright, but he had a slightly strained look on his face. When I looked around, I could see that our ranks had swollen. As Christmas was almost here it meant that a lot of staff would be having time off, so the hospital had had a re-shuffle. The ward, which had to be permanently manned, was topped up with people from the not so important wards. Our intake was about eight little old ladies and I mean little and old. However, they were not out of it by any means. They were funny to listen to as they all wanted to speak at the same time. I took Markie over to the windows and we settled down quite close to two tables full of these lovely people.

All talking, all grey headed and all small and fragile looking and all very, very hungry as one of them kept saying,

"Wens dinna cumin?" in a very strong local accent.

They fell silent when dinner finally arrived, as they all got down to enjoying their 'Sunday roast'.

I looked and smelt the food and I must say I could have happily joined in, but what did Markie think? Could he smell the food? Could he have enjoyed a proper plated meal? I looked at him but he just sat there expressionless, no deep breathing to smell the food, just nothing came from him. At times like this, you get to wonder just what Mark must feel. He can't do anything for himself, he can't communicate in any way. Can he smell things, can he hear anything, can he see anything, his eyes are open but what does he see?

"Oh God, you want to shout, where are you? Please come and help our Markie."

Suddenly we were all startled into the present. It was Mark who did it, he had let go such a loud sneeze that it made everyone panic. It was a sneeze but it was similar to a very loud shout. It certainly snapped me out of my painful thoughts.

All the little old ladies had taken off from their seats, some were standing and all were staring at Markie. What did Mark do? Absolutely nothing, yes!

Nothing. He just sat there with a 'who me' look on his face. I had to laugh, as it was so funny.

"Bloody hell, Mark, where did that come from?" I said aloud. This brought about a tittering from all the little grey ladies. Some even had a laugh.

"That wer loud luv," one shouted.

"Corse it wer loud, he's a big strong lad," said another.

Back in the real world, I decided that I should not ask myself questions about Mark's demeanour or what he has or hasn't got. I must compel myself to think positive and get on with the job in hand and that job was to get Markie back, 'come hell or high water'.

Went back again at night to see Markie. This time he was on his bed and seemed quite alert. What should I tell him? I get lost sometimes as I forget what I have told him and what I haven't. If he does understand what I am saying he must get hell of confused at times.

What about the time I met my elder brother in Malta?

"Mark, Granville my eldest brother, who is senior to me by 12 years, went into the navy when he was 18, so I would have only been six. I was in Malta at the time serving with 40 Commando and Granville was serving on the Ark Royal.

One day I got a letter from him saying he would be calling at Malta and suggesting that we meet up. He would be put ashore at the Naval Air Base on the island for important maintenance to some of the aircraft.

The day came and it was a Saturday. Just as well as we were going to have a jar or two. The rendezvous was to be on the esplanade in front of the NAAFI club in Valetta, a place I often used, as near the club was a very tiny bar. Malta, and especially Valetta, is built like a big fort. In fact, there are forts all around the island. The tiny bar I frequented was part of the battlement built to house about ten defenders. Anyway, Joe's Bar was small, very small. It was full if you had six people in there, and that is standing up, as there was no space for stools or anything. I don't know why I adopted that bar. Perhaps it was more Joe adopting me. He was probably 20 years older than I was and a great guy to listen to. He was small, round and noisy, I wouldn't have thought he could have whispered, even if his life depended on it.

I was early for the meeting with Granville, so I had a couple of beers with Joe first. I told him my brother was coming and he insisted that I introduce him to Granville. That agreed, I went over to the club, got myself a beer and settled down on a low wall in front of the club entrance.

One o'clock, the appointed time, came and went. Two pints later and now almost 2 o'clock. There was still no sign of Granville.

People were coming and going all the time. In fact, it was quite busy. Suddenly I thought,

"What does Granville look like, is he taller than me, fatter than me, what's the colour of his hair? Oh dear! I have a problem."

I had not considered when I last saw him. I thought back and I reckoned it must be at least 12 years as I was about eight.

Perhaps another half hour went by when I got the strange feeling I was being watched. I let my eyes go around all the faces in an attempt to find one looking at me.

"There he is." I thought a guy was looking at me, or was he. No, he turned away and walked into the club, was it him? Again I looked around but as I did so I noticed a man sitting about 10 to 12 feet away and he too was looking around at people, just as I was.

Then our views coincided, our eyes locked on each other and instantly something clicked. It was Granville and I knew it. He too knew it was I as he came over, put his arm over my shoulder and gave me a big hug.

"Bloody hell, you've grown," he said.

"I should hope so, its 12 years since I last saw you."

"Come on, Granville, I have a good friend who has insisted that I introduce you to him."

We crossed the square to Joe's place and went in.

"Joe, this is my brother Granville."

Joe immediately emerged from behind his bar and stepped down from it. I suddenly burst out laughing. I had never seen Joe other than when he was behind his bar and he looked short and fat then.

"Wata u lafin at, Pedro?" his name for me.

"Sorry, Joe, can't help it, I didn't realise you were stood on a fucking box when you were behind the bar. You are even shorter than I thought."

"Ura cheeky bastard, Pedro, yes, a cheeky bastard."

By now we were all laughing out loud, Granville more than both Joe, and me he had put his arm around Joe and looked down at him.

"Hiya, Joe, I'm Granville."

"Dona get cheeky, Granville, dona get like yur baby brother."

When we had got over laughing, Joe said,

"Come on boys, letsa lock the bar and hita da town."

Hit the town we did, Joe took us to places I didn't know existed. We went to an eating place only frequented by the Maltese and it was first class. Wherever we went Joe introduced us as his best friends and everyone made us more than welcome.

The night ended with the three of us sitting on a kerb edge, drunk to oblivion and burbling over each other and finally going our separate ways. I think I got back to my camp by taxi but cannot recall it.

MONDAY 18TH DECEMBER, 2000

Mark had a good lie-in today, to allow him to be awake for carol singing in the dayroom. This started at 14 00 hrs and all who were able to attend did so. It was good and very moving as some of the poor sods in there were trying their very best to join in and sing. One man had suffered a really bad stroke and lost the use of his right side, but not totally as he could walk with the assistance of a carer or nurse. Before having his stroke, he had been a very clever man who had lectured all over the world. I have no idea what he lectured about, as he was reluctant to tell anyone.

He sat for a while, watching the singing, not taking part as he rarely spoke. All of a sudden he shouted out,

"Oh God, why me, why have you struck me down this way? I am a good man, I loved you God, why me, why me?" He collapsed back into his chair and burst into tears. His actions had brought about an eerie silence, the lady playing the guitar stopped playing and everyone sat in silence. If all of the people felt as I did, then they were feeling so sorry for him.

He gestured to the nurses and shouted,

"Take me to my cell and let me die there."

When he had cleared the room, the lady with the guitar started to play and sing, soon to be joined individually by the rest present, as it seemed to take time for each person to recover from the sad, yes very sad, incident.

We were all present, Julie, Wendy, Lauren, Georgina, Marion and I. It was the first time we had all been with Mark at any one time since his accident and it felt good.

There was a good party-feeling and someone had provided food in the form of cakes, crisps, sweets and, very much to Georgina's delight, a big jar of Jelly Babies.

Funny how visiting Mark has never really been a problem for Georgina. She readily accepts people with problems and disabilities, but there again she knows no difference as she has been amongst such people from being a baby. There is one thing she excels at and that is bringing joy and happiness to all around her, especially me.

TUESDAY 19TH DECEMBER, 2000

Mark is having a very lazy day today. At 11 00 hrs when Julie visited, he was dressed but sleeping on his bed and try as she may he refused to wake up. I got to him at 15 00 hrs only to find that there was no one to give Mark physio. Shortage of staff was the excuse, oh well! Suppose it has to happen sometimes. It's just a bit annoying when you put yourself out to be here and all is called off. Read Mark's notes. He has been up for a short period, up at 11 45 hrs back to bed at 14 35 hrs.

Wendy has left Georgina with Marion. I don't doubt that the pair of them are having a customary walk along the bypass, or at least Marion will be as Georgina will be in her pram. Reading Wendy's entry is a little touching. Like us all, we have good days, bad days and really terrible ones when you know you are getting overpowered with grief. Sadly, you don't know when it is going to hit you, Wendy has written.

Mark was sleeping on his bed when I arrived but woke up when I spoke to him. I cleaned up his face and chattered to him to try to keep him awake. All of the time he was looking at me. It felt strange to have such good eye contact. I just wish I knew what he could see or what he sees. Mark had a slightly pained expression on his face but still maintained eye contact, then he started making strange moaning sounds. I feel he was trying to say something to me but all that came out was the moaning sound. It made me feel very upset and a bit excited. He finally nodded off, so I left him to sleep. Marion and I at 19 05 hrs. Jacqui and Karen had just got Mark up and they were setting up his drip feed. They have to start his feed as early as they can as it takes 16 hrs to give his daily requirements.

Gave Mark a cup tonight and tried moving his hand up and touched his mouth with the cup. He did offer some assistance but it was very little. Never mind, must keep trying.

WEDNESDAY 20TH DECEMBER, 2000

Mark off to E.N.T. and the results were satisfactory. The infection he had in his right ear has almost cleared up. His vocal cords are intact, according to the view from the tiny camera, which was pushed up Mark's nose and down his throat. The view on the monitor is unreal, seriously unreal. It's like taking a crawl down the throat, everything is on the move around you, tiny muscles expanding and contracting all the time, saliva making its way down the tunnel passes the camera and engulfs it for a split second. Then the journey back out makes you feel like you are being pulled out feet first. A most interesting trip, I assure you. However, one I wish I had never had to take but I couldn't let Mark go to E.N.T. on his own. I like to think that, on such occasions, a member of the family should be with him.

The only minus on the E.N.T. visit was that Mark's jawbones are very stiff. Not surprising really as he hasn't chewed anything for nearly 6 months. I am making a mental note to manipulate his lower mandible on my mouth exercises. Should have thought of that before, as it is pretty elementary. No, being unfair with myself, I feel that I should have been made aware of it by someone, or did that someone forget to tell me? That is, there is a someone. Confusing I know but all of this excursion is confusing. There is a severe lack of advice and transfer of information given out to people in our plight. We are not specialised in any medical fields, as we have not been trained. We have walked in off the street into a very painful nightmare. Maybe someday, someone will have the foresight to publish something on the matter or will they, as the fear of being taken to task for misinformation is getting greater by the day?

Linda Bloomfield and her lad Alex called to see Mark in the evening. Poor Mark, as Linda can talk for England and she knows it. She says he was tired and barely opened his eyes whilst they were there. She does say that Mark looks a lot better than he did on her last visit and that his skin is in a near normal condition now. I suppose she is right. Events such as this are a slow process, making it hard to notice change on a daily basis. A bit like watching a baby grow I suppose.

THURSDAY 21ST DECEMBER, 2000

Eye test today as Mark has had a noticeable red spot on his left eye. Their report reads,

'Patient needs a certain degree of communication to perform an eye test. With Mark as he is, no tests could be carried out.' So much for that. No mention of red spots or anything. Strange, the test should have been today and even stranger that his left eye was clear on my evening visit and his right eye is red. Think I am losing it a little, I will check back in the diary in the hope of proving it was his left eye and to confirm that I am in fact sane.

Not a good physio today, perhaps it was due to being in a different room. O.T. says that Mark switched his radio on and off three times today. I was present and I am sorry to say I think it was 'pot luck', as I was convinced that Mark was far from being conscious at the time. Mark's Uncle Fred with him when I got to him. He was giving Markie a good talking to and Mark was responding with a lot of guttural sounds and a positive waving of his left arm. He did the same for Wendy when she was here in the afternoon as she has noted,

"He turned straight to face me and mumbled something when I kissed him on his lips."

Julie cleans Mark's teeth every day now and throughout the procedure she says he gets easier on a daily basis. She is also quite convinced that Mark knows he has to co-operate to ensure he keeps his teeth. I am pleased to hear, as I understand that being fed that strange formula via the PEG gives Mark all he needs but I am led to believe that a side effect of it is to rot the teeth.

FRIDAY 22ND DECEMBER, 2000

Julie got a nice surprise from Markie today. When she entered the room, Mark was facing away from her. However, she said "Hello, Markie". She says he turned his head right round and looked at her only for a couple of seconds then he turned away again. She decided to give it another try and sure enough it worked. She is well chuffed.

I got a good buzz from Markie as well. Physio was well supported today, by Rob, Andy, Leanne and myself. We decided that, after getting Mark relaxed, we should go for a stand.

"Let's go for it on three," said Andy.

We were all in position and when "three" arrived, up went Mark. He was great, legs and body straight up, feet flat on the floor. Andy said it was going so well that we would keep him up as long as we could and we did. I didn't time it but I would estimate a good 10 minutes, it certainly beat all previous episodes.

Mark also got a great treat today. Kellie brought Dannielle in to her Dad. Wendy was present and she says,

Mark was very tired and I was about to ask if he could go to bed, when Kellie and Danni arrived. As soon as Kellie spoke, he pushed his head up and opened his eyes wide and stared at them, it was a treat to see. Little Dannielle is still finding it difficult to cope with seeing her daddy like this. So Kellie only brings her in when she asks.

Good move, Kellie, a wise decision as we don't want that little 'pocket rocket' (as I call her) to get distressed.

That night saw Markie reasonably alert so I took him back to my time in jail.

Bang, bang, bang on my cell door woke me with a shock. I jumped out of bed and sat back down quickly. The room was spinning around and I couldn't quite work out where I was and what was going on. Seconds later and reality flooded back by means of my favourite Corporal bursting into my cell shouting,

"Get up, Holroyd, you idle bastard, its 6 o'clock and time for Walkies."

I quickly dressed and ran along the metal balcony and down the stairs. Two other inmates were doing a copy of me. The Sergeant pointed to the floor in front of him, so we lined up to face him.

"We are going to do a little rifle drill to run up an appetite for you."

One of the Marine Guards came out of the office with three rifles and passed them to us. As is customary when you are given a weapon, the first thing you do is carry out a safety check to ensure it is not loaded or have any rounds (bullets) in the breach. The sergeant checked the weapons and declared them safe.

"No ammo. Holroyd, you look quite disappointed but then again I don't think you would have the bollocks to shoot anybody, even me."

I wondered why this bastard had it in for me. He didn't know me, I had not seen or heard of him so why me? Is it second nature to people like him to be a true bastard?

"Right! Outside and fall in at the double."

When we were lined up he looked at me and said "Rifle" and he put his hands out. I whipped the rifle up and opened the bolt to prove it safe and handed it to him.

"You will adopt this position and double around the building and keep doubling until I give the order to stop."

He took the rifle in both hands and raised it over his head.

"Savvy," he said, then threw the rifle at me.

"Rifles up, double march!"

We set off line astern, me at the rear, as I didn't want to be the one to set the pace. Round and round we went and heavier and heavier the rifle became. On checking the clock in the tower, we had been going round for over an hour when it started to rain and did it rain? Torrential, big blobs, bounced on the stone flags. Within minutes we were soaking.

The Sergeant stood in the shelter of the prison doorway and shouted abuse at us as we passed by him. I never knew the names of the other two prisoners at that point in time, as we were forbidden to speak to each other.

"Williams, you fat little 'git', hold the rifle right up."

So Williams was the little one at the front of our trio. I don't doubt he will abuse the other man before much longer, I thought and I thought right.

"Benson, you fucking wimp, keep that rifle up as high as you can."

Round and round we went; by now my mind had gone into autopilot, I tried to switch off to the weight and the pain of that rifle. I seemed to manage to lock my arms somehow and keep the rifle aloft.

Food arrived whilst we were going round and round and I felt sure he would call a halt but no.

"The bastard will wait until it is cold before we can have it," muttered Benson when we were round the rear of the building.

He was right. At 08 30 hrs he called us to a halt and ushered us inside at the double.

"Get your eating irons and mess tins. You have 15 minutes to feed."

Cold scrambled egg, beans bonded together into a ball and two (burnt) sausages. It was wonderful as I was absolutely starving; no luxuries like tea or coffee but as much water as we wanted.

"Holroyd, you are the new kid on the block, so you have the pleasure of cleaning up and I mean cleaning up."

Fifteen minutes up and we set about our delegated tasks. Benson was sent to clean out and 'stoke up' the boiler, Williams had to 'slop out' the heads and I was taken to the ancient kitchen or what had been the kitchen. All that was in there was a long stone slab and two massive sinks big enough to sit in, I reckoned.

The food had arrived in two big stainless steel fannies (metal containers with a sealed lid and trays within them to hold the food). They were not the cleanest of containers when I started but they were the cleanest in the world when I finished, two and a half hours later. I learnt later that the galley would search the kitchens for the dirtiest fannies they could find to send food to the prison to ensure that they would come back as good as new every time. Good move, I suppose.

After my first attempt at cleaning, a Sergeant grabbed it, took me outside and threw a load of ash from the boiler house into it and said,

"Call that fucking clean, I wouldn't let a dog eat out of that. Now get in there and clean them. I want to be able to shave using them as a mirror when you have done."

Job done and passed I felt quite proud, but no compliments were forthcoming, just a scowl and a nod from my mentor.

All three of us were summoned to muster by the office.

"You will parade in number ones at 14 00 hrs and you had better be perfect."

Number ones are best blues, Markie, like I was dressed when I saw the C.O.

I was determined not to give this man anything to pick me up on so I cleaned all of my buttons, cap badge, belt brass ware three times. Even the two little buttons that held the chin strap on my hat were gleaming. Boots were perfect and gleaming. I felt good as I made my way to the office.

A new corporal was on duty today. I had watched him skulking and lurking about, not saying anything, just watching and noting my every move. He made me feel uneasy.

"What's that bastard up to?" I thought to myself. I was soon to learn that this man was not nice to know and for some reason he had it in for me.

The sergeant had left and the new corporal was now in charge.

He called us to attention and lined us up one arm's length apart. Slowly and very methodically he looked us up and down.

"I feel I need to introduce myself to you scum bags, my name is Corporal Howard, I have a reputation for being a mean bastard and I am getting better at it. When I address you, you will spring to attention and sing out your name, understood?"

"Yes, Corporal," we replied in perfect unison. He stopped in front of me, weighed me up and down, and then screamed.

"Name?"

"Marine Holroyd, Corporal."

"You don't like me, do you, Holroyd?"

I paused, not knowing how to reply. Should I say yes or no? What sort of answer was he looking for?

"Well?"

"I don't know you, Corporal."

"I didn't ask you if you knew me. I asked you if you didn't like me. Well, do you like me, yes or no?"

Again, I was stuck for words, he was goading me into saying something that I couldn't really answer.

He moved on to Benson.

"Name?" he screamed.

"Marine Benson, Corporal."

"You like me don't you, Benson."

"Yes, Corporal."

"Name?" he shouted into William's face.

"Marine Williams, Corporal."

"Well, Williams, do you like me?"

"Oh yes, Corporal," he replied loudly.

He moved back to me.

"It seems to me that you are the only person who doesn't like me, Holroyd. Now why would you dislike someone you don't even know."

Again, another silence from me, his questions were double edged. Did he want me to say yes or no? The bastard was reeling me in, trying to make me say something I would regret.

"Well, Holroyd, do you like me or not?"

At last a positive question, he had got me. I would have to answer him. My thoughts were racing back to my childhood days.

"What would my Mam want me to say?" I thought. She had always been a very honest person and she had been very firm with us all on the subject of being truthful, one of her famous sayings came to me.

"If ya ave to lie to save your arse, yu must have done somat really bad."

The Corporal closed in on me and his face was only inches from mine.

"Well, lad, what's the answer?"

210

It was then that I realised that he was a professional bully, he was smaller than me, in fact a lot smaller than me, and in real life I wouldn't tolerate being treated in this manner especially by a little runt like him. He was using his rank to bully people and was successful at belittling others. I had made up my mind; I looked down at him and stared into his eyes.

"No I don't fucking like you, you are a little bastard. I reckon your Dad would be proud of you if you knew who he was."

"Oh shit," I thought, I have done it again. Why couldn't I have said, of course I like you corporal and left it at that. Again, I blamed my upbringing and again I realised that being honest is not always the best policy, but again I thought of your Grandma, Markie.

I was not prepared to lie to save my arse, as she would have put it.

"What would you have done, Markie?"

I was looking straight into Mark's face.

"Is he understanding me? Are his glazed eyes seeing me? Does he understand any of my stories? Am I wasting my time? Should I go on?"

All these thoughts were racing through my head as I stared into his face. Then something hit me. From whom or where this came was not clear but suddenly I put my arms around Markie and said,

"Come on, son, come back to me. You don't know how much I love and miss you."

I hung onto him and prayed. I whispered the Lord's Prayer into his ear and meant every word I was saying.

On the drive home, I had to stop in my usual lay-by on Barden Lane, as my emotions had overcome me again and I cried and cried.

"Why Mark, God, why my Markie?" I remembered shouting out loud.

SATURDAY 23RD DECEMBER, 2000

Double birthday celebrations today. Frank and John, both patients, are having a good day. Lots of happiness as plenty of visitors are calling to see them with well wishes. We are all gathered around them both and singing Happy Birthday. They responded by revealing a big chocolate cake. Where it came from I don't know but I do know where it went as everyone enjoyed it.

Mark had a 'down to the bone' haircut today, Marion and I witnessed the operation and we are both in agreement that Mark suits his hair short. Don't know what he feels about it as he has had long hair for such a long time. He will probably smack me if he realises that his hair has gone.

"I didn't do it, Mark, I only held your head steady whilst the deed was done," I said.

SUNDAY 24TH DECEMBER, 2000

Mark is a tired lad today and I think he is coming down with a cold. He was up and in his chair at 11.30 and we sat out in the dayroom.

Julie came in with Steve, her on, off, on, off boyfriend, nice guy and clever with it, just wish they could get together but I doubt it. Still it's good to have a nice friend.

Mark went back to bed at 14 30 hrs, as he was shattered, not bad he managed 3 hours.

Two of his friends called this afternoon, Entie and Albert, but sadly Mark was very sleepy, so doubt if he acknowledged their presence.

Marion and I arrived at 19 30 hrs to find Mark in a very deep sleep; shame to disturb him but it is for the better, as he needs lots and lots of rest as all head-injured people do.

MONDAY 25TH DECEMBER (CHRISTMAS DAY), 2000

Not many people in the home as a lot have managed to go home over the festive season. But what we lack in quantity is made up by the quality of those left behind.

I left home early today, as I wanted to walk and get some fresh air. 11 45 hrs when I got here. I was followed by Entie, then Marion, then Julie and Lauren, and on their heels came Wendy and Georgina.

The nurses had clubbed together and bought presents for all who were staying. They came out with the presents and it was very touching. Markie was given a T-shirt and two pairs of socks.

Sarah joined our company, as her dad had not been able to get in to see her. Like Mark she is a head-injured person and has been for several years now.

We all gathered around the big table. Present were John, David, Frank, Desmond, Craig, Sarah and Mark, all from Rakehead. Visitors included our little gang and Hazel, John's wife. Soon, the nursing staff joined us and when all were present, we sang Christmas Carols.

We all gathered again in the evening as the galley had sent down lots of food. There were meats, pies, prawns, cheeses, biscuits, salad and bread and butter. We all gathered around the big table again and had a good time whilst we 'stuffed' ourselves. A good atmosphere abounded and I found it difficult to know why. Here we all are, it is Christmas, a time of festivity, it is cold and wet outside. All of us, I assume, have our own thoughts and I, for one, had a very heavy heart. I looked around and tried to imagine what could be going on in everyone's mind. I was watching David, an ex-stroke patient, his face was expressionless, and here was a man who had given up completely. I had talked to him in the past and I even went out of my way to drag him back into the real world but all he wanted to do was chain smoke himself to death. It came as a shock to me when one day, whilst trying to encourage him to eat something, he looked me straight in the face and said,

"Peter, I know your intentions are great, I have watched you with Mark, but I am not like Mark. I am a man who has had enough, all I want to do is die and they won't let me. I thank you for your concern and care, but save it for your son. I don't deserve it and I don't need it."

He just sat at the table, pushing the small serving of prawns and salad around his plate.

"Does he really want to die?" I thought to myself. Only David knows the answer to that one.

My view turned to Craig. Regardless of being badly distorted and unable to do anything for himself, he was having a whale of a time shouting, laughing and enjoying the food his mother was feeding him.

Then I looked at Markie and I tried to imagine what was going through his mind. He was sitting in his chair quite motionless, his eyes were open but he wasn't looking, his face was devoid of expression. He just sat there oblivious to what was going on around him. I wanted to go to him and love him but I knew he wouldn't want that, as he had always shrugged off actions such as a cuddle or squeeze.

I looked at Marion and I could almost feel the pain radiating from her as she too was looking at Mark.

"Oh God, where are you?" I said to myself.

"This is your day, God, please come and help us all and rid us of our terrible pain."

"A penny for your thoughts, Peter, you look miles away. I hope it's somewhere nice."

This came from Hazel, John's wife.

"Sorry, Hazel, they are not for sale love, at least not at the present time."

"It's painful isn't it?"

"Painful, it's purgatory but we have to hang on in there, as I can't find the way out yet, but I will, mark my words, I will."

"I know you will, I am sure of that."

She fell silent then and just looked at me, knowing what I was feeling. It made me feel better to know that I had support of someone who was almost a complete stranger.

Mark brought the party to an end by doing his 'I snore for England' act and some performance it was. So, the carers kindly took him away from us to settle him for the night.

TUESDAY 26TH DECEMBER, 2000

Yomped in again today and it was a good one, fields a bit too wet, so I was somewhat 'shop soiled' when I got here. Found Markie in his room on his bed with two nurses fussing around him and getting him dressed. No mean task as Markie is 6'2" and weighing in at about 12 stone. That done, we set off on our tour of the corridors only to find we have a wheelchair problem. On the handlebars that you hold to push the chair along are two levers, just like the hand brakes on a pushbike. These are not brakes: they control the angle of Markie's chair-back. When he is alert and sitting, you can have him sitting upright but, as he tires, you can recline him back a little to help him maintain an upright posture. If you didn't, he would 'flop' forward and become very difficult to handle. Our problem was that one of the levers had a fault. Automatically, it would release that side of the chair, causing Mark great alarm as it left him at a crazy angle. Carried out temporary repair, as to call in the 'chair people' over the festive period may have proved a bit of a task.

I decided that, when all the 'jolly's' were over, I would investigate as to why we were still in an old worn-out chair made up by my begging, borrowing and even on two occasions stealing to keep Markie mobile. I checked back and found that it was 5 months ago since Mark was measured for his chair. Why, what can cause such a long delay? Simple answer, money I thought, but later realised that it was not just money but gross inefficiency on the part of just a few people, no names, no pack drill, but not good enough. I decided to continue on my wheelchair crusade.

I let Markie have a sleep at 14 20 hrs, but he got little of that as at 15 15 hrs a raiding party in the shape of Marion, Julie, Lauren, Dannielle, Wendy, Georgina and Entie. Markie's 'cat nap' must have done him good, as suddenly he appeared revived. All had brought in presents for Mark and they took turns unwrapping his presents and handing them over to Markie, it was wonderful, all of us with him bearing gifts. It made me realise how much we all love and miss Markie. With a family like this, how can we fail to get him back, but who knows? If we get him back some quality of life and some form of communication, I would be content, not happy, just content.

I stayed on with Markie that night, as he appeared to be aware of my presence.

"Guard, arrest this man and place him in his cell." The corporal bellowed into my face. Out came the two guards or warders and took me by both arms and led me to my cell.

216

"Mind your fingers, lad," said one of them as he slammed the cell door.

"What now?" I thought as I stood there, all dressed up and nowhere to go.

Suddenly, the door was wrenched open and I was ordered from the cell at the double.

"Inspection time, Ollie, let's see what sort of 'Crabbie' bastard you are."

The Corporal, glowing with anger, made me take off my belt first.

"Strip it," he ordered. So I carefully removed the brass buckles and slides and held it in front of me. He examined it with 'a fine tooth comb', then threw it to the floor.

"Hat!" I removed it and handed it to him, again a very close inspection, paying special attention to the chinstrap buttons, he gave a grunt and dispatched that to the floor.

"Tunic!" This removed and it got the very same amount of scrutiny before that too ended up in a pile.

"Boots!" I carefully removed them one at a time and placed them in front of me.

"Not bad, not bad at all," he said as he moved closer to me. Suddenly, he raised his foot and crashed his studded boot down onto the toecap of each of my boots in turn, shattering the highly polished toecaps. By now, he was so close to me, I could smell his smelly breath, he was goading me and I knew it. The two guards closed in on me ready to pounce, should I make a move.

I was on the boil, a coiled spring ready to pounce and yet I was in control.

"Don't smack him, Pedro, it's what he wants. If you smack him, you will be out of the mob," I told myself.

So I stood there looking down into his eyes thinking,

"This little runt has just ruined hours, no days, of polishing, it would take weeks to get my boots back to their original shine, what a little shit house he is."

"Trousers!" I duly removed them.

"Socks, vest and kecks!"

I deftly removed them and stood there in front of him, stark naked but to attention.

He walked around me, bent down, picked up my socks and sniffed them before sending them to the pile. My underpants or kecks suffered the same treatment.

We came face to face again and he was still glowing red.

"You're on a charge, Holroyd. I have made arrangements for you to appear before the R.S.M. in the morning, so you had better get busy and clean this filthy pile of shit before then."

217

He walked to my clothes, stood on them then stepped back to watch. I went over, gathered my gear and set off towards my cell. I suddenly got an urge to retaliate, but stopped, turned round and walked backwards towards the stairs to go to my cell.

"Mustn't throw caution to the wind, must we corporal, one can't be too careful in a situation like this?"

I quickly turned, shot up the stairs and slammed my cell door shut.

A few hours later one of the guards brought me some food, some sort of beef stew and a chunk of bread.

"You certainly know how to win friends and influence people, Ollie, he is fucking fuming down there, it was great to see the little bastard lose it," he said in a low voice.

With that, he shouted one or two obscenities at me and slammed the door.

Up at the crack of dawn and once again 'dressed to kill', stupid statement that, why would one say 'dressed to kill'? Especially in my situation more like 'dressed to be killed' or a fate almost as bad.

No breakfast forthcoming and I can remember my stomach reminding me every 2 to 3 minutes or was it the butterflies in my stomach, another stupid statement, how the hell could I have butterflies in my stomach?

Thoughts like these were going through my head as I waited and waited for someone to summon me, march me away to meet my executioner. Well, not really executioner, but one who had a 'hell of a lot of clout', and one who would be laying the plans for my future existence. The R.S.M., that man I really respected, that man who had got me out of the shit on this occasion, that man who I felt had higher hopes for me, that man I had let down badly. What would he feel about me now? I know what he will feel. He will feel I have let him down and I have, and I know it.

"Clank, clank, clank," the sound of studded boots on the metal staircase and my landing. The sounds stopped outside my cell and the door was pushed open. Hardly any light got past the body that entered the cell. He was another giant of a man but one I knew from a couple of lectures he had given us on the Special Boat Service, explaining what it was all about. One of the badges on his arm said it all, it was crossed canoe paddles with S.C.1 on it. This means swimmer, canoeist No.1, a badge rarely seen but one that said what it meant. This colour sergeant was a No.1 in my books and one that I envied, as he had achieved all that I wanted to be.

"You must be a special lad or a bad bastard as they have placed you in my care today. Take my advice, don't think of doing a 'runner', as believe me you won't make it."

"Yes, Colour Sergeant."

He went on to give me a very close inspection and concluded that I was okay to proceed to see the 'boss' as he put it.

"You won't need your hat, lad, prisoners are not allowed to have that pleasure. Right, jump to it and get down those 'dancers' (stairs) and fall in with the escort."

Four corporals were in the escort.

"This must be some occasion, a Swimmer Canoeist Colour Sergeant and four corporals," I thought to myself as the big oak gates started to swing open. It looked like another world out there; my short but eventful stay in jail had felt like a month away from the outside world.

"Prisoner and escort quick march!" Our feet crunched on the stony gravely surface of the prison compound, once clear and onto the tarmac we made our way down the road towards the administration block. It was early and lots of men were coming and going to the mess hall for breakfast. I could feel a thousand eyes gazing at me, so I kept my head up, eyes straight forward trying my hardest to stand proud but it was hard, very hard as my heart was in my boots and it was being pounded as we went down that road.

"Crunch, crunch, crunch." The sound of our boots lulled me a little but not for long.

"Prisoner and escort halt!"

We had arrived outside the door that went into the administration building where R.S.M. had his office.

We were left there, all standing to attention whilst the colour sergeant pushed open the double doors and vanished inside. Less than 2 minutes later he re-appeared.

"Prisoner and escort right turn, follow me quick march!"

Outside the R.S.M's office, we were halted and stood at ease.

"Mam, I am sorry, honest. I am sorry I have let you down once more, I am sorry if I have brought disgrace on the family name. I am sorry for letting down dad, who I feel is watching over me." My thoughts were snatched from me as the Colour Sergeant brought me down to earth with a crash.

"Prisoner and escort shun, quick march!" We wheeled round and brought to a halt in front of the R.S.M.

Not the R.S.M. who had been sound with me before. It was the same man but a changed man. He sat there glaring at me, and he made me feel so uncomfortable as he looked into my face.

We all stood rigidly to attention for what seemed a long time, and then the R.S.M. broke the silence.

"Dismiss the escort, Colour Sergeant."

"Escort about turn, quick march!"

I was left alone in front of the R.S.M. The colour sergeant was close, very close behind me, perhaps hoping I would make a move.

The Corporal of the prison, who had pressed the charges against me, marched in and he was asked to read out his charge, a little glossed up, no mention of how he had asked me impossible questions, no mention of how we were ill-treated by him. Only the side of the incident that he wanted to portray and that was to make me look as charged, both insubordinate and offensive behaviour to a Senior Rank. Now that sounded bad and it was, but it was not true in the true sense.

I was not given the opportunity to give my side of the story; in fact, I was not asked a single question.

This was a trial all right, a trial with only one sentence and that was guilty. To my surprise, another witness was called. It was the guard who had brought me my supper. He was questioned by the R.S.M. to some length and he answered very truthfully and accurately,

"Have you anything to add to your statement?"

"Yes Sir, it is probably not relevant to what Holroyd did but as I am leaving the Corps in 3 days I feel this is a time when I should be truthful with myself. If I had been in Marine Holroyd's shoes I would have not been able to control myself as well as he did." The Colour Sergeant interrupted him. "Silence Marine, silence, you are right, and as you say it is not relevant."

"Hang fire, Colours, let him say his piece," said the R.S.M. as he turned to the witness.

"If you had been in Holroyd's position what would you have done? Come on, be honest with yourself. How long have you served in the Corp?"

"Nine years, sir."

"Well, trained soldier, what would you have done?"

"I would probably have smacked the bastard as in my opinion Ollie, sorry I mean Holroyd, was forced into an impossible situation and to take it on the chin as he did is something I don't consider I could have done."

Silence befell us, as we all seemed to let his comments 'sink in'. This silence was broken by the R.S.M.

"Admirable the way you have defended Holroyd, especially if you have never met him before, or have you?"

"No sir, I have never met Holroyd up until now."

"Yes, okay, but as both you and the Colour Sergeant agree it is not relevant in this instance. I have to say, however, that the Corp is losing a good and honest Marine and I have to admire your attitude. It is very important in life to be honest especially to yourself, dismiss him, Colours."

"Witness dismissed."

My saviour snapped to attention and marched from the room, head held high and perhaps a slight smile of satisfaction on his face.

Again, silence seems funny how, when your head is on the chopping block, even a short silence seems like eternity.

"Holroyd, it seems to me that you are not going to conform to the Royal Marine way of life; either that or you are a very unlucky person. I cannot begin to know where you are coming from. I have looked at your service record to date and in such a short period you have proved that you are not a man to stand in the wings. I have read of you and your mate stealing from the carousel owner, a humorous tale I have to agree but not behaviour becoming of a Royal Marine. Then we have the encounter with the Naval Shore Patrol where you could have killed one of those men or even both. Now, we are face to face again charged with insubordination, a very serious offence. The N.C.O. who has brought these charges was right to bring them, as you broke the rules. May I remind you that provocation is no excuse for retaliation. If you had 'smacked', as your friend the guard puts it, the corporal, I would have had no hesitation but to have you Court Marshalled and driven from the Corps. Bear in mind, Holroyd, you are in jail serving a 14-day sentence, you are not on a 'banyan' somewhere. I have confirmation of your posting now and I have to make a serious decision. Do I let you go off to 40 Commandos in Malta or do you feel I should extend your stay here in our local prison. What do you want me to do and how can you give me any justification to let you take the easy route? Now is your chance, Marine Holroyd, as what you are about to say is going to draw the map of your future."

"Sir, I need to stay in the Royal Marines as it is all I have wanted to do for the past 10 years. Sir, in civvy street I could feel my life wasting away and I know that I would have no future should I have to go back there. Sir, I owe it to my Mam, as she broken-heartedly signed the consent form for me to join. I convinced her that to let me go would be the making of me. Sir, I am so proud to have the honour of being able to wear my green beret and I want to make to you my solemn promise that, if you let me stay, I will channel all my ambitions and frustration that I find myself subjected to in the direction of making me a far better Marine than I could have been had I not had these excursions. I feel, Sir, that the lessons I have learnt are going to make me a better Royal Marine, one that I am sure you will be proud of, should you give me just one more chance."

Silence and this time long enough to make me wonder where all of what I had just said had come from. It flowed from me, or from someone within me. Was it my Dad influencing from above? Or was it my Mam waiting at home with her famous leather-picking strap to give me a good thrashing, should I be dismissed?.

"Holroyd, an admirable speech and one that I feel came from your heart. With that in mind, I will give you one more chance, but believe me, step out of line again and your feet will not touch the ground until you are carried from this place and put down in civvy street. I will find an appropriate task for you to carry out during your incarceration here at Eastney. In fact, I already know

221

what it will be. It is a task to prove the worthiness of your words and such a task that some day you may be able to show your grandchildren and say,

"Do you see that big Sheet Anchor over there, well that's my handiwork. That's as much as I am going to say about that, you'll find out more later."

"Take him away, Colour Sergeant."

"Prisoner attention, right turn, quick march!"

The escort joined us and I was marched back to jail feeling a lucky man, yes, a very lucky man.

WEDNESDAY 27TH DECEMBER, 2000

Julie first in today, a little later as she confesses that she had a fight with the bed and the bed won.

Physio was at 15 00 hrs, Mr G., Leanne and me today. First, we worked on Markie's body, as Giles thought that Mark required some trunk exercises, so, a little like a contortionist, Mr G. manoeuvred his body so that Markie's bottom was on his knees and his legs were bent up almost to his tummy. Once Mark had accepted this strange position, Mr G. commenced to gyrate Mark's legs from side to side, causing his hips to swing from right to left. This continued for a good 10 minutes and Markie appeared to accept it, or even enjoy it, as he made no protest sounds. Mr G. appeared happy with Mark's demeanour, so much so that he announced.

"I think Mark's ready for a stand now."

Single-handed, Mr G. got Mark onto his knees and he kept explaining to him exactly what he was doing and why. He also persuaded asking Mark to 'go along with it' as he put it.

"On three Markie, one, two, three!"

Up they went into a 'cracking' standing position. I just stood there and watched and poised to pounce, should something happen to Markie, like a stagger from Mr G. or an imbalance, as Mark was much taller and heavier than Mr G. My fears were thankfully not justified as, after about 7 minutes, Giles sat back on the plinth with Mark still firmly on his knees. By now, Leanne had returned from seeking out Markie's chair. Mr G. stood Mark again and with me supporting one arm and Mr G. the other, Leanne moved around the back of Mark with the chair. Once in position we 'plopped' him in his chair.

"Markie, that was brilliant," said Mr G. and both Leanne and I echoed his remarks.

"Mr G. calling Markie, Markie, that's good," I thought. A positive gesture that he is getting more attached to him. Perhaps Mr G. has been reading our diary as it was he who said that he knew of my displeasure over Mark's wheelchair and he promised he would 'chase it up' for me. That evening, Marion brought in two cassettes. One was Jim Reeves and the other Patsy Cline; she knows that Mark dislikes both of these. I agreed to pass them over to Sandra the Occupational Therapist girl, as it was her who asked for them. She is of the opinion that Mark may react better to a singer he dislikes rather than to one he likes, we will see.

I showed the tapes to Markie and said,

"Look what your Mam has brought in for you. You will be the envy of all others when they see what you have got. You lucky little devil."

Not even a flicker of acknowledgement from Markie, just a blank stare or was that a smirk?

THURSDAY 28TH DECEMBER, 2000

Another good performance in physio. We went for a stand again but the first attempt was a disaster as Markie's feet slipped on the carpet. My fault entirely, as I had not made sure his slippers were on properly. Slippers firmly in place and up we went, another perfect performance and he stood virtually unaided for a good 5 minutes.

During the session I asked Mr G. how we could progress with Mark's eating and drinking, as right from day one he had been receiving his food and water via a plastic tube. At first, this was a tube inserted via his nose into his stomach, but as Mark progressed it was changed to a tube put into the stomach, directly through his abdomen. The tube emerged from Markie's body just above his belly button, it finished with a plastic clamp with a multi-connection point. Every few hours a nurse would come along with a big jug of water accompanied with a massive syringe. When Mark was connected up, the nurse would relax the clamp and send a measured amount of water straight into Mark's stomach. During the night this pipe was connected to a drip-feed bottle, assisted by a small pump on a stand by his bed. Then, for hours, a highly concentrated fluid was fed into him. I am told that the food contains everything that Markie needs to remain well and healthy.

Mr G. said that Mark must remain 'Nil by mouth' until the specialists had carried out tests as to where his food and water would go, should it be administered via the mouth. The big danger is some intake going into his lungs. This could result in Mark contracting pneumonia, a severe illness. Pneumonia is when the air sacks in the lungs fill up with pus causing a dangerous infection, which can cut off of oxygen supply into the blood circulation. He went on to explain that the pus was a greenish, opaque liquid, which was made up of dead white blood cells and bacteria mixed with tissue debris and serum.

"Thanks, Mr G., you have made me a much wiser man," I remember saying to him.

I went on to think just how complicated our bodies are. Just a simple act of eating or drinking can be so much of a matter of life or death, should it go 'down the wrong hole' as my Mam used to say should you choke on a bit of food.

Mr G. explained that Mark would have to undergo a swallow test during a continuous X-ray. A luminous fluid would be sent down his throat and the X-ray would follow its progress to ensure it took the right track. If this was proved okay, then very small amounts of fluid or 'sloppy food' could be given to him.

"I wouldn't be too eager to go for an oral intake yet, Peter, as Mark's accident is very much in its early stages and with an injury such as this you will find that progress proceeds at a 'snail like pace', so slow that you rarely see it, especially if you are ever present as your family tend to be."

"Yep! I know what you are saying. It's just a new road to us, unlike you, as we never realised that this road existed. I just wish we did not have to take this route at all."

"Sorry, Peter, I wish I could do more for the family and Mark, of course, but believe me I can't. You will have to re-examine the meaning of the word patience."

That night, I took his advice and looked up the meaning of patience and learned that it means,

"The capacity to tolerate delays, trouble or suffering without becoming angry or upset."

"Good one, Mr G., that's it in a nutshell," I said to myself.

FRIDAY 29TH DECEMBER, 2000

Woke up to find lots of snow today but thankfully the 'gritters' had made an early start and the roads were safe to travel on. When I got to Markie, he was out of it, apparently he had developed a urine infection and the doctor had recommended Mark on a course of antibiotics. Must have been a powerful one as it put Mark's 'lights out' for the whole weekend.

MONDAY 1ST JANUARY, 2001

Mark still out of it, but not to worry as this place is like a 'graveyard with lights'. Not surprising as it is a public holiday. Nevertheless, Mark has still had as much attention as he would have got should he have been well. Tom, a cockney porter who Mark used to pal up with, called to see him. I know what Mark would have said to Tom had he been able to communicate and that would probably have been,

"Hello, you cockney git, what are you after?"

It had been about 3 months since Tom saw Mark and he was pleased with what he saw.

"Bladdy 'el, Mark, ur looking a lot better."

Music to my ears as I could not see much change, but I accepted what Tom was saying and I don't think he was just being a nice guy to make us feel better.

TUESDAY JANUARY 2ND, 2001

Mark had a visit from Kellie and Dannielle in the morning but I am afraid he slept through it. I can't help wondering what Dannielle thinks when she sees her dad like that. It must hurt her. She is a very quiet child and often she just looks and listens to what is going on around her. Maybe someday I will be able to ask her but the time is not right yet.

It's a Bank Holiday in Scotland, so Betty and Karen have arrived on a flying visit. Good to see them and it is great moral support that they bring with them and we very much appreciate that. Karen went in with Wendy and Georgina in the afternoon but, by the sound of things, Mark was a tired lad.

At 15 00 hrs I trundled Mark off to physio on his bed. I am getting quite an expert at this one-man circus act, not easy negotiating passages and swing doors with a 12 stone man in his bed. Off the bed and onto the plinth for a quick chill out. That done, we decided that standing should be the thing to focus on for the immediate future, and stand we did. Only Mr G. and Andy to get him up, with Mark offering quite a lot of assistance. It was one stand but a long one finishing with Mark being seated in his chair straight from his stand.

Back again at 19 00 hrs with Mark's Aunty Betty. Betty gave Mark a good talking to but true to form he completely ignored her and went off to sleep.

Tom called again to ask Mark if he would snap out of it and go on a trip to India with him in a fortnight's time. All expenses paid, as Tom had planned on taking his girlfriend with him but sadly they had had a big falling out do and she had 'kicked poor Tom into touch' and told him what to do with his trip to India.

WEDNESDAY 3RD JANUARY, 2001

Mark a little more active with his left hand today, as when Wendy put her keys on his wheelchair table he took hold of them and wouldn't let her have them back. Wendy says his psoriasis is back with a vengeance; his head, chest and back have lots of pretty nasty patches. Don't think there is much they can do with that problem, but I will ask.

THURSDAY

Mark was a treat in physio today or should I say he had a treat. He had been extending his legs this morning so Leanne set about massaging them. I felt that Markie knew it was Leanne's magic touch or was it the fact that she was working on his thigh muscles that made him very co-operative? Did I notice a trace of a smirk on his face? Perhaps not but there was something different radiating from him. On the evening visit, my brother Fred said he could see a great improvement in Mark over the past fortnight. He has purposely not been in to see Mark, due to having had a bad cold.

Mr G. gave me an update of the progress of Mark's chair, or should I say lack of progress. The chair people at Preston have all been struck with a terrible problem. All of them have been hit with a very strange ailment, which has left them all deaf and dumb, leaving them all unable to take or make telephone calls.

I suggested that I go and visit them to help them in their plight but Mr G. begged me not to do so, as I may compound the problem and extend the waiting time. I agreed but not happily, as the whole wheelchair incident is now well beyond comprehension.

FRIDAY 5TH JANUARY, 2001

Markie at his best ever today. Physio was a treat. Roby, Andy, Jayne (an auxiliary nurse) and I were present. Up went the plinth and without hesitation Mark moved into a perfect stand, which he held for over 10 minutes. Wendy arrived whilst Mark was stood upright and the look on her face was one I will always remember. It was a look of love and endearment but mixed with it was a confident, slight grin of feeling proud of Markie.

Back in his chair, I asked Markie if he would show us he was aware. I asked him to scratch his table with his fingers. He just sat there staring straight at me, as if to say,

"I hear you Dad and I am trying, honest I am."

I adjusted his left arm and raised it clear of the table, leaving his fingers free to move.

"Come on, Markie, please scratch the table."

The look on his face changed to one of slight confusion or frustration. However, I could feel a twinge in my wrist that was supporting his hand. Suddenly, I felt it again and it seemed stronger.

"Come on, Markie, I know you are trying and I can feel it coming. Just scratch the table son, please I know you can do it."

The room was eerily silent as everyone concentrated on Mark, willing his fingers to move.

"Oh! Markie," Wendy shouted, "Do it, Markie, please!"

That I feel was Markie's trigger, he continued gazing at me and slowly one finger moved, followed by another then the third one. He was scratching the table. Still silence. If everyone felt as I did, they would have been unable to utter a sound, due to a massive lump of emotion cutting off the ability to speak.

"Mark, that is amazing," said Andy

"Markie, do it again," begged Leanne.

"Oh, Markie! That was wonderful," I heard Wendy say.

All eyes were now transfixed on Mark's hand and his table and all were willing his fingers to move.

"Mark, can you scratch three times?" asked Andy. Slowly Markie's fingers moved all three in unison, his nails scratched the table, once, twice then a third time.

It was too much for me and I felt tears running down my cheeks, but I didn't feel embarrassed as I was not alone. I looked around and there wasn't a dry eye in the room.

"Well done, son, well done, I am so proud of you," I heard myself croak.

"And so you should be, Dad, that was brilliant, Mark, well done." It came from Rob as he patted Mark's back. Suddenly the room was filled with a buzz and everyone was so pleased with Markie's amazing performance and they all told him so in their own way.

Jayne was with Mark when Marion and I arrived for our evening visit and she was still on a high as she explained to Mum just what Markie had achieved. I was glad she did it, as her interpretation was far better than mine was, as I had tried to play my version down a little just in case it was a 'flash in the pan'.

I felt Markie was still on a high as he was very vocal and he made lots and lots of eye contact with his mum. The mumbling sounded very much like "Mum, Mum", but they came out "Mom, Mom".

"What a day," I said to Marion, she just nodded in confirmation.

Saturday 6th January, 2001

Lots of traffic for Mark today, first Mum at 11.30 to 13.45. Pam, my sister, has been and made her comments in the diary.

"Markie is making some nice noises during his sleep, you can see his eyes moving under his lids, he is dreaming, I do hope it is something nice and peaceful, maybe he is with Dannielle, I hope so." She wrote that Julie and Wendy have also been but it seems that Mark was very tired during their stay.

The Ambush

On my evening visit I found Markie quite aware so I decided to take him back to the Dhala Pass in Aden.

Laying in wait in the God-forsaken place of the observation post that we occupied was not easy. Heat gets almost unbearable; you are constantly thirsty, but very wary to drink too much water, as you need to conserve every drop, should something go wrong. I have tried several ways of controlling my intake of water, and I find the best for me is to wait until I am holed up or at least at rest before I take a few sips. Some of the other lads have their own methods. Biff, our big minder, takes small drinks almost on the hour and that seems to work for him. One thing we don't do is complain about the shortage of water; you have to put up with it when out on a trip. To even think of moaning is taboo, so it never gets a mention. The water shortage is due to its weight, and because you are loaded down with many other essentials needed on an outing, such as your weapon, ammunition, camouflage gear and scrims, food, mortar bombs for your defensive mortar, batteries for the antique radios, as they do not last very long due to the their age.

"Ragheads haven't moved for over an hour now and I am not happy. It's as if they know we have them eyeballed and are keeping their heads down. I suggest we get some 'shut eye' before the shit hits the fan. Do you mind if I crash out first, I am absolutely knackered?"

"Not at all, pal, be my guest. What about the convoy, when are they due?"

"Don't know, no news from them, and we are maintaining radio silence until we can hear them approaching."

Robbo wriggled himself into a more comfortable position and was soon sleeping, or 'power napping' as one of our instructors referred to it, when he explained that you must learn how to switch off to a situation and get some sleep as and when you can. I had got quite adept at this and I can still do it today. Twenty minutes of deep sleep is sufficient to recharge me, then comes the problem of waking me up, as when I do come round I tend to make a lot of noises. Not a good thing when your life depends on silence. My hour of watching seemed to pass quickly. I was at my best, carefully observing for any movement or change from our rag-headed enemy. I was alert the whole time, as were my comrades also on watch, knowing only too well we were the eyes and ears for your resting mates.

I bent over Robbo and whispered into his ear, "Wake up, darling, its time for work." Slowly he opened one eye and looked at me, then nodded that he had got the message.

"All's quiet on the western front, Robbo, and it's your turn to watch over me, while I catch up on my beauty sleep."

" Go for it, pal, beauty sleep is something you definitely need, you ugly 'git'."

I didn't need to be told twice and, within minutes, I was off to Noddy Land.

Robbo pulled me out of my sleep the only safe way he knows how. He placed his hand over my mouth and two fingers pinched my nose. I opened both eyes and 'bang' I was back in the real world. Pity really as, for some reason, I had been dreaming of home.

"We've got company," Robbo whispered into my ears. It took a few seconds for me to take it in but that was all. Robbo was peering forward from our safe sanga. He looked poised ready to pounce, I noticed the veins on his neck and temple were standing out, he was giving 100% concentration on what he espied. Our communication line became active, two positive tugs; I crawled to observe the sender, it was Biff. First he put up three fingers, then one, then five, followed by a nod of the head. I signed back to him three, one, and five. He nodded confirmation; compass bearing 315 degrees was the message. I moved cautiously now, as obviously, as Robbo put it, we were about to have company.

Peering out of my observation hole, armed with my compass, I watched as the needle slowly spun round, now to get the hairline to 315°, almost there now.

"Fucking hell, Robbo, that's not company it's more like a fucking army,." I heard myself whisper as I eyeballed our visitors.

One by one, I carefully observed our rag-headed friends and on each head count I could feel my adrenaline start to pump. Like Robbo, I was ready, or almost. I groped around for my rifle, located it and gave it a firm grip to restore some of my confidence. We watched in total silence as they carefully made their way over the rocks in a very sure-footed manner.

"They're only kids, most of them, some can't be much more than ten or twelve."

Robbo was right but young or old they were all on a mission as they moved down towards the road.

"Those buggers eat, drink and shit this game, so treat them all the same, Robbo, their age is not important as they know nothing better than to fight."

Biff came sliding down into our 'sanga'.

"Dusty says we will have to break radio silence before much longer and alert the convoy of what's in store for them. As soon as we hear the trucks approaching, he will give us the okay to open fire on our visitors for a few minutes before we leg it out of here." Robbo nodded to Biff and off he went.

I continued my head count and was happy to find it was only 32, add to that the original 6, 38 in total. Not bad odds, 6 against 38, only 6 and a bit apiece.

From our commanding position we were reasonably safe, as by now the rag-heads were well below us. We watched over them as they moved slowly and cautiously over the rocky terrain to establish their ambush position.

It was a good 10 minutes before I heard the sound we had been waiting for. Engines could be heard approaching; as the noise became louder, I realised it was not the familiar sound of Bedford three 10-ton trucks. It was a much higher pitched noise.

"Ferrets, that's Ferrets coming, they must be leading the convoy," said Robbo.

We were disturbed by four tugs on our line. I looked and saw Dusty gesturing to me. He raised his hand and put it on top of his head.

"Come on, Robbo, our master requires our presence." Without hesitation, we stuffed our 'worldly goods' into our packs, and crawled away from our temporary home to join up with the rest of our team. We huddled together whilst Dusty gave us a quick precise briefing.

"Time to make a tactical withdrawal, gentlemen," we sniggered in unison, as a tactical withdrawal was a military way of saying, run like bloody hell away from somewhere before the old proverbial hits the fan.

"Ollie, Robbo, stay here and give us covering fire if you have to. We will get nearer to the top of the ridge. As soon as we go to ground, we will cover you while you leg it out of here. Right, Paddy, break the good news and let's get ready to announce ourselves to our uninvited company."

Paddy moved over to one side and set up the radio. The rest of us crawled away and got ourselves into positions where we could overlook the ambush site.

"Orient Express, Orient Express, this is Hawkeye, this is Hawkeye, how do you read me, over?" We all heard the loud reply from the convoy.

"Hawkeye, Hawkeye, this is Orient Express, you are loud and clear, loud and clear, over."

Paddy quickly and perfectly announced the situation to the convoy. He was not whispering any more as the situation had almost reached its climax.

"Big Rat, Big Rat, this is Hawkeye, affirmative Yellow 47, I repeat Yellow 47, out."

Paddy was now in contact with the Ferret Commander to confirm the ambush location.

Bang, Bang, Bang, Bang, shots came in on our position. They were not coming from the ambush site at Yellow 47 position but from much higher up than that, not above us but more or less at the same level as us. I got sight of two men as they moved position and bawled out that I could see them.

"Open Fire." That was what I wanted to hear as Dusty gave us the all clear to return fire on the enemy. There were more of them now, I could see them as they scrambled up the rocky sides of the valley opposite us, in an attempt to gain the high ground where they would have a dangerous advantage over us. Only one man was giving them covering fire. He was firing into our position trying to keep our heads down. I watched as four of them scrambled upwards as fast as they could. Taking careful aim, I squeezed the trigger, and I kept on firing at them until I had emptied my magazine. I quickly re-loaded and got back into my firing position only to find that the four were no longer to be seen. They had either gone to ground or been hit. I waited then, as I had no target to shoot at. Then the man lower down opened up on us again; his rounds were a little too close for comfort now. It was obvious that he knew my where I was, so I moved my position. I crawled about 30 feet away, and adjusted my 'shemagh' to cover my face, then slowly and carefully peered over the edge. There he was, still firing in at us but not at me. It was crucial that he had to go. I manoeuvred myself into a perfect firing position and took very careful aim and slowly squeezed the trigger; I watched as he lurched backwards, and started writhing about on the rocks, then he stopped and lay still.

Silence, other than the pounding of my heart as it pumped away keeping me 'on a high'.

"Was that one yours or mine, Ollie?"

" Yours, Robbo," I said, as I was not in the game of scoring points. At that moment in time staying alive was my main priority.

We must have taken them all out or they had gone to ground and were staying there. In the distance I could hear the sound of the approaching convoy. So I turned my attention to the ambush site; I was able to see the enemy as they lay in wait. They were well hidden but, from my commanding position, I could see them tucked between the rocks. Two in particular caught my eye, one was holding a rocket launcher, close behind him was his colleague, rocket in hand, waiting to re-load the launcher after it had been fired. I attracted Robbo's attention and he crawled over to my position.

" There's a 3.5 rocket launcher team below, let's smack 'em."

" I'm all for that, pal, wait till I get in position."

Robbo was first to open fire and he robbed me of my target, the man with the launcher. I was about to squeeze my trigger when I heard the retort from Robbo's weapon. Down went the man, still clutching his precious weapon; I switched my aim to the second man as he rushed forward to recover the rocket launcher. He was about to pick it up when my rounds hit him. He stumbled forward and fell on top of his friend. I withdrew from my position and moved another 10 feet or so. This was perfect timing, as no sooner had I got in a safe spot than gunfire came raining in on Robbo and me. This came from the men on the high ground that we thought had been despatched; they were alive, angry and hell bent on a bit of vengeance. Suddenly, the sound of approaching vehicles was filling the air. It was the Ferret Armoured Cars. Two of them rounded the bend close to the ambush position, their hatches closed and their .30-calibre machine guns blasting into the enemy as they scurried for cover. The leading vehicles were closely followed by two more and they too joined in the attack.

" It's getting too fucking busy round here for me," shouted Robbo as we both cowered behind the rocks protecting us.

"Come on lads, we need to move out. Ollie, Robbo, stand by to give us covering fire."

"Okay, Dusty," Robbo shouted back. He looked at me and said,

"Come on, Ollie, let's show these buggers who's the boss."

He jumped to his feet and started blasting away in the direction of our rag-headed attackers, his positive action 'kick-started' me and, scared as I was, I leapt to my feet and joined him in the firefight. We remained standing and firing, only dodging for cover when we had to re-load. Soon, we could hear fire coming from the other four; they had taken on our assailants to give us the opportunity to withdraw.

"When are we doing the tactical withdrawal?" shouted Robbo with a silly grin on his face.

"Now," was my reply as I leapt to my feet and ran for my life, bobbing and weaving from side to side as I raced across the open ground.

We dashed past the lads giving us covering fire, and the bullets hit the ground some hundred yards from them. It was pretty open terrain and cover was a bit sparse, so I forced my body into the ground, and adopted a firing position, resting my rifle on my pack ready to give covering fire for our mates. Suddenly, there was silence, again no incoming fire. What a relief I thought as I felt my heart pulsating in my chest. Then came the pounding of feet as our mates raced past us.

" Don't like this, Ollie, I would rather have some action than this bloody silence, I bet the bastards are waiting for us to make our move."

"Your turn, Robbo, I'll give you a start just in case you are right."

Thankfully, he was wrong but I adopted my evasive running technique just as I had before. I was scared, bloody scared, as I raced after Robbo as fast as I could.

This action was carried out again and again, until Dusty finally called us to a halt. We plonked down and formed a circle, all of us carefully observing in every direction to ensure our safety. "Right lads, time to stop playing ragheads and get back to being shit-scared bootnecks," shouted Dusty.

With no more prompts, I stuffed my shemagh in my pack and replaced it with my beret. Dusty and I set about checking our position to enable us to guide the pick-up team back to our location. That done and double-checked, Paddy relayed the information back to 'Mother Hen', our transport co-ordinator.

We settled down for the wait, still watching all round, feeling reasonably safe where we were as this spot offered the only decent cover for miles, plus it was the only elevated 'lump' we could see.

"Don't relax, lads, we are not out of the frying pan yet, keep an all-round watch as these buggers can appear from nowhere, as you well know."

An hour later a dust cloud appeared from just north of west, the right direction for our transport to appear from. Another 10 minutes and the grinning faces of our bus drivers and conductors arrived.

Allan Woodcock, a corporal better known as 'Timberdick' to his friends and all who knew him well, but he objected to strangers calling him that:

"Sounds like you buggers have stirred some shit back there, are you all okay?"

We affirmed that with a few handshakes and hearty pats on our backs.

"Old Timberdick had the right name this time with 'Mother Hen'. I have been straining at the leash to get back to my 'little chicks'. Come on," he said, "let's get you back to Grandma." With that, he jumped into the Land Rover and settled behind the Bren gun mounted on the bonnet in front of the passenger seat.

"Thank you, Mummy," shouted Biff out loud. This brought about fits of hysterical laughter, as Biff was the last guy you would expect to come out with something like that.

"Paddy, call Grandma and ask her to run the bath, and tell her we are all coming home."

More laughter, was it funny or was it relief, maybe both?

Mark was snoring for England by the time I had finished the tale. I wondered when he had fallen asleep.

"Sorry, son, I got carried away again," I said as I left for home.

MONDAY 8TH JANUARY, 2001

Julie first in today and she is not a happy girl as Mark's chair back seems to have got worse. For no apparent reason it suddenly 'clicks' and the back framework moves, not much, but enough to make both the chair pusher and poor old Markie stumble. Who knows what it does for Markie, she has written.

Wendy here at 16 00 hrs and after the chair faltered on her, she went on the warpath. After contacting G. she bawled him out and cornered him into ringing the Disabled Service Centre at Preston. Finally, she put the screws on tighter and eased a contact name out of him. She has achieved in half an hour what I have been after for weeks, no months, and that is a name.

I will take up the battle now, as I don't want Wendy to be charged with G.B.H. or something worse. I will bear her in mind in the future just in case I need to let the heavy gang loose on someone.

JUDGEMENT DAY

Mark's assessment today and it was, as before, not really an assessment more a statement of affairs and a decision they had reached with none of the family present. Judge and Jury assembled in the meeting room and I was prepared to air some of my views if the meeting went the same as the last one. Dr A. in the chair. Mr G. (Physio), Sandra (Speech), Debra and our Senior Nurse Sarah (a great person), last came Mr M. (Social Services). I had to sympathise with this man, as it was obvious that he is Public Enemy Number One. I have yet to find anyone who likes him. His job is probably the most difficult one as we all want money from him and he has nothing to give away, that is without an inquisition with his Lords and Masters who are safely locked away somewhere.

Shock upon shock came when we were invited to join the meeting, as the end result was exactly what we wanted. They were all in agreement that Mark was making sufficient progress to justify a further period of rehabilitation.

Mark got an extra treat today. My sister Norma must have been in to see him; her notes in the diary are as follows:

"Hi, Markie, called to see you. Fast asleep, you woke for a few seconds and smiled at me. You looked so comfy that I decided not to sing but I will get you next time. Oh, did I tell you that I love you?" Auntie Norma XXXX

Sarah caught me on the evening visit and told me that Mark has got another screening for the M.R.S.A. disease tomorrow. She feels we will get the all clear.

Wednesday 10th January, 2001

Markie did his table scratching today for Wendy. She said (to use her words):

"I was well chuffed."

Even got some action from his right hand, not a lot but action all the same. To say action, one could imagine him waving it about. Not so, as even the slightest of moves are action but it is something, and something small as it might be is far better than nothing.

Physio today was good. Andy, Rob, Leanne, Sandra, another lady and I. Rob decided that, as Markie appeared stiff around his middle, we should perform some rotation of his hips. Good to watch as Rob got the small of Mark's back onto his knees; Leanne held his legs whilst Rob swung Mark from side to side. I felt he was enjoying the change as he was well relaxed and went with the flow of the action. The session was concluded with a good 10-minute stand to which Mark contributed around 80% of the effort. We all agreed that Markie deserved a very well done, and we told him so.

I watched Rob throughout the physio session using his special quality. Not sure what it is other than his ability to gain Mark's confidence by talking to him and encouraging him all the time. Of them all, I reckon Rob brings out the best in Mark. I sound like I am knocking the others; I certainly don't mean to. It is just that I know how Markie 'ticks' and he was and still is the sort of person who would move the world for you if you asked him in the right manner.

Thursday 11th January, 2001

Julie tried a new approach today. Instead of touching Mark on her arrival, she just spoke to him

"Good morning, Markie," she said and it worked. He opened his eyes and looked up at her, not straight as his head is not responding to much side-to-side movement; yet another area to exercise, his neck, not a problem as I can do that in his chair. Got Markie off his bed, onto the plinth, using the patslide. Then had to call a halt, as Mark was wet through. A swift investigation highlighted he had bypassed the catheter. One of a few reasons could cause this: a kink in the pipe, excessive pressure when 'weeing' or a blockage. Whatever it was resulted in physio having to be called off for the day. Back onto the bed and off to his room where Michelle took over and sorted Markie out. She assured me she would watch the 'leak' and let me know what the cause was, if any, on my evening visit.

When Marion and I arrived for our evening visit, we were greeted by Michelle, who told us that Mark had remained dry since the afternoon incident. When we got to Mark's room, we found he had a visitor. It was Joe, a long-term friend of Mark as they had grown up in our village together. This was Joe's second visit and he said that Mark looked so much better than the last time he saw him.

My brother Fred also called and he too was very pleased with Mark's appearance and he was only here last week, so there must be some changes visible with Mark. Hard to notice when you are with him on a twice a day basis.

FRIDAY

O.T. have responded to the occasional notes I have been leaving in the diary to ascertain when and what she does with Mark. She has written that she is working on a timetable for Mark and that she will contact us shortly.

"It's here, it's here, Mark's chair has finally arrived." It was Wendy on her mobile phone at about 14 00 hrs. I rang her back and told her to pat herself on the back, as I felt it was the constant harassment she had given all concerned that had resulted in it finally turning up. Wendy has acquired very much of my 'make-up', only she has mastered the art not to 'hit' everybody. Mr G. refers to her as being just like me with the 'bulldog' taken out and a 'poodle' put in its place.

Markie in bed but looking quite alert when I arrived at 18 10 hrs, so what can I tell him tonight? Should I start with the time when I was one of the bodyguards to Prime Minister Harold Macmillan, or about the rioting army in Tanganiki, as that occasion was probably one of my scariest moments? Or maybe how, when in the Falklands, with only a team of four, including myself, managed to foil 20 odd dissidents who had high jacked an internal flight in Argentina and forced the pilot to land it on the Race course in Port Stanley?

Lots of my excursions were rushing around in my head but one I felt I must complete was the time I was jailed at Eastney Barracks and how this 'touch of porridge' changed my whole life in the Royal Marines.

"Prisoner and escort, quick march!" bellowed the Colour Sergeant. I was on my way back to prison. We took the route that led down the main road of the Barracks. I noted several of my friends attracted by my appearance. They lined the roadside jeering at me as we marched by.

"What did you get, Ollie? Are you being kicked out?" I recognised the voice, it was Derby's. Unable to reply, I marched on keeping my eyes straight to the front. I had a terrible desire to shout out that I was staying but sense prevailed. I was in enough trouble without compounding my situation.

We approached the prison and the huge gates were swung open. The Corporals on duty sprang to attention as we passed by. Bang, the doors slammed shut behind us once we were inside the courtyard.

"Prisoner and escort, halt!"

"Escort, dismiss."

They did a smart turn, crashed their feet to the ground and marched away from me.

Standing there alone, it was when all that the R.S.M. and the Colour Sergeant had said to me started to strike home. I was getting another chance, yes, another chance and I was buzzing with the thought of heading to change my ways. The Colour Sergeant speaking to me interrupted my thoughts:

"You're a lucky man, Holroyd, a very lucky man. The R.S.M. in his wisdom has made his decision and, if you want my opinion, a dodgy one. Don't even think of letting the side down. He has put his neck and his arse in a sling for you. Why? Don't ask me. I can see you have something: what, I am not sure, but like the R.S.M. I feel you can go places. So, pull your finger out lad and go for it, cos if you become unstuck again we'll use your guts for garters." He moved in very close and glared arrogantly straight into my eyes until I could feel I was getting upset. I didn't want to cry but the urge to do so was quite overwhelming. He was still glowering when I felt a tear roll down my cheek. I was overcome with emotion. Here I was being given a chance of a lifetime to continue to be in the Royal Marines and this chance had come from two more than eminent men, heroes, or my heroes at least.

"Have you anything to say, Marine Holroyd?"

"Yes, Colour Sergeant," I croaked in an almost inaudible manner.

"What lad?" he whispered, mimicking me.

"I promise I will make you and the R.S.M. proud of me. I don't know what else I can say other than thanks."

Another tear, I felt so bloody humble. More silence and more 'eye balling'.

"I know you mean that, Holroyd, grab your future by the bollocks and go for it lad, you can do it, I know you can. Now, when I shout, go, you will vanish from my sight but be aware I will be following you, lad."

"Go," he bellowed into my face and I bolted through the prison door, up the steps and into my cell. Feeling both physically and mentally drained, I sat on my bench and started to sob and there was nothing I could do about it.

It was sheer relief, as how could I have gone back to Burnley and how the hell could I have faced my Mam or our Fred as he was so proud of me being a Marine Commando. What about my mates? They would have really given me some 'stick'.

"Could you not stand the pace, Ollie, was it too tough for you?"

I could almost hear their words.

I crashed back into the real world with a startled Benson shaking me.

"Come on, Ollie, or you will be in more shit. I've been detailed to show you the ropes in the boiler room."

After a quick changing act, we went along the landing, down the metal steps and snapped to attention outside the guard's office.

Out he came, my favourite Corporal Howard, dressed to kill in his best blues and he looked good even if I said so myself.

243

"You're a lucky man, Holroyd, a very lucky man. If I had had my way, you would have been banged up for 6 months, then kicked out of the corp." He continued strutting around me looking me up and down, I kept my gaze straightforward and completely avoided any eye contact with him.

"That's it," I thought, "don't look at him, he is trying to reel you in. At all odds don't lose your rag."

Strangely enough, Markie, he didn't affect me, he didn't even make me simmer, let alone reach boiling point. I had cracked it, I am changed, I am not getting annoyed, I am feeling good, and yes, that's it, feeling good. I could almost laugh but that was definitely not the order of the day. He continued bawling at me but by now it was going in one ear and out of the other, without even comprehending what abuse he was giving me. As far as I was concerned, he was rambling and I accepted all he had to say with a 'pinch of salt'.

"I have some good news for you, Holroyd." I heard that as he had stopped strutting and he was looking into my face.

"Would you like to hear it?"

"Yes, Corporal," I shouted into his face.

"Well, today is my promotion day, in just 1 hours' time I will be Sergeant Howard and I am moving on to greener pastures, away from this shit hole and all the arseholes I have had to put up with for the past year. Now that's good news isn't it?."

"Yes, Corporal," Benson and I shouted in total unison.

"Now get out of my sight and stoke up the boiler, it's bloody freezing in here."

With that, one of the guards opened the door and Benson and I were led around the building to a small door. He opened it to reveal about ten steps leading down into the boiler room. What a bloody dirty hole it was as it burnt a mixture of small pieces of coal and coke. This arrived into the boiler room via a stone chute from the courtyard, which was closed off with a big metal trap door.

Benson showed me how to 'riddle' the fire bed to extract the spent ash. The ash was set on one side to cool and then taken from the boiler room, up the steps and 'dumped' in a walled-off area by the top of the steps.

"The main thing you need to know, Ollie, is the amount of draught you give the fire. Too much and you can boil the system, not enough and the bloody thing goes out, so remember to keep touching the pipes to ensure that our 'Robin' is okay.

"Our Robin, what do you mean?"

"That's his name, look." He guided me to the boiler fire door and pointed to the writing on the cast door. Clearly, I could see Robin Hood boldly displayed on the door.

244

"So look after our Robin, won't you. I am out of here in a couple of days, so he is your baby now. By the way, I'm well chuffed that you didn't get thrown out."

"So am I, Benson, so am I. You don't know my Mam, but she would have bloody killed me if I had turned up back at home and I would have had to go back to working down the pit.

"The pit, what's that?"

"The coal mines you 'dork'. Where do you think coal comes from? It is not the best of jobs but the money is good and most of my mates are still mineworkers, but not for me now, I have turned over a new leaf thanks to the R.S.M. and Colours. They have put their faith in me and the last thing I will do now is let them down."

We stoked up the boiler, took the now cold ash up the steps and dumped it, then went to the prison door and pulled on an ancient lever by the door which was connected to a sparkling shiny bell on the inside. I became quite close to that bell, as it was another of my daily tasks to keep it clean.

"Markie, Markie, come on son, it's not bedtime yet," I reiterated.

"Oh! Yes it is, it's nearly 9 o'clock," came from Sarah.

"Time to turn and water Markie and settle him for the night."

"Thanks, Sarah, got a bit carried away tonight, good night, love."

"Night, night."

On leaving Markie I sensed he was in the safest place in the world, a good feeling when your face is hard against a brick wall and you cannot turn away from it.

SATURDAY 13TH JANUARY, 2001

Steve Dawes, another childhood mate, called today, he hasn't much to report other than when he asked Mark if he thought he could still beat him at pool. The reply was a loud grunt and a few "Mom, Moms", before drifting back to sleep.

Diane, Joe's mum, called to see Markie as well and she has noted that, when she gave Markie a good cuddle, he responded with good eye contact and got quite verbal, nothing comprehensible, but still noises.

Lauren and Julie also came but Markie very tired so they didn't stay long. Wendy followed them and her comments are:

"Mark is having his normal weekend sleep, sleep and a bit more sleep, not to worry as he looks very much at peace."

MUM AND DAD AT 19 10 HRS

Mark in his chair when we arrived but he looked quite agitated and stressed. He was also quite verbal, eye contact good but still verbal.

"He is trying to tell us something," said Marion "I think he wants the loo."

"Me too, I'll sort it."

With the assistance of a male nurse called Jim, we whisked Mark away and prepared him for the night but not before we had placed a big 'nappy' underneath his bottom. He went silent then and was still silent when Mum entered the room

"It's okay Markie, go on son, have your bowel movement. We know it is alien to do it in bed or in your trousers; your actions and noises have demonstrated to us that you are aware of that. Don't feel ashamed, son, you should feel pleased with yourself as you have made very positive communication tonight. You have told us you need the loo and both Dad and I are so pleased you have done that." Markie was still silent but more at peace now.

"Markie, well done son, we are now in touch and that is one hell of a plus. Soon we will be able to put you on a toilet or a bed pan but not yet, Mark, as you are not well enough. Go on, son, have your bowel movement and don't feel bad." I bent over and pecked him on his forehead and handed him over to his mum, knowing she wanted time with him. I waited in the corridor; soon she appeared, looked at me and said,

"Thanks," that's all but we understood each other.
"Another big plus, Marion?"
"Yes."

SUNDAY 14TH JANUARY, 2001

Walkies to see Markie today, the weather was bad but at least the trip was exhilarating. Arrived at 11 30 hrs, just in time to catch Markie being lowered into his chair. I have brought in my adjustable spanner, as I must do some fine adjustments to the chair, footrests not quite right as his knees hit the underside of the attached table when his feet are on the rest, plus his thighs are not resting on the seat. Lowered both rests about 2 inches and it made all the difference to his sitting. He looks more comfortable and I hope he feels so.

J., one of the principal nurses, reported that the night staff had reported that Mark had had a bad night, so that probably accounts for his inability to keep awake. Tried just about every trick I know but failed badly, so I reclined his chair back and let him have a short nap. Left him with Marion at 13 00 hrs and trudged home. I say trudged, as I took the long route as I was feeling a bit 'pissed off' and sorry for myself. When I get like this I find it better to have time alone.

MONDAY

I failed to return to see Markie on Sunday evening so I read the entries the girls had made when they went in.

Julie has noted that she asked for Mark to go to bed for a couple of hours at 14 30 hrs as he was shattered. When Marion arrived at 18 00 hrs Mark was sitting out in his chair again and looking good. She managed to keep him awake until 20 00 hrs, not bad considering he must be getting tired now due to his 'body clock' being disrupted on Saturday night.

MONDAY 15TH JANUARY, 2001

Julie with Mark early doors as he was up by 10 40 hrs. She called me at work to let me know that physio would be at 13 00 hrs. She also said someone had written in the diary, saying that Rob (physio) was an ex. Royal Marine. That made me feel good as I had a strange bond towards Rob, and Mark certainly has. Perhaps Mark can relate to a similarity between Rob and me, possible I suppose as we have both had the same 'operation' that the corps carries out to convert near normal people into Royal Marines. Marion has often said that she does not know what they do to Royal Marines during training but she has commented on lots of occasions that we are given a 'bootneck transplant' which makes us all 'tick' alike.

Big change again in physio routine today. G. has introduced a big exercise ball, it is about 2-ft in circumference. Rob behind Mark to support him, Mr G. in front and me standing by to push the ball under Mark's bottom when instructed to do so by Mr G.

"On three, Peter, one, two, three."

Up went Markie and I placed the ball underneath him, down he went sitting on the ball, supported by half of the Ex-Royal Marines present.

"So far so good, Mark, we are going to gyrate your body and bounce you up and down on the ball, with the intention of you regaining your sense of balance. We will also be rotating you to relax the muscles around your waist."

This went on for a good 15 minutes and I honestly felt that Mark was enjoying it. He certainly didn't put up a fight in any way.

From this exercise, we went to standing, just one stand but a long one, probably 10 minutes before we placed him back in his chair.

Occupational therapy now, so I accompanied Mark. S. the O.T. girl had prepared several pots with different contents. First we tried Mark's hand in sand, then lentils followed by beads and marbles. To be honest, there was little or no response. Then we tried passing bright objects across Mark's line of vision. He did show a slight reaction but I felt it was because we were very close to his face and that it was instinctive.

S. wanted to dismiss this as automatic but I gave it more thought by asking myself,

"If Mark is blinking automatically, what is making him do so and where is the message coming from?"

On my evening visit, Mark was bright-eyed and bushy-tailed.

249

"More stories, Mark?" No reaction, so I had to assume it was yes.

THE TAXI RIDE

On one trip back from the Radfan or Dhala Camp in Aden, we were housed out at Little Aden on an old oil refinery about 20 miles from Aden Town.

A small gang of us decided we should have a 'run ashore' for the day. I teamed up with 'Bungie Williams', an old chum, so armed with a bottle of 'Pusser's Navy Rum' we boarded the back of a Bedford 3-ton truck with bench seats down the sides. Before leaving, we were subjected to a 'Pep talk' by the Provost Sergeant. His advice was all good stuff and pretty much common sense, like,

"Don't get pissed out of your brains."

"Don't eat any local food, especially the curry on the Arab Market Place. If you do, you can guarantee a very sore arse for a few days. Believe me, I have been there and done that.

"Don't get involved in any punch-ups or the local police will bang you up. Two, don't miss the transport home or you will be in deep shit. Last, but not least, don't move about in less than threes, remember there is safety in numbers."

All good stuff, Bungie and I agreed as we cracked open the rum and had our first 'swig' from the bottleneck. About half an hour's journey, down past Khourmaksar, which was where the R.A.F. were based. Then another 15 minutes out to Steam Point, this was where most of the 'think tank' lived and worked, it was also where a big NAAFI Club was situated.

The club was big and sported just about all you needed, booze, a swimming pool, darts, snooker and, most of all, girls as Steamer Point was where all the girls were billeted; there were Women's Royal Army Corp, Women's Royal Air Force and Queen Alexandra's Nursing Corp. I don't know how many in total but certainly not enough to go round. I reckon a male to female ratio of about 100 to 1, and the girls certainly knew it.

The club was really the only place for the girls to go, as it was the only place under constant guard and protection. Hence it was the only place the boys used to go. They would hang around, leering at the girls as they paraded about in the designated area, set aside just for them. They didn't have to be separated from the boys but the bulk of them chose to do so, as it left them in a situation to relax without the ever-watchful eyes of the boys and the guards. The guards were ever-diligent over the safety of not just the girls but the boys as well. The club was a perfect target for anyone who might want to cause a catastrophe for us and inflict a lot of casualties in one hit. There was also another area for the families of serving personnel and that was always

250

packed with wives and children, and, as expected, was strictly out of bounds to single men.

"I'm bloody starving," one of the lads said, "Anybody fancy a wander into the civvy area to see what's on the menu?"

The Civvy or Civilian Area was where all the local shops were and it was really just the main road leading from Khourmaksar and Crater City to Steamer Point, which is not just the H.Q. but also where all the ships on passage through the Suez Canal and the Red Sea docked. Passengers and crew would go ashore to stretch their legs and do a little shopping whilst the ships re-fuelled.

Probably ten of us streamed out of the NAAFI Club and headed for the shops and the odd bars.

"Remember, lads, don't get split up and certainly no less than three of you. We are about as welcome as a fart in a space suit with some of the locals, so watch your backs," one of the corporals reminded us.

"Don't forget we will be picked up at the club at 21 00 hrs sharp ... savvy."

"Oh yes, Corporal," someone shouted back, this caused a good laugh as whoever it was put on the voice of a pansy.

"I could eat a scabby dog," said Bungie as we wandered along the dockside.

Johno, one of the lads with us, had been down this patch before, so we looked to him for inspiration.

"Come on, Johno, where would you go for somat to eat?" I asked.

Without any hesitation he replied,

"Only one right place to go down here and that's where all the gentry go, come on follow me."

Off he went with four of us in tow. Down the main road about 200 hundred yards, sharp right turn, another 50 yards and then a left turn brought us into a big square which was the locals' market place. He led on through some stalls and halted at a long table with bench seats down both sides.

"This is it, boys, the finest curry house in the whole world. Believe me, I have been all over and I have yet to find a curry to beat this one."

We stood there just looking around in dismay. Seated around the table were about ten to fifteen Arabs, all at different stages of feeding from brown bowls. There were several trays set out at intervals on which Naan bread was piled high.

"Come on, never mind what the Provost Sergeant said, I have eaten here loads of times and never had the shits."

Like lambs to the slaughter, we followed Johno to the end of the table to be greeted by a guy who looked like he was on a pair of 'stilts' under his long robe. He was tall and very thin, obviously African and Somali.

"Gentlemen, welcome," he put out his hands in greeting. Not an accent whatsoever, his English was perfect, and he explained that he had been brought up in a home in Somalia run by Irish and English Nuns, from being a child. His full-time employment was in the British Embassy. This 'side line', he explained, is his bid to get enough money together to allow him to go back to Somalia and help others who, like him, were abandoned as babies and left to orphanages. I couldn't get over the height of him, he was at least 6'6" and scrawny with it, his arms were longer than any I have seen and his face was that of someone who has been starved. I found out later that all Somalis look like this.

"He'd make a bloody good painter and decorator. He could do the ceilings and I'll stick to the skirting boards, we could make a fortune," said Bungie.

He led us to the end of the long table where a big earthenware pot was on top of a makeshift heater made from a steel barrel that had been cut in half.

"Gentlemen, please help yourselves," but only after we had paid him and received our personal bowls. Johno took the ladle and stirred up the contents of the pot.

"Get it from the bottom that's where all the juicy meat is," he advised us.

My first impression was the smell, it was great, my second thought was, I wonder what it is going to taste like, and my last one was, I wonder what's in it.

Too late to change my mind, so I took the ladle off Johno and filled my bowl. One by one we helped ourselves then sat down on the bench in one long line, our backs to the wall and facing into the market.

"We have the best seats in the house, lads, I said, and the only ones where we can see who is knocking about."

Suddenly, I felt a bit vulnerable. Up until now the fact that I had no weapon with me had not entered my head, none of us had, as we were not allowed to go ashore with them.

"What if we get smacked here by some bastard?" I thought to myself. I must have sent a telepathic signal to the others or they were feeling just as vulnerable as I was.

"I'm not too happy with this set-up, I feel fucking naked without my weapon," said Bungie. Trust him to sow the seed of doubt.

With a certain amount of tension, we settled down to eat. Johno threw pieces of Naan bread to everyone and we got stuck in.

"That's what I call bloody good curry," said one of the lads.

"I'll second that," I said, as I got a mouth full of the excellent dish.

Two bowls later and several, no, lots of water down the hatch, we all sat there in a row with that gloated, contented smirk that you acquire when you are full and satisfied.

"Oh shit, Red Caps," said Alec.

Sure enough, some Army Military Police were making their way towards us, led by a short but stocky sergeant.

"Who's in charge?" he said as he halted, facing us at the other side of the table.

"No one's in charge, sergeant, we are not working. We got some time off so we thought we would have a picnic."

"Picnic, my arse," he said, "this is the last place on earth anyone with even a little bit of sense would choose for a picnic."

"We know that," said Bungy, "In fact we were hoping someone like you would come along and rescue us. You see we were lost and very hungry when we stumbled upon this place. It was only after we had eaten that we realised how foolish we had been."

The sergeant mellowed at that as he looked us up and down, then came a smile, then a laugh. This proved infectious as all of us burst out laughing, much to the surprise of our Arab neighbours who were enjoying their meals.

"Okay, lads, let's have you away from here. This nice sergeant and his merry men will get you to a safe haven."

We filed out of the market and we were escorted back to the main road.

"The NAAFI is down the road that way ..., okay?" The sergeant was pointing with his stick in the direction of the club.

"Three cheers for our heroes," shouted Johno.

"Hip, hip, hooray," we echoed three times, to the dismay of the policemen.

"Thank you, Sergeant Robin and your merry men, we will never forget you for saving our lives. Come on lads, let's rush home before we meet any trouble," Bungie again.

"This man is bloody mad," I thought.

With that we joined hands and skipped down the road towards the club, leaving the Sergeant and his men watching us in disbelief.

Back in the safety of the N.A.A.F.I. club we settled down to some serious drinking. By 16 30 hrs I was full and I wasn't on my own. All of the 45 Commando lads had taken over the area close to the bar. Usual performances that you get when a gang gather together, lots of singing, shouting and party performances from those of us who could manage to stand up.

At 18 00 hrs, much to our surprise, a big gang of girls arrived, a mixture of Army, Air Force and some Nursing Corps. Silence befell the Marines as they watched the girls file in, no more shouting or singing, just the odd muttering amongst ourselves, as we sang out the attributes of each girl in turn.

To give the girls their due, they came over and joined us, or most of them did. Chairs and tables were quickly rearranged as we gave up space for our unexpected guests. Drinks began to flow again and slowly the noise got louder, but not the bawdy behaviour we were displaying earlier but more of 'I need to impress these girls to see if I can have one for myself'. I looked and watched the lads as they strutted about the club, a bit like a bunch of roosters, all vying for the charms of these lovely lady chicks.

"Bloody hell, Ollie, this is something isn't it. I never dreamt we would be invaded by a bunch of beauties. Just look at them, not an ugly one anywhere. Okay, some are a bit better looking than others but all are beautiful. Just a sniff would do me, let alone the other job."

"Dream on, Bungie, dream on, I bet they do this every night, can't see many of them getting the drinks in, can you?"

"No, but I don't give a shit. I don't care if I end up skint, just as long as I get a sniff, yeah! Just a sniff would do as I have almost forgotten what a bird smells like." With that, Bungie set off to try to score, or at least get a sniff.

"Markie, are you still listening?" I said as I pulled my chair closer to his bed. He was, or he appeared to be. Now what I am going to tell you is something your Mam doesn't know, so think on when I have got you back with us, it's our secret. Mark was sat upright and still quite alert.

I suddenly realised I was on my own, as all the lads were chatting up the girls, when a female voice said,

"They always say the quiet ones are the worst, is it true?" I turned, looked and looked again. It was a girl and she was talking to me. I looked away again, and then back to her. She was smiling at me now. I was speechless; here I was with a girl smiling at me when the odds of even getting near one of the females were so remote that I hadn't even considered trying.

"Would you like to sit down?" I croaked, as it didn't want to come out very clearly.

"Yes please."

I jumped up and offered her my seat; again that gorgeous smile, as she sat down. I grabbed another seat and sat by her. Then her scent smacked me, Bungie was right, just a sniff would be enough, yes just a sniff.

"Can I get you a drink, err, err, sorry what's your name, mine's Peter." I was rambling and I knew it, I also felt quite nervous as I fumbled about.

"A coke would be nice, thank you, … Peter." Again, I was caught off guard, she had called me by my name, I could hear it again, Peter.

'Right, one coke coming up."

I went on to the bar, got a coke and quickly returned to her. She took the drink and again that dazzling smile as she replied.

"Helen, you asked me my name, it's Helen, aren't you having a drink, Peter?"

Again, I hesitated before replying, she had called me Peter again.

Soon we were getting on like a house on fire but not before I had got over the shock of actually speaking to her. I had been caught completely off guard and I was feeling like a little lad on his first date.

We nattered on and on, what about, I don't really remember but I was brought back to reality by the man behind the bar ringing a bell loudly.

"Girls, it's 20 30 hrs," he announced.

"What's that all about?" I asked Helen

"Sorry, but for this posting we are all early birds, even Cinderella got until midnight but our curfew is 9 o'clock. It's understandable as we are classed as something of a rare commodity."

"You can say that again," I said and I meant it.

"You can walk me back if you like, our place is only 10 minutes away."

"My pleasure, madam, my pleasure indeed."

I stood up and announced my departure to the lads as loudly as I could. I grasped Helen's hand, stood up on a chair and shouted for silence. It worked and they went quiet.

"Sorry lads, I must say farewell as I am off to escort this beautiful creature home."

Talk about jeers and banter, I got hold of Helen and looked at her, she was bright red, and must have felt terribly embarrassed. When we got away, I stopped, looked at her and apologised.

"Sorry, Helen, I shouldn't have done that, I just wanted to show off and have some crack with my mates."

"It's okay, seriously it's okay, I understand as I am in communications and I know just what you lot at 45 Commando have to endure, honestly it's okay." With that, she gave me a peck on the cheek and said. "Come on, I can't afford to be late."

She was right, her camp or Barracks was only 10 minutes away. It was a large building set behind a very high fence and well guarded, I was pleased to observe.

A nice cuddle close to the entrance and a promise that we would meet again and off she went up the steps. I waited until she turned and waved, then I set off back to the club.

"Can't afford to miss the truck, got an early start tomorrow," I told myself as I started to increase speed. Almost there, just another 200 yards. Heart pounding, I approached the guardroom and our pick-up point. No truck, perhaps it hadn't got here yet, hang on no-one about, quick time check, 21 06 hrs. I rushed towards the guardroom but was halted by two guards pointing their weapons at me.

"Sorry lads, 45 Commando, where are the boys and the transport?"

"They've gone, left at nine on the dot. Do you want to see the guard commander?"

"Yeah, please."

I was escorted into the guardroom to be greeted by a Royal Engineer's Sergeant.

"How the hell have they managed to leave you? We did two head counts before the truck left and we were sure that we had got everybody. There was a lot of banter and a lot of pissed marines, but we were sure we had a full number of heads. Sorry lad, all I can do is ring Little Aden and let them know you are here and safe, they will probably pick you up with the mail wagon at 09 00 hrs in the morning. Well that's what they usually do, as you're not the first to miss the boat home."

I plonked down in a chair and put my head in my hands in despair.

"Would you do that for me, Sergeant, please?" I asked.

"I'll just go back to the club for half an hour, if that's okay."

"No problem, lad, I will reserve your cell number two, and I'll fluff up your mattress for you."

"Cheers, Sarge."

On the way back to the NAAFI Club I had to pass the road that led to the Officers' mess. Suddenly, I got an idea. I recalled that our officers came down here on a regular basis and always returned home by taxi. I have watched when I have been on guard duty as all taxis had to drop the passengers at the barrier in front of Little Aden's guard room.

"That's it, that's the answer, get a taxi," I told myself as I made my way towards the Officer's Mess. There were three taxis waiting outside the building when I got there, so I approached the leading one, only to be told to wait whilst they checked if one of the cabs was available to take the hour's trip out to Little Aden.

After about 5 minutes another taxi arrived and it drove around the three waiting taxis and stopped by me. The driver got out and asked,

"Commando?"

I nodded and he waved for me to enter, as he opened the back door.

"How much will it cost?" I enquired, but he just looked at me stupid, obviously he was not an English teacher. He left me there and went to talk to the other drivers. One came back with him who could speak English, to a degree. Eventually, we communicated and I paid the man, got in the back of the cab and off we went.

The two guards on the barrier, glanced at the cab, lifted the barrier and waved us forward. I went to wind down my window but there was no handle, so as we passed them I banged on the glass, then waved to say bye, bye.

Their response was a little strange as they both waved back frantically, not in an up and down manner, but more of a rapid wave across their bodies, strange, I thought but no alarm bells rang.

I settled back in the back of the cab and started to doze off.

"Markie, Markie, you have done it again you have gone to sleep on me," I said as I looked at him. His bed was still propped up to allow more of a sitting up position, so I slowly lowered the bed head, made him comfortable and covered him up.

"Don't worry, Markie, I'll bring you up to speed on that tale later. Must leave now or your Mam will think I have got lost. God bless you, Son, see you tomorrow."

MONDAY 15TH JANUARY, 2001

Got here at 13 15 hrs for physio, to find Mark balancing on the big red gym ball, not alone I must add. Mark's head and shoulders were on the plinth, held there by Rob who was squatting behind him. Mr G. sat to Mark's front with his knees between his legs, and both hands on Mark's thighs, pressing firmly down on them to ensure his feet remained firmly on the floor. I stood and watched as they carefully gyrated Markie's trunk from side to side.

"Good one this, said G. "What I am trying to do is 'separate' Mark's body from his hips. It may feel a little alien to Mark but it should assist in keeping him nice and supple. That way he will be easier to handle and, hopefully, he will not feel quite so stiff."

"Come on, Markie, let's twist and shout," said Rob as he gyrated Mark from side to side.

The 'show' went on for a good half hour and I watched Mark's face for any signs of reaction. Nothing, just a blank expression, not even a movement of his eyes or head.

"What is going on in Mark's head?" I thought. "Does he know who is present? Does he know I am here, watching him and begging for some sign of recognition? If only he would look at me, for a second, or even a glance of acknowledgement, anything, anything but please Markie, give me something."

I was snapped out of my thoughts by G. saying,

"Well done, Markie, you have performed like a little soldier, as your friend Rob would have put it."

"Hang on G., correction, correction, Mark has performed like a 'boot neck'. However ,you are not allowed to call him that." He moved around to look into Mark's face.

"What do you think, Mark, can Mr G. call you a boot neck?"

We were all looking at Mark, hoping for something.

"Sorry, Mr G., but Mark, his Dad and I, after careful deliberation have decided that 'boot neck' is a word you are not to put in your dictionary. You may use Marine, or preferably Royal Marine but certainly not 'boot neck' and definitely not, 'little soldier'."

I looked at Rob and had to smile. He had a cheeky grin on his face, just like a little lad who had got away with a naughty prank, and he had, as G. was his boss and he had just had the pleasure of 'telling him off'.

Mr G. took it all on the chin and even managed a little chuckle.

"Okay, Marine Markie, you have performed like a true hero today but only with a little help from your," he paused, looked at Rob and me in turn then said, "'boot neck' friends."

"Thanks 'G'., said like a true little soldier!"

That tickled me and I was shaking inside with hidden laughter. Rob too must have had the same problem as he kept spluttering with short bursts of laughter.

Sandra from Occupational Therapy broke the ice when she entered; she had come to take Mark for some treatment.

"What's tickled you two?" she said.

"Nothing, absolutely nothing," said Rob, "well, nothing that any normal person would understand."

Still chuckling, Rob and I lifted Mark into standing to allow Mr G. to carefully take him from the front and sit him into his wheelchair.

Mr G. stood for a while, carefully weighing up what had occurred. Sandra was watching the proceedings with a vacant look on her face. I was waiting for a comment from Mr G., who was still fighting to contain his inner laughter. Mark just sat there, expressionless in his chair.

"Can you tell me just what happens to a normal person when he joins the Royal Marines?

I am confident that something is removed and replaced with an uncanny cloning device, one that puts them on the same wavelength. You two are like 'two peas in a pod'. It's strange and I find it very difficult to comprehend. Something happens that is not normal, what, I don't know but it's not normal. Come on Rob, we have work to do."

"Certainly, boss," said Rob after giving me a nod and a wink.

"What was all that about?" asked Sandra as we made our way to the Occupational Therapy room.

"Nothing, Sandra, believe me nothing. I think Mr G. is losing the plot."

In O.T. Sandra tried various tasks. She used bowls of different products and she placed Mark's hands in them. " This is rice, Mark, can you tell it is rice? This one is full of sugar, can you feel it? What about this one, Markie, it's thickened water, does it feel like jelly?" She went on trying various methods to get a reaction out of Mark. Finally, she looked at me with a pained expression on her face and said. "Sorry, Peter, but I feel I am just not getting anywhere, perhaps another day when he is more aware, we can try again."

"No problem, love, you have done your best, please don't despair, you just rest assured that we will get there, won't we, Markie?" With that Mark and I went off to his room, to allow me some space to recover. I felt sad, so very sad, and I needed to be alone with Markie.

WEDNESDAY 17TH JANUARY, 2001

Off to physio at 13 30 hrs. Leanne was present today so we wheeled Markie off to the treatment room on his bed. Off the bed, and ready for treatment. We carefully manoeuvred him into the sitting position on the edge of the plynth, flanked either side by Leanne and me. We were ready to accept our pre-arranged visitors.

At 13 45 hrs the lady from the eye department arrived. She had called earlier to 'rubber stamp' a little time with Mark to get a preliminary assessment of his ability to see, or not see, whatever the case may be.

She started with a torch shining the light into Mark's eyes. Her findings were not too promising. She did, however, say, "Mark appears to have limited reaction to light."

"Better than nowt," I thought, but I was feeling a little disappointed inside.

Then came the 'rotating cylinder'. This was a homemade contraption, or at least it looked that way. It was a cylinder painted with black and white stripes on the length of it, very much like a paint roller, but bigger. She placed the cylinder in front of Mark's eyes and rotated it. As it spun round, it was a little like watching a car's wheels on a film, where at one point they appear to slow down, stop, then start moving in the opposite direction. Mark's reaction to this was nothing, in fact he started to 'doze' off.

"Maybe he is totally mesmerised with the roller," I thought for a minute but I knew that was not the case. Her verdict on this one was similar to the light test.

"Mark appears to have limited reaction to movement but not very significant, I'm afraid."

Again I felt a little sad and I have to confess a little angry. Here we are in this modern day and age where all sorts of remarkable achievements are being made. Then along comes a lady to assess my son's ability to see after a traumatic accident. Armed with a torch and a home-made rotating cylinder. Don't get me wrong, I am more than grateful for her presence and her assessment but to me it all feels a little 'Mickey Mouse' to coin a phrase.

"Mr Holroyd, you seem concerned at the results. I would like to stress that this is only a glance of what is a much, much bigger picture. She paused, then moved to confront me face to face. As our eyes met she continued. From this visit we will progress in a more positive manner. From what I have seen today, I can produce my report for assessment along with my recommendations.

Soon, and I can't say when, Mark will receive an appointment to go for further exploratory examinations using much more sophisticated equipment than I have used today, so rest assured that we have Mark's interests in mind, and we will go forward. Please take my word for that, I won't let you down."

I felt bad, really bad, here is this lady carrying out her important duties in such a professional manner and here am I, with no knowledge of her expertise, doubting her. She can

sense my feelings and my frustration. Perhaps my reaction was one she had seen on many occasions and one that she had often dealt with in the past.

I moved to Mark's side, put my hand on his shoulder and said to the good lady,

"Thanks for coming, both Mark and I are very, very grateful."

"A pleasure, believe me." With that she turned and left, leaving me feeling quite humble.

Our evening visit was quite good, as Markie seemed to have had a 'kick start' from somewhere and his left arm and leg were very active, maybe he was trying to kick my arse over my behaviour today, who knows?

The next few days were all of a similar pattern as we continued with quite concentrated physio on Markie. Lots of balancing with the gym ball in the small of his back and more time standing Mark. On each session we tried to extend the time he was bearing his own weight but all the time we had to be very conscious that he could lose concentration, relax his effort to stand, and let himself fall. Trying times for Markie but even more of a test for us, as to let Mark fall would have been a major disaster and a hell of a setback for everyone.

True to her word, Stephanie the eye lady came up trumps, not on the matter of Mark's ability to see but to carry out tests to find out if he can hear. She has arranged an appointment with the Audiologist for Wednesday 24th January.

The day soon arrived and, accompanied by a nurse, Mark and I were taken to the Main Hospital's Hearing Department. After a lot of careful manoeuvring, we all managed to cram ourselves into a tiny room, which was full of so much equipment that there was hardly any room for us all to fit in. A conducted introduction as to how things worked and the lady audiologist set about the task of wiring Mark up for the tests.

Long wires extended from the main machine, the ends of which were fitted with tiny receivers or small microphones. She carefully attached these to the back, front, sides and top of Mark's head. Headphones were placed over his ears and for a good hour he was subjected to a series of mixed sounds. As Mark received these signals, they were registered onto the machines, which recorded his reactions. The monitor clearly showed that Mark was hearing something as the screen showed peaks and troughs as the sounds were received by him.

The end result, Mark can hear. His right side is good, very good. The left side is impaired, according to the examiner. To confirm her results, I explained that prior to his accident Mark had received a good 'clout' from someone resulting in his left eardrum becoming perforated.

On our return to Rakehead, I decided that the results of the tests must be made clear to all concerned, so my entry in the diary reads:

" Take heed one and all, that Mark may appear to be shut in a box and oblivious to all that goes on around him. Be wary, as that is not so. Mark can hear every spoken word. So please take care not to make any negative statements in his presence. Only statements of encouragement are acceptable from now on as I am convinced that those are what Mark wants to hear."

Thursday 25th January, 2001

Julie in nice and early today. She notes that she arrived at 10 00 hrs to attack Mark's teeth prior to the dentist calling. She has, thankfully, taken over the role of dental carer, not that she wants to steal someone's task, but more because she wants to. It is Julie who has pushed for Mark to have a good dental check-up and her insistence has paid off, for the dentist arrived and gave Mark a good examination. Her findings are that she is very pleased as to how clean Mark's teeth are and said he needed no immediate treatment. Julie is up and down with a 'grin from ear to ear', and so she should be as she is doing a great job.

Got a note from Julie on my evening visit to say that Mr M. of Social Services had been looking for me with an aim to having a meeting. I can't understand why he cannot ask me in person, as I see him most days when I call for physio. He seems a little strange to me, not strange to laugh at but strange in his manner. He scurries about, head down, avoiding eye contact whenever our paths cross. I felt like doing a bit of homework on him by asking one or two of the staff, but thought better of it, as it is against the rules to disclose information about staff or patients to anyone. I did, however, have my own feelings about him, a sixth sense perhaps, a feeling that was confirmed when we finally got our heads together.

Knock Knock

Great day today, another first from Mark. I 'yomped' in this morning and arrived looking as if I had done a '20-miler' across Dartmoor. I had taken the scenic route over the fields and found it to be a bad decision. Mud almost up to my knees, so I had to wash it off in the quadrangle garden before I could go in to see Markie. He was not looking good, right arm rigid and left leg straight out. Having watched Mr G. and company 'chilling' Mark out, I set about him. Julie arrived to find a 'happy' Dad and a very relaxed brother. As she greeted Mark, she was rapping her nails on the table attached to his chair. She noticed Mark watching her hand movements and he appeared to be listening to her knocking; taking his left hand she rested his wrist on her clenched fist leaving his fingers to dangle and free to move.

" Come on, Mark, see if you can tap like me," with that she started to knock on the table. "One, two," she said as she gave the table two distinctive knocks.

"Come on, Markie, go for it, see if you can knock twice," I said to encourage him.

"Go on, Markie, have a go, just two knocks, see one, two," she rapped on the table twice.

"Look, Dad, look, he's trying to knock."

I stared at Mark's left hand and sure enough it moved, very slowly he raised his fingers, then 'bang' he hit the table. Julie and I were locked out of action, we just watched and willed Markie to do it again.

The wait seemed an eternity; silence was noticeable only by its absence. Slowly, up came Mark's fingers again and again he knocked on the table, not just that once but another four times.

"Five knocks, Julie, five bloody knocks," I shouted out. "Five bloody knocks, well done, Markie, that was bloody wonderful."

My shouts brought members of the staff running to see what it was all about. Julie told them as well as she could, as like me she was overcome with excitement, and her words were interspaced with little sobs.

"Come on, Markie, knock for us please," this came from Jayne, an auxiliary nurse and a very caring person.

"Please, Markie, knock for us," said Vileda a student nurse, new to Rakehead but again a lovely person.

We all waited and watched for a repeat performance but it was not to come. Mark's fingers were draped over Julie's hand and were resting on his table. His head was down, chin almost on his chest.

"It's okay, Markie," I felt myself say, "honest, it's okay, be at peace, son, that was wonderful." I could say no more as I choked up, unable to speak and almost in tears. I wasn't on my own, as in total silence the girls wandered off to perform their duties.

I left Julie with Mark and walked back home, regardless of the foul weather that had moved in. I was oblivious to the driving rain and the muddy tracks as my thoughts were with Markie and the remarkable act he had performed.

Knocking became Mark's 'party piece' after that, but only when he wanted to do it and this was usually when there was no audience to impress.

On February 8th another big first.

Debbie had rang me on the 7th to ask how Mark had progressed with his swallowing during the oral exercises that I had been carrying out on Mark over the last few months. I explained just how much saliva I could create in his mouth and how, with a little encouragement, I could get him to perform a positive swallow.

"Do you feel he is ready for a swallow test?" she had asked to which I had to reply.

"Debbie, by trade I am a plumber, so if your question is as how well he is doing, my answer has to be that, when I ask Mark to pull the plug on his mouth full of saliva, he does it and as far as I can tell the water goes down the right hole."

"No coughing?"

"No coughing, I assure you."

"Good, then tomorrow we will put him to the test. Is 3 o'clock okay?"

"Perfect, we will be ready and waiting."

Straight after physio, with Mark comfortably seated in his chair, we met up with Debbie and one of her colleagues.

"Markie, I am going to see how well you can swallow, is that okay with you?" she waited for his response but none was forthcoming.

"I am going to try you with some yoghurt, is that okay?" Again, a blank.

Debbie removed the top and placed the tub on the wheelchair table. Carefully she dipped the end of her little finger in the yoghurt, only up to the depth of her fingernail.

Mark seemed to pre-empt what was about to happen as, when she moved her finger to his mouth he opened it. Debbie looked at me and smiled.

"So far so good, Peter, let's press on."

With that she placed the end of her finger into Mark's mouth, then withdrew it leaving behind the yoghurt. We watched and waited but no reaction from Mark, not even a movement of his mouth.

"Not enough eh, Markie, let's go again."

Debbie took a teaspoon offered by her colleague, and dipped it in the yoghurt part-way and again offered it to Mark. Again, he seemed to know what was coming but unlike the first attempt he allowed the spoon to go into his mouth. Debbie slowly removed the spoon after he had closed his lips about it.

"Bingo," Marks face suddenly contorted and his mouth moved rapidly in a chewing motion, his eyes part closed, all this in response to a half-spoon full of yoghurt.

"Always get the best response with lemon yoghurt," Debbie said with a big grin on her face.

We watched with baited breath as Mark 'chewed' the yoghurt then performed a perfect swallow.

"Don't cough, Mark, please don't cough," I prayed to myself as we watched and waited.

"Brilliant, Markie, brilliant," said Debbie as Mark's face returned to normal, one more and that will be a sufficient test to satisfy me."

This time a little more on the spoon and the result was just as the first run, distorted face, rapid chewing, and then that perfect swallow. I felt wonderful and again a big lump crept into the back of my throat and tears welled up in my eyes. This time some of them escaped as I could feel them run down my cheeks. Thankfully, I was not alone with my emotions as Debbie and her friend were both tearful.

Debbie broke the silence by saying "Mark, that was great, you coped with that extremely well. The next move will be to request a medical swallow test with the Ear, Nose and Throat people. I will get the wheels in motion now and request that we would like it as soon as possible. "Meanwhile, Dad," she said, turning to me, "you must try to step up your activity in Markie's mouth. You need to generate as much saliva as possible and increase the number of swallows you can get him to do."

A nod of affirmation from me and she left with her friend in tow. I just stood there looking at him, speechless and full of great emotion. I put my hands on Markie's shoulders and looked into his face. I wanted to speak but I couldn't. I was full of tears and there was no holding them off. Eventually, when I was able to take control of my feelings, I said to Markie,

"Well done, son, you were great, we have got to go on from this one, as I want you off that nightly drip feed and tucking into proper food, we will do it, Markie, I know we will."

After leaving Markie, I wrote a text message in my phone and sent it to Marion, Wendy, then Julie to give them the good news. I did this as to try to tell them verbally would have been far too difficult. A coward's way out I know, but I'm not ashamed of that.

Mark continued very slow progress for the next few weeks, giving us quite a few interesting highlights.

His physio was improving all the time, as he got stronger and more confident in the way he was handled. His standing was getting better and he was able to withstand the full weight of his body with a little support from the handlers. The diligence of the physio staff never relaxed as they were constantly poised to leap to Mark's assistance, should he falter in any way. A fall at this stage would have set us back months and we were all too aware of that.

Other things, trivial to anyone else, started to happen such as reaching out for objects on occasions. One evening, Mark put his finger up his nose in a positive motion, on another occasion he put his thumb in his mouth. This was something he had done from childhood. It had always been a comfort to Mark, even as he got older. All of the family and friends knew of his thumb-sucking. He was very difficult to catch in the act, as he performed it in such a very 'covert' manner.

Mark's posture and his general appearance were slowly getting better. His Auntie Norma, who loves Mark dearly, probably put it in a nutshell by saying,

"You know I haven't seen Markie for over a month now, but what a change, I don't know what it is but, by heck, he looks well, confident is the word I think; aye, that's it confident, an I'll tell ya what, he doesn't half make me feel good."

This general picture came from lots of people. Family and friends alike were giving off these same positive 'vibes' and it built up a lot of confidence in us all.

BACK TO REALITY
THURSDAY 1ST MARCH, 2001

Mark not well at all today. Katriona, his principle nurse, has decided that, due to his running such a high temperature, he needs to be kept in bed.

Doctor called to see Mark and has prescribed something to reduce his overall temperature until we can 'put the finger' on his problem.

Didn't take long, as on our evening visit we noticed that Mark was lying in a very wet bed. Margaret, senior nurse on duty investigated and found that Mark was bypassing his catheter. Conclusion was obvious; the catheter was blocked at its pick-up point in his bladder. Margaret said it was not an uncommon problem and could be rectified in two ways. First, she would attempt to back flush the pipe and disturb the built-up sediment, thus clearing the tube. The second alternative is to replace the catheter.

"Please God, let the back wash work," I thought.

No such luck, it didn't work, so the next day it was decided to remove it, give Mark a couple of days to get over the trauma and when ready replace it with a new one.

Markie's temperature rose considerably over the following day after the removal, and understandably so. One cannot perceive just how this sort of procedure can be, but it must be very painful and traumatic.

The family took on the caring vigil of trying to be by Markie's side over this bad period. I found it very difficult to imagine how it must feel to have a tube inserted down the penis and the thought of what Mark had to endure was very, very painful for me, mentally.

Tuesday 20th March, 2001

Mark had the catheter replaced today and, to my surprise, he looks very much at peace. No respite with the physio people as we launched Markie back to where we had left off and he performed as if there had never been an adjournment.

Wednesday 21st March, 2001

Big day again for Markie as at 09 00 hrs he was taken off to the E.N.T. Department for a full assessment and a swallow test. The test consists of a camera sent up the nose and down the throat. Once in position, a white fluid, milk in Mark's case, is administered via a spoonful to the mouth. The passage of the fluid is 'watched' as it flows past the camera. Mark was very tired for the test but thankfully he passed. Debbie was quite pleased with the result and, on the strength of the results, she was given the 'rubber stamp' to introduce small amounts of ice cream on a daily basis. This must be done with great caution and at the time when Mark is at his best. It was agreed along with the head nurse, Katriona, Mr G. of physio and taking the family's observations into account, that the best time would be after his physio, daily.

Thursday 22nd March, 2001

Another great physio today and again another first. First sitting on the ball, rocking from side to side with a slight twisting movement thrown in.

"Mark, we are going for a stand with a difference today, we are going to bounce you up and down on the ball gradually increasing the height on each bounce. When I feel you are ready, we will give you one hard bounce and take you up into standing. Here we go, Markie, with a one and a two and a three and a four. Again, a one, a two, a three and a four. This time, Markie, on the four, with a one, a two, a three and a four, up you go, Markie, up, up, brilliant, Mark, hold it, hold it, that's perfect."

Mark was stood tall now and looking great, better, much better than ever before. I felt so pleased and proud of him that I wanted to shout out,

"Look everybody, look at my lad, what a fucking stand, brilliant, Markie, brilliant."

Thankfully, I only shouted in my mind but the urge to do it for real was so strong I don't know how I controlled it.

I manoeuvred to get in front of Mark. I managed to get a full 'eyeball' from him. Now we were eye to eye and connected in a strange way.

Mark knew it was me, I am sure, as I felt I was within him and I know he was saying to me,

"That's my best, Dad, my very best."

"Markie, that is wonderful, thanks son," I whispered. We held this position for a good 3 to 4 minutes, in total silence, not a sound from anyone, as we all were aware of this amazing contact.

"Chair please, Leanne," said Andy

Leanne brought the chair to the back of Mark and gripped it firmly in the required position.

"We are going for a sit, Markie, on three please, one, two and three." Mark bent to this command and we placed him into his chair.

"Perfect, bloody perfect, thanks, Markie, he's all yours, Dad." With that, they filed from the room in silence leaving Mark and me together.

"Can I come in?" that ice-breaking voice came from Debbie. "Come on, Markie, it's ice cream time and the stage is set." Off to the dayroom we went and sure enough a small crowd was waiting for us. Marion, Katriona, Margaret and a couple more of the staff were all waiting for the big moment.

"Markie, just take your time with this, I am going to let you have a small taste and, if it meets with your approval, you can have a little more."

Debbie removed the top from the tub of vanilla, took about half a teaspoonful from it and offered it to Mark's mouth.

I stood back and watched as the spoon approached his face. 'Butterflies' raced into my stomach.

"What if he won't open his mouth or even worse, what if he coughs and chokes on it."

Then humour hit me, as I noticed each and everyone present were so intent on the action that they too were opening their mouths in readiness for the spoon full of ice cream. Mark was ready and so was everyone else. As the spoon was inserted, Mark's lips closed and Debbie removed the spoon. Almost instantly, Mark started his chewing motion and within seconds he made a very positive swallow, much to the relief of all watching.

A short wait, then Debbie offered Mark another taste and again everyone, even Debbie, opened their own mouths as if to encourage Markie on the test.

"That's it, Markie, no more today, don't you dare cough."

A buzz started amongst all present, as unbeknown to me the crowd of observers had swollen to include some other members of the staff. Even the two cleaning ladies were present and all were so pleased with Markie.

"Cough if you dare, Markie, but you will make a lot of people unhappy if you do," said Debbie as she carefully and caringly wiped Mark's mouth.

I was feeling great, what a day, excellent physio and a very successful swallowing exercise. However, my elation was not to last.

"Can I interrupt you, Mr Holroyd?" It was Mr M. from Social Services. "Do you think I could have a word with you and Mrs Holroyd in my office?"

"Now?" I enquired.

"If you don't mind, it won't take long."

Katriona took over Mark and Marion and I followed Mr M. to his tiny office, where we seated ourselves in front of his desk.

"Difficult to know where to start really, such a delicate subject, especially in your situation. He paused, shuffled a few papers around on his desk, then said, "Your Case Assessment is due in a few days and I have to report on the progress you have made in finding Mark alternative accommodation. You see, we are only allowed to keep someone a maximum of 6 months and that is in extreme cases. I am sorry I have not been able to help you on this matter but as I am not a well man in myself, I have found it almost impossible to find time to get this meeting together."

"Hang on, are you telling us we have to find Mark alternative accommodation. Why? When? This is a Rehabilitation Unit and that is what we are doing. We are all working on getting our Markie back. Are you trying to say that it's pack your bags you're out of time?"

"No, no I'm not saying that at all."

"Well, what are you saying?" Marion asked him in a much more controlled manner than I could have done.

"Well, it's a matter of finance really. You see in a case such as yours there is a lot of funding to be found for the patient like Mark." He paused and looked at us as if we knew exactly what he was saying.

"You are trying to tell us that it all boils down to money, aren't you? Or are you saying, sorry Mark, you have not recovered in your 6 months allocated to you, so off you go lad, where you go is your problem, but you can't stop here, we can't afford to spend any more brass on you?"

He could see I was getting agitated, as he kept moving the papers around on his desk and tugging at his tie. He was nervous and it showed.

"No, Mr Holroyd, that is not the case. What I am saying is that I have to put together a package for Mark. One that will draw money from Social Services for some of the cost and the rest of the costs will come from the National Health Service. All very complicated, I'm afraid, and something that I cannot explain in one brief meeting."

"Put in a nutshell, Mr M., what you are saying is we have to go, is that what you are trying to say?"

"Yes, but not right away. It depends a lot on the case assessment next week. If the findings of the assessment are that Mark has reached a level plateau, then we will have no alternative but to relocate him."

"Level plateau, level plateau, can I assume that is a nice word for it's the end of the line for Markie? Get your gear together, lad, we can't help you anymore, come on chop, chop, on your way."

I stopped there as I could feel myself getting angry, bloody angry. I glanced at Marion as I could feel her trying to connect with me, her eyes were full but her body language was calm and some how it 'cooled' the temperature that was building inside me.

"If we have to go, or when we have to go, where do we go to?" Marion asked.

"This may not be what you want to hear, but I am prevented from advising you as to where you can take Mark. There are lots of Nursing Homes in the area, I am sure you will find a home more than willing to take him on."

I put my head down in my hands and tried to absorb what was being said. How could they let us down now, especially as we are getting remarkable results from all the efforts everyone is 'pouring' into Markie? I was struggling to accept that it was all to just stop.

"What if you are wrong? What if it is decided to keep Markie and press on with his recovery? What if he somehow suddenly breaks out of his box and speaks? Come on, Mr M., can you say that, if Mark suddenly comes back, you will still ask us to leave?"

"No, I am not saying that, but to be honest with yourself and the family you have to accept that nothing short of a miracle would have to happen for any of your hopes and wishes to occur. I wish most sincerely that I didn't have to be the bearer of such bad news, believe me, it is the worst part of my job and a part that hurts me, deeply."

"Where to from here, Mr M., where do we get help in finding somewhere for Markie?" Marion said calmly.

"The law forbids me from recommending anywhere, and to be honest I cannot think of any place that could cater for Mark's needs. You must be aware that it is a full-time task looking after head-injured people. You know and understand that Mark needs at least two very able-bodied people to carry out simple everyday tasks, such as putting Mark to bed; getting him up and placing him in his chair; not to mention the personal hygiene side, like bathing and going to the toilet. I am, however, prepared to stick my neck in the noose and say to you: do not consider taking Mark home, I have seen it tried only too often and the failure rate is high and the cost on family pressure gets unbearable, so much so that probably nine out of ten, no, more than that, 99 out of a 100 result in disaster."

Head down again and pressing my hands over my ears. "I don't believe I am hearing all this. It is not happening. Please God, make it go away, snap me out of this nightmare."

"Come on, Peter, let's go home now, we need to sit with the girls and see where we can go from here." Marion was very much in control at that moment and I knew what she was saying was right. We have to investigate all aspects of the problem and somehow find an answer, or locate the elusive miracle.

Marion and I decided that night that we would not alarm the girls at this stage. After all, we had only got the news from Mr M. and he was not the person who would make the final decision. We both wanted to stave off the inevitable for as long as possible, but we knew it was lurking around the corner.

Determined to find Mark an equal if not better home was now my order of the day.

"Where do I begin? Who can I ask for advice? What are my guidelines? And does a place exist for Markie?"

All these questions are racing around in my head but answers are certainly eluding me.

Not sure how or where to turn, so I decided I needed to get away and be alone for a while to 'stew over' all my options and try to formulate a plan of attack.

FRIDAY NIGHT

"Markie, sorry son but I will not be in to see you tomorrow. If you don't mind, I feel it is my turn to 'chill out' so I am off to Fleetwood tonight as tomorrow the tides are perfect for a trip out."

I was watching Markie for some reaction but he just lay there, head to one side, a position he adopted a lot now. I moved my chair to the other side of the bed to enable me to get eye contact with him. I could see into his eyes now.

"I'll miss you tomorrow night, son, but rest assured that my escape for a couple of days is what I need, I have to get away from all and everything, just for a short period, I just need time to myself, honest."

That night after leaving Mark I drove straight over to Fleetwood to where 'Sea Soldier', my boat, was moored in the Marina.

"Hello, my chum," I said to the boat but only after carefully looking about to ensure no one could hear me, or they might have thought I had lost the plot.

I stowed what little gear I had brought and set about preparing the boat for sea. Not a short task as we had not been out to sea for months, and over that period I had only had a few short visits to ensure that all was 'shipshape'. It wasn't, as I had been carrying out some small necessary repairs that needed attention and I had not stowed away my tools. I had left them strewn about on the deck of the wheelhouse.

With everything stashed away and my bed made up, I decided that I deserved a pint so I walked down the pontoon, over the lock gates and out of the marina via the exit close to town. Two pints later, and with a contented feeling inside, I made my way back to the marina. I confirmed the high water time on the tide table posted outside the Marina Office.

"Eleven o'clock, just right," I muttered to myself, "up for seven, breakfast for eight, sails in place and safely stowed for nine and read to go by ten, that is if the lock keeper opens the gates an hour before high water as is the normal practice." With nothing more to do I settled down for the night.

Sleep eluded me most of the night. I kept wakening with a jolt, wondering where I was. This I feel was due to being in a different environment, as I hadn't slept on board since Mark had had his accident. The strange thing was that, when I 'found myself', it was Markie that sprang to mind, and I felt that I shouldn't be here. I should be with him.

I awoke to the alarm ring from my phone, stowed away my bed and bedding and prepared a simple breakfast of toasted bread, two eggs and a pint of tea, all set out on the table in the seating area, which encircled the well deck. It was just coming dawn and the sky looked good, slight chill in the air from a gentle south-westerly wind force 3 to 4 was the forecast and a quick check on my wind indicator confirmed that.

I sat there for some time, steeped deep in my thoughts and pondering what the future might have in store for us.

Would I find somewhere for Markie to stay? Would he continue to get the much-needed treatment? Would he continue to improve, slow, as it might be, but improvement never-the-less? All these thoughts raced through my mind as I sat there alone awaiting tide and time.

"Woof, woof," loud barks coming from a dog brought me down to earth, as it bounded down the pontoon, placed its paws on the gunwales of my boat and stared at me, tail wagging and asking in his own special way for me to greet him.

"Good morning, where's your Dad?" silly question really, as Peter, the Marina Manager, was stood behind him.

"About time you blew some cobwebs off her. Sheer waste her laying here doing nowt. Anyway, how are you and how's that lad of yours comin' on?"

In the briefest of explanations, I brought Peter 'up to speed' with Markie's situation. I purposely omitted my inner problems and tried to make it seem much better than it really was.

"Off on this tide then?"

"I certainly am."

"Back on the next?"

"Yep, but I wish I wasn't."

Now, why did I say that, I thought, why did I say "I wish I wasn't?"

"Enjoy yourself and bring her back in one piece as I love this lady more than you know."

"Thanks, Peter."

With that, he made his way to the Marina Office with dog wagging his tail in tow.

Hoisting the sails took longer than I had anticipated as they had not been hauled up for some time. Eventually I got them raised and lowered again, reefed in ready to unfurl and hoist, once clear of the Marina.

Clank, clank, clank, the sound of the inner lock gates opening resounded throughout the marina.

"Fleetwood Harbour, Fleetwood Harbour, this is Sea Soldier, Sea Soldier for a radio check, over."

"Sea Soldier, this is Fleetwood Harbour you are loud and clear, do you wish to lock out on this tide?"

"Fleetwood Harbour, that's affirmative, may I proceed?"

"Sea Soldier, that's okay, you may proceed."

"Fleetwood Harbour, thank you. Sea Soldier listening on 12 and 16 out."

Formalities completed, I slipped my mooring lines and made my way into the lock. Two other boats joined me in the lock before the inner gates were closed. Slowly, the outer lock gates started to open, a slight delay to allow water levels to become equal, and then they opened fully to reveal the channel that would allow me passage to the open sea. Up went the revs from the engine as I eased the throttle forward, and back came the lovely reassuring throb you feel in your feet as Sea Soldier took me away from the harbour.

I carefully made my way down the well-marked channel, targeting buoy after buoy in a zig-zag fashion until I approached Lune Deep Buoy, the first or last buoy you encounter when coming to, or going from, the main channel to Fleetwood.

I set the auto-steering on a course to hold the passage straight and safe, then set about hauling the sails. Mizzen sail first as this would assist the boat in holding a straight course, then the fore sail. So far so good, now the main sail. This was housed in the boom and it went up remarkably well considering it had been in 'wraps' for quite some time.

Back in the wheelhouse, prepared for the bit I love best, the closing down of the engine. I pulled the stop handle, peace, sheer peace, as the engine stopped. I rested my hands on the wheel, placed my forehead on them and stayed there enjoying the silence, or near silence, as all I could hear was the water rushing along the hull and a slight whistle from the shrouds as the wind drove us forward.

It seemed a long time but in reality it was only minutes, three, maybe five at the most, but it was wonderful. I felt so much at peace for those few minutes and it was lost to all the goings on in my mind. I was at peace

With auto pilot set, I left the wheelhouse and went out onto the upper deck to relish the sound of the wind rushing through the sails and the racing noise of the water passing along the hull as it cut its way through the sea.

"Wonderful, fucking wonderful," I shouted aloud, then I stood there, face into the wind, savouring every minute of it.

I went below to reset the auto-steering. This time I was on a course for Peel Island, a straight line to my proposed destination, providing I had no other vessels to consider or avoid. I made passage for just 1 hour, before I had to 'snap' myself back into my real world.

"Come on, Ollie, that's it, we have to head back now, that's your lot for this trip," I said aloud, "it's time to head back."

I wanted to ignore what I was telling myself, I just wished I could sail on and on, where to, I didn't know and I didn't care. I just had a terrible urge to go, get away from everything and everyone.

I looked up into the sky, looking for help and shouted.

"Why me, God, why Markie, why us?"

I slumped down onto the seating in the well deck and fought to stop my tears and compose myself. Eventually it came, some kind of inspiration hit me, from where I didn't know, I just heard myself shout.

"Markie, Markie, don't worry son, I'm coming home."

I went below, gripped the wheel with both hands and turned Sea Soldier slowly into the wind and waited for the fore sail to show signs of 'backing'. I moved back out onto the upper deck and watched as the sail took the wind and started to bring the bows round onto our new course. After securing the sail on its new setting, I dodged below and set the auto-steering on a bearing to send us back to the Lune Deep Buoy and home.

"Home, I thought, home to the pain of what we were encountering." My thoughts went out to Julie and Wendy. What have they done to deserve a sentence of worrying for Mark?

Marion, like me, is finding the trauma almost unbearable at times. He is her baby and always will be. She is so brave in the way she handles events and so strong, much, much stronger than me. Then me, I love and miss Markie so much that I want to hit out at something, but what? There is nothing to hit that would change anything. I stared down at the sea rushing past the hull, feeling low, so very low but determined to fight to get my Markie back.

For no apparent reason, my thoughts went out to a friend of mine, 'Doc'. He had been good friends for many years. We first met when I was on passage in a merchant vessel. He was the Senior Communications Officer on board the ship, and his ability and skill in communications were amazing, especially when it came to high-speed Morse Code, a skill that he had mastered over several years. This proved a great asset to me and of paramount importance during our first brief encounter.

Prior to Mark's accident he telephoned me one night:

"Hi ya, Pedro, been trying to get you all day, can you talk?"

"No problem, Doc, what can I do for you?"

"Not good news, pal, been trying to avoid contacting you lately as I have not been very well. Anyway, it's out now, I've got the dreaded."

"Not surprising, knowing the sort of company you prefer, don't worry, cock, a few jabs and you'll be back to your old self."

"It's not that, you prick, I've got cancer."

"Fuck off, Doc, you don't joke about having cancer."

"I'm not, 3 weeks at the most, will you be an executor to my will?"

"Doc, stop it, it's not fucking funny."

"I know, Pedro, will you do it, please? I just want to be sure my lads get some of my gear and I know you will see to it."

He was serious and I knew it.

"Doc, course I will, I'll come and see you and sort it out."

277

"No, please don't, I'm not a pretty sight now. Just say you will do it for me, then I can go in peace."

"Doc, listen to me, of course I'll do it, but let me come and sort it out."

"No, Pedro, please and thanks, see ya." With that he hung up.

He called me again the day before he died:

"Pedro, just had another shitty day in paradise," his voice was low but clear, "think I'm off this time as the pain has stopped; you will sort out the boys for me, won't you, pal, please?"

The connection gave a 'click'.

"Doc, Doc are you there? I will, you know I will. Doc, can you hear me, Doc?"

The phone was silent, Doc had hung up.

The next morning I got a phone call to say he had died during the night.

As Lune Deep Buoy neared, I felt a change in me. I felt that Doc's visit has got me back, back from feeling sorry for myself, back from feeling sorry for the girls or Marion. I felt lifted and inspired. Doc had put trust in me to see to his last wishes and he was helping me now.

As I rounded the buoy, I fired up the engine and pushed the lever to 'full ahead'. The wind picked up and was blowing hard from the south-west. It filled the sails to full capacity.

The journey back was fast; as I passed the 'Ro Ro' ferry dock, I nipped out on deck and lowered my sails. Once lashed down and secured, I returned to the wheelhouse and called Fleetwood.

"Fleetwood Harbour, Fleetwood Harbour, this is Sea Soldier, Sea Soldier, may I enter the Marina, over?"

"Sea Soldier, this is Fleetwood, you are clear to enter, out."

Firmly alongside and secured to my mooring, I called Marion.

"Hi, love, enjoy your sail?" she enquired.

"Bloody right I did. Do me a favour, Marion, give Markie a message from me, will you?"

"Yes of course I will, what do you want me to tell him?"

"Tell him I've been in contact with my old 'chum' Doc, and that he has brought me down to earth with a jolt. Let Markie know that he has kicked my arse and told me to stop feeling sorry for myself and get out and find the key."

" Doc?, Peter, Doc? He's gone, Peter, he's dead and you know that, and what's this about a bloody key? I think you have lost the plot or banged your head. Are you sure you are okay?"

"I'm fine, love, honest, just tell Markie that I'll find the key to his box, he will understand."

"I hope so, as I am lost, what key? And what bloody box are you on about?"

"The key is for Markie's box, love, Markie's box!"

I hung up then as I knew she would go on and on with her questioning. The problem was I could say no more. I was on a 'high' and hell bent on getting on with the fight for Markie's return.

June 2005

(By Peter Holroyd's Daughter,Wendy Holroyd)

Whilst on holiday in Tenerife in October 2004, Dad was struck down by what appeared at the time to be a mystery to the doctors. After several doctor's visits to the holiday apartment they diagnosed him with Sciatica and he was hospitalised. After a week of treatment, it was discovered that his bowel had perforated and was leaking poisons into his body and he had surgery to remove a large portion of his colon. This done, the amount of poisons in his sytems was too damaging and resulted in total organ failure. He had septic Shock to his organs and Scepticaemia as well as having contracted MRSA in his blood and wounds.

He was taken to intensive care at University Hospital, Santa Cruz, Tenerife, where he lay there on a life support machine. The drugs that were administered were to effectively paralyse him in the hope that a barrage of antibiotics would kill the extensive poison in his system. The questions we all asked ourselves were echoes of Markie's accident. Can he hear us, can he see or feel us and how aware was he of what he was going through?

He was taken, by air ambulance, at the end of December 2004 to an intensive care unit at Wakefield, Yorkshire. As he was back in this country his treatment could now be changed and the drugs that were paralysing him were discontinued. It was in the lap of the Gods as to his recovery. No doctor could say if he would ever move or communicate again. The damage to his body was tremendous but there was also the question of what all this could have done neurologically. He had further stays in two more intensive care units, each time getting closer to home, but still remained on life support machines. It took time and great determination to battle on but the machines were eventually removed.

Because of extensive muscle wastage, movement has been a major hurdle to jump, but time has proved that he had no lasting neurological damage. At this time, June 2005, he is in a Rehabilitation Centre and is trying with all his mind, body and spirit to regain his muscle power and at present is walking in a limited way. Thankfully his hands have come back to the fore and he is putting them to very good use by writing a second book.

Because of his tragic situation, Dad has not been able to see Markie for several months, which must cause him a great deal of pain and anguish. One thing that has never dimished through everything is Dad's total determination and enduring humour.